# 365
# MOTORCYCLES
# YOU MUST RIDE

DAIN GINGERELLI
JAMES MANNING MICHELS
and CHARLES EVERITT

First published in 2010 by MBI Publishing Company and Motorbooks, an imprint of MBI Publishing Company, 400 1st Avenue North, Suite 300, Minneapolis, MN 55401 USA

Motorbooks titles are also available at discounts in bulk quantity for industrial or sales-promotional use. For details write to Special Sales Manager at MBI Publishing Company, 400 1st Avenue North, Suite 300, Minneapolis, MN 55401 USA.

To find out more about our books, join us online at www.motorbooks.com.

ISBN-13: 978-0-7603-3474-4

Editor: Darwin Holmstrom
Design Manager: Kou Lor
Layout by: Chris Fayers
Cover designed by: Rob Johnson

Printed in China

**On the front cover:** *Photo by Kevin Wing*

# 365 Motocycles You Must Ride

## Contents

# 365 Motocycles You Must Ride

**Sometimes motorcyclists get stuck in a rut.**
Sometimes we get so caught up in our own tiny little corner of the motorcycling universe that we think that's all there is. If we ride big V-twin cruisers, we can't fathom why people would fold themselves up like pretzels and ride high-powered sportbikes. If we ride big adventure tourers, we don't understand why anyone would want to fly through the air on a motocross track, tackling double and triple jumps. If we go big rubbery ones over our antique motorcycles, we can't understand why anyone would want to ride a "soulless" modern machine. We focus on our own little motorcycle community with such laserlike intensity that sometimes we don't get subgenres within our own genres, as, for example, when a group of sportbike riders who roam urban areas in large packs can't understand why other sportbike riders

commute two hours just to spend an hour strafing twisty rural byways.

The thing is, it's all fun. It would behoove us all to look outside our own comfort zones to see the amazing variety of motorcycles out there, and for the most part, they're all good. Sure, some are better than others, but even the worst motorcycles provide certain entertainment value. In this book, we've tried to provide as broad a cross section of motorcycles as possible, ranging from the spectacular to the sublime to the downright silly.

This book was a massive undertaking and an absolute beast to put together. Collecting photography of nearly 125 year's worth of motorcycles proved the most challenging. In some places we've had to approximate the bikes as best we could. For example, we might discuss a racing

motorcycle but illustrate the entry with a street-going version of the same machine. Or vice versa. In other instances we may not have been able to get the exact year or variation being discussed. Fortunately we had a great deal of assistance. *Cycle World* magazine provided the bulk of the photography from their amazing archive, and much of the rest was filled in by manufacturers; from the largest manufacturers like Harley-Davidson and Honda to the smallest, like Fischer and Mission One, everyone we contacted jumped on board. Harley proved especially helpful, providing images of motorcycles so rare that the only place they exist is in the Harley-Davidson Museum. It's located at 400 Canal Street in Milwaukee. If you haven't been there yet, go. Now. It contains the most amazing collection of motorcycles ever assembled in one place.

We had an incredible amount of help from *Minnesota Motorcycle Monthly*'s grand pubah, Victor Wanchena. *MMM* is a fantastic magazine, one of the best regional motorcycle mags in the country; it always features the coolest and most unusual motorcycles around. We also raided the archives of some of Motorbooks all-time greatest photographers, like Randy Leffingwell and Jerry Hatfield.

Some of our picks will make you smile, and of course you'll disagree with many of our choices and conclusions, but in the end we hope you enjoy the book. Better yet, we hope this book inspires you to get out there and ride some of these machines yourself.

 ## Did You Know?
Presents interesting facts and information about the motorcycle.

 ## The Perfect Ride
Tells the reader where the authors would go on that particular motorcycle in an ideal world.

 ## Claim to Fame
Points out the most notable aspect of a given motorcycle.

 ## Rebel Factor
All motorcycles are rebellious; this feature simply points out how rebellious a particular motorcycle may be.

# AJS

## E-90 Porcupine

**Without its supercharger, this porcupine didn't have much of a sting in its tail, but it still won a world title**

Twin-cylinder powerplants haven't seen the grandest of fortunes in motorcycle road racing's blue-riband class (500cc Grand Prix as it was called then; now MotoGP), occupying the top end-of-season slot but a single time. It was 1949 when an AJS E-90 Porcupine, ridden by Les Graham, did the deed. Why so little success for the configuration? Simple, really. Insufficient development resources, the same reason that lies at the heart of most famous failures. In the specific case of AJS' Porcupine, the E-90 was a prewar design, intended to take on a supercharger. But sanctioning bodies made such devices illegal postwar, a decision akin to a company death blow, not only to AJS, but to several U.K. firms that had similar designs. For many manufacturers of racing bikes, the banning of superchargers signaled an automatic game over.

 According to some sources, AJS made only four of the second-generation, E-95-style Porcupines.

 AJS' E-90 Porcupine marked the first and only time a twin-cylinder-powered motorcycle won the 500cc road racing world championship.

 European racetracks, of course. Preferably nothing too fast, or the Italian four-cylinder bikes would blow the doors right off this English machine.

 ★★
By banning superchargers postwar, motorcycling's sanctioning bodies robbed the Porcupine of its key element, one that would have made it stand out and maybe even win more than a few races and a single title. Not hardly.

Engine: Air-cooled, DOHC, four-valve, parallel twin
Horsepower: 50 at 7,600 rpm
Top Speed: 120 miles per hour
Weight: 320 pounds
Value Now: $$$$

### The bikes from Brazil

If a motorcycle magazine uses the following words or phrases in its test of your flagship—"crude," "primitive suspension," "amateurish," "evil," "carelessly sculpted," "unwieldy," "directional stability is a problem at almost any speed," and "by any engineering standards, even those of the Third World, it's a disaster"—you can figure you've got a problem or 10 on your hands. That was the case for the VW-powered, Brazilian-built hyper-tourer known as the Amazonas, which seemed to be poised to take a run at the U.S. touring market in the mid-1980s. Fortunately, cooler heads prevailed, so to speak, and the Amazonas threat never materialized. Just as well; the bikes from Brazil really were so slow and awful that they could have put American youth off motorcycles for a generation.

 The Amazonas was originally intended to be a police bike for Brazil.

 Just being one of the biggest ships of motorcycle touring's state ever, for starters. For more, it becomes a matter of how much time you have on your hands. The Amazonas was also hailed as having one of the biggest fairings in all of motorcycling, yet it achieved no real benefit from it; fit and finish were atrocious, and so on and so on.

 To another brand's dealership, so you could trade it in on a truly functional motorcycle.

 ★ ★ ★ ★ ★
The Amazonas rates 5 jackets simply for being hard-headedly, self-destructively, and needlessly different.

Engine: Air-cooled, eight-valve with pushrod-actuation, horizontally opposed four
Horsepower: 50 at 4,000 rpm (claimed)

¼ Mile: 17.96 seconds at 76.27 miles per hour
Weight: n/a
Top Speed: 91 miles per hour
Value Now: You would want one?

# Aprilia

## RVS1000R

### A new Italian marque emerges

The Master Bike Shootout is an annual event held to select the top sportbike in the world. In 2006, after 16 motorcycle magazine editors completed more than 1,000 laps around Jerez Circuit and wore through countless tires in the process, Aprilia's RVS1000R was deemed the winner. One publication praised the RVS1000R, saying, "It takes a good two laps to learn how to ride it, and then a completely different bike emerges. The big V-twin motor doesn't need revving; it just grunts its way from corner to corner, while the slipper clutch works brilliantly at masking all that engine braking when you barrel into tight corners."

 Many consider the RSV1000 to be one of the best-handling motorcycles ever built.

 First non-Japanese bike to win a Master Bike Shootout.

 Jerez Circuit in Spain, where the Master Bike Shootout takes place.

 ★ ★ ★ ★
Aprilia should rate some cajones by going head-to-head with rival Ducati.

Engine: Liquid-cooled, 998cc, four-stroke, 60-degree V-twin
Horsepower: 143 at 10,000 rpm
Top Speed: 171 miles per hour
Weight: 408 pounds
Value Now: $$$

# Aprilia

## Tuono

### A more civilized RVS1000R, if you will

Horsepower wins races, but torque wins smiles for everyday applications on the street. Aprilia engineers obviously understood that when they revamped the RVS1000R engine for the new Tuono by trading horsepower for torque. Not that the factory engineers exactly castrated the Tuono's powerplant; it should almost be capable of hoisting the front wheel in the air, should some miscreant choose to behave in such a socially irresponsible manner.

 Aprilia is headquartered in Noale, Italy, a town of about 15,000 citizens.

 Race-bred technology distilled for the street.

 Take the Tuono through the back roads of Malibu in Southern California, and you'll appreciate the engine's linear power curve.

 ★ ★ ★ ★ ★
Ride the Tuono fast, and you'll begin to feel like a superbike racer.

Engine: Liquid-cooled, 998cc, four-stroke V-twin
Horsepower: 139 at 9,500 rpm
Top Speed: n/a
Weight: 408 pounds
Value Now: $$$

When the RSV4R's tachometer needle sweeps to 7,500 rpm, hold on, because that's where the engine's power really kicks in.

 The RSV4R shares the same ride-by-wire technology found on Max Biaggi's factory superbike.

 Mugello Circuit near Florence, Italy, where the bike was unveiled.

 ★ ★ ★ ★ ★
Possibly as close to a superbike as you're going to get for the street.

Engine: Liquid-cooled, 999cc, four-stroke, 65-degree V-4
Horsepower: 180 at 12,500 rpm

Top Speed: 180 miles per hour
Weight: 405 pounds
Value Now: $$$$$

### A superbike for the masses—on the street

The RSV4R is nothing short of a superbike-spec racer with lights and a license plate. Yet, while this Aprilia takes much of its technology from its World Superbike kin, its purpose is to be a streetbike. Here's what *Cycle World*'s editors had to say about the RSV4R: "Destined to reshape public perception of Italian sportbikes, this liter-class V-Four RSV superbike marks Aprilia's arrival as a leader in both engine and chassis design. The track-bred racer-replica has an incredibly compact stature, competitive power output, and unmatched liter-class agility, all while possessing Italian style that is music to the eyes and a V-Four exhaust song that is music to the ears."

# Aprilia

## Moto 6.5

### Egg-shaped for eggheads?

Aprilia launched the Moto 6.5 at the height of the dot-com era, back when geekdom was something to which all young hipsters aspired, which might help account for the bike's rather unusual nomenclature, not to mention its unorthodox styling. The bike's angles and curves, penned by Philippe Starck, seem to flow one into the other, much as you'd expect a computer or other desktop device from the dot-com era to do. In fact, the Moto 6.5 bore a remarkable resemblance to the iMac, the trendiest computer of the era. The two even came in similar pastel colors. There's a reason the dot-com bubble burst, and it's probably the same reason why we don't see the Moto 6.5 in Aprilia's lineup anymore.

 The dictionary describes the word *nerd* as slang for a socially inept, foolish, or ineffectual person.

 Appeared in the Guggenheim's Art of the Motorcycle exhibit. And pretty much nowhere else.

 Take a lap around the parking lot at Microsoft HQ, and you're sure to draw a crowd of computer nerds.

 *
You can bet the jacket will have short sleeves, and perhaps even a token pocket protector.

Engine: Liquid-cooled, 649cc, four-stroke, single-cylinder
Horsepower: 42 at 6,250 rpm
Top Speed: 115 miles per hour
Weight: 331 pounds
Value Now: $

The Square Four is often referred to as the Squariel.

The Square Four was produced in 500cc, 600cc, and 1,000cc displacements from 1931 to 1958.

Cruise the streets of London, with the final destination—where else?—Trafalgar Square.

★ ★ ★
Edward Turner, who was responsible for Triumph's popular twin, also designed the Square Four.

Engine: Air-cooled, 497cc, 597cc, and 997cc, four-stroke, square four
Horsepower: 45 at 5,500 rpm (997cc)

Top Speed: 105 miles per hour (997cc)
Weight: 465 pounds (997cc)
Value Now: $$$$

## Square today, gone tomorrow

Few engine designs have evoked as much curiosity as Ariel's Square Four. The engine's unorthodox cylinder layout presented a bike that was fast and smooth—and different. But one major problem kept the Square Four from greatness—as you might suspect, those two trailing cylinders didn't receive adequate air over their fins, so overheating was always a concern. Ariel spent decades trying to perfect the design and solve the cooling issues, but ultimately the square four engine concept was one that was not compatible with air-cooling.

# Ariel

## Red Hunter

**Proof that the hunt could be more rewarding than the trophy**

Like just about every other company trying to survive the world's economic downturn during the early 1930s, Ariel encountered financial hardship, temporarily closing its doors until Jack Sangster, son of Ariel founder Charlie Sangster, reorganized the company. And the first order of business was to market the Red Hunter design, in both 350cc and 500cc configurations. The engine proved to be fast and reliable, and with periodic updates to this single-cylinder engine, Ariel enjoyed success for many years to come—even after BSA bought the company in 1944.

 Ariel was one of the world's first motorcycle companies, formed before 1900 by Charles Sangster.

 The engine design that saved Ariel during the Great Depression.

 Abbey Mill Lane in St. Albans, England, with a stop at Ye Olde Fighting Cocks, possibly England's oldest pub.

 ✹ ✹
Yet another fast and reliable British thumper.

Engine: Air-cooled, 350cc and 497cc, four-stroke, single-cylinder
Horsepower: 26 at 5,600 rpm (497cc)
Top Speed: 82 miles per hour (497cc)
Weight: 375 pounds (497cc)
Value Now: $$$

# Benelli

Kel Carruthers won the 250cc World Championship for Benelli in 1970.

Remarkably accurate replicas.

Isle of Man Mountain Course—nothing else will do.

★ ★ ★ ★ ★
Wear a silver helmet in Paso's honor.

Engine: Air-cooled, 350cc and 413cc, four-stroke, inline four
Horsepower: 50 at 14,000 rpm (350cc); 65 at 14,000 rpm (413cc)

Top Speed: n/a
Weight: n/a
Value Now: $$$$$

### Imitation is the sincerest form of flattery

Englishman George Beale has been part of the Grand Prix road-race scene since 1971, and in 1976 he formed George Beale Motorcycles, a company that supplies reproduction parts to vintage-bike racers. But perhaps one of his most remarkable contributions has been the re-creation of Benelli's four-cylinder racers that were ridden by the late Renzo Pasolini in the world championships during the late 1960s. Beale offers variations of Paso's 350cc and 413cc (500cc Class) Grand Prix racers, and the attention to detail is breathtaking, to say the least. The repli-racers have the same type of Ceriani forks, dry clutches, even seven-speed gearboxes used on the factory bikes (350cc factory bike shown below) of the late 1960s.

Benelli 350 GP · 1970
Pilota: Mike Hailwood

# Benelli

## Sei

### A bike to help you rediscover the joy of six

Based on its curbside appearance, the Benelli Sei looks heavy and cumbersome. In truth, the 485-pound motorcycle feels rather agile and light, especially considering its overall size. But the Sei's signature is the exhaust note that chimes from those six megaphone mufflers. To quote the road test that appeared in the August 1974 issue of *Cycle World*: "Were a dealer trying to make a sale to an undecided customer, merely starting the engine would have the guy running for his Parker T-Ball Jotter [pen]." No doubt, in the true Italian spirit of motorcycling, the Benelli Sei offers pure, erotic six appeal.

The Benelli motorcycle company was owned by Alejandro De Tomaso, an Italian aristocrat with an automobile company that bore his name.

The first transverse, inline six-cylinder motorcycle engine to be mass-produced.

Who cares about the ride; just fire up that six-cylinder engine so that we can listen to it purr.

★ ★ ★
You'll enjoy the ride, but remember to keep your earplugs in your pocket. This engine's exhaust note is, in typical Italian fashion, music to the ears.

Engine: Air-cooled, 747cc, four-stroke, inline six-cylinder
Horsepower: 71 at 8,500 rpm
Top Speed: 126 miles per hour
Weight: 485 pounds
Value Now: $$$

# Benelli

## Tornado Tre 900

Though first shown in 1999, the Tre didn't actually start rolling off production lines until 2003.

The Tre's groundbreaking technology is further proof that Italians know how to make exotic motorcycles.

Can you say Italian Alps?

★ ★ ★ ★
As the wind rushes past you and the Tornado spools up to speed, you'll understand fully what it means to ride an exotic motorcycle from the boot-shaped peninsula.

Engine: Liquid-cooled, 898cc, four-stroke, inline three-cylinder
Horsepower: 140 at 11,500 rpm

Top Speed: 167 miles per hour
Weight: lbs. 436 pounds
Value Now: $$$

### Sexy styling through aerodynamics

Leave it to the Italian stylists and engineers to figure out a way to allow form to lead function. In the case of the Benelli Tornado Tre 900, careful attention to the bike's body lines allowed engineers to place the radiator in the low-pressure area under the seat, which allows for more efficient heat exchange. It also makes for a smaller, cleaner, even more aerodynamic frontal area. Where most sportbikes have bulky radiators at the front of their fairings, cluttering the lines (and fouling aerodynamics), the Tornado Tre's front section is smooth and inviting to the eye. Two vertical intake ducts draw cool air in, directing it to the under-seat radiator.

# Bimota

## YB4 EI

### Another replica racer for the street

Federico Martini designed the original YB4-R as a racer to contest the 1987 TT Formula 1 World Championship series. Virginio Ferrari, riding for Bimota, responded by winning the championship, and for good reason: the YB4-R was considered to be the best-handling motorcycle of its time. Its twin-spar aluminum frame offered near-neutral steering, and the five-valve FZ750 Yamaha engine generated plenty of power. Shortly after winning the F1 title, Bimota produced the YB4 EI, using an FZ750 engine with proprietary electronic fuel injection.

 The YB4 EI was the first production motorcycle to have electronic fuel injection.

 The bike that won the TT Formula 1 World Championship.

 Misano Adriatico World Circuit, near Cattolica, Italy. This is where Massimo Tamburini crashed his Honda 750, prompting him to form Bimota.

 ★ ★ ★ ★
If the YB4 is good enough for Virginio Ferrari, it's good enough for us.

Engine: Liquid-cooled, 749cc, four-stroke, inline four
Horsepower: 121 at 10,500 rpm
Top Speed: 170 miles per hour
Weight: 398 pounds
Value Now: $$$$

# Bimota

## SB8R

### Suzuki's big V-twin finally finds a good home

Ever since the birth of Bimota, the lads from Rimini, Italy, have grafted a variety of engines originating in Japan into exquisite-handling frames of their own design. Perhaps the most unlikely to be featured in those exotic aluminum frames was Suzuki's TL1000R V-twin, since the donor bike was a massive failure in every respect. Every respect except one, that is; in spite of all its many failings, the porky TL-R possessed a fantastic V-twin engine.

 The name *Bimota* was created by combining the founders' names to form a word (from Bianchi, Morri, and Tamburini).

 This is the most affordable Bimota. Even so, it remains costly compared to most other brands.

 Highway 89 from Jackson, Wyoming, to Salt Lake City, Utah, where you can experience gentle curves and long straights to stretch the SB8R's legs.

 ★ ★ ★
The reward is a spirited ride that contains loads of engine torque from the V-twin Suzuki motor.

Engine: Liquid-cooled, 996cc, four-stroke, 90-degree V-twin
Horsepower: 138 at 9,500 rpm
Top Speed: 170 miles per hour
Weight: 392 pounds
Value Now: $$$

# Bimota

## Tesi 3D

**An Odd Duck**

Trellis structures incorporated into the Tesi's front and rear suspension create a truly cutting-edge chassis, one that you'd expect from Bimota. Factor in the unique hub steering and carbon-fiber body panels, and you have one of the most compelling motorcycle designs of all time. Although the Ducati engine is rather conventional, a conventional Ducati engine is no bad thing, especially when it's wrapped in familiar red, white, and gold Bimota livery. It all adds up to remind us why the Rimini, Italy–based company is so special when it comes to presenting something new and provocative to the motorcycle market.

 *Tesi* is Italian for "thesis," which is fitting because designer Pierluigi Marconi based his original 1990 Tesi 1D on his university thesis.

 Only 30 numbered 3Ds were to be built, each costing about $38,400.

 We'll head to Southern California's legendary Rock Store to hang out and show off. Keep your full-coverage helmet on, and somebody might mistake you for Jay Leno.

 ★ ★ ★ ★ ★
That hub steering warrants at least a couple of extra jackets, no?

Engine: Liquid-cooled, 1,078cc, four-stroke, 90-degree V-twin
Horsepower: 95 at 7,200 rpm
Top Speed: n/a
Weight: 370 pounds
Value Now: $$$$

# Bimota

## V-Due

### The one (and only) Bimota engine

The V-Due was a good idea gone bad. Horribly, horribly
bad. Like Damien in *The Omen* bad. The good idea was
that the V-Due should represent Bimota's first proprietary
engine, and not only was it a good idea, but it was also an
ambitious one. Bimota decided its new engine would be
a two-stroke, resurrecting the oil-burner concept by using
sophisticated fuel injection to help the ring-dinger engine
meet modern emissions standards. The idea went bad when
the two-stroke's fuel injection proved faulty and costly to
repair. Indeed, the costs to repair customers' recalled bikes
became so prohibitive that Bimota eventually filed for
bankruptcy in 1999.

 The various engine recalls eventually cost Bimota so much money that they led to the company's bankruptcy.

 The V-Due represented Bimota's (failed) attempt at engine manufacturing.

 To your local Bimota dealer (good luck with that one), so their technicians can tend to the current recall notice for your bike.

 *
You'll need that jacket to stay warm while the mechanics repair your V-Due's engine.

Engine: Liquid-cooled, 499cc,
   two-stroke, 90-degree V-twin
Horsepower: 110 at 9,000 rpm

Top Speed: 165 miles per hour
Weight: 354 pounds
Value Now: $$$

Each DB-7 is hand-built by only two technicians.

 The V-Due buried Bimota in debt and eventual bankruptcy in 1999; the DB-7 helped resurrect the company seven years later.

 This ride is reader's choice: select your favorite stretch of twisty macadam and then have at it with the DB-7!

 ★ ★ ★ ★
The DB-7 is considered one of the best-handling motorcycles in the world.

Engine: Liquid-cooled, 1,098cc, four-stroke, 90-degree V-twin
Horsepower: 165 at at 9,000 rpm

Top Speed: 160 miles per hour
Weight: 375 pounds
Value Now: $$$$

### How to improve on an already great bike

How do you improve on a Ducati Testastretta, anyway? If you're an engineer hunkered in the Bimota works factory at Rimini, Italy, you do it very carefully. Step one is to lift out the Testastretta engine, setting it aside while you build one of your patented no-flex frames made of alloy and carbon fiber. Next, equip the frame with a fully adjustable Marzocchi race-spec 43mm inverted fork and an Extreme Tech rear shock absorber, and then insert the engine. Your 379-pound package is now one of the best sportbikes on the planet. Now that's Italian!

# Bimota

## Mantra

**Today's mantra: this is really a Bimota, this is really a Bimota . . .**

Two things you need to know about the Mantra: Its bold lines were the work of French designer Sacha Lakic, and in the ancient Indic language of Sanskrit, *mantra* translates to "tool of thought." Perhaps Lakic conceived the Mantra as Bimota's answer to Ducati's Monster, but that's not how the motorcycle-buying public saw it. When the Mantra was revealed for the first time at the Cologne show in 1997, many people *thought* this was a concept bike. It wasn't; Bimota actually produced the insectlike machine. Unfortunately, the company didn't really sell very many, marking the start of a decline that eventually ended in receivership. Hey, even Ted Williams struck out every now and then.

 Bimota used engines from Japanese motorcycles for its early designs.

 Considered by many Bimota fans (called "bimotistas" by the faithful) to be the redheaded stepchild of the Rimini-based family.

 You should only ride this at night, and keep the dark shield down on your full-coverage helmet.

 *
And people blame the V-Due for Bimota's bankruptcy!

Engine: Air-cooled, 904cc, four-stroke, 90-degree V-twin
Horsepower: 85 at 7,000 rpm

Top Speed: 125 miles per hour
Weight: 423 pounds
Value Now: $

**Okay, we'll say it—this is a Wolf in sheep's clothing**

On paper, the Wolf should handle like a dog. A wheelbase of nearly 84 inches coupled with a combined steering head angle (neck and raked triple trees) of 45 degrees should be the ingredients for a rather unwieldy bike. And let's not forget the 23-inch (front) and 20-inch (rear) tire diameters. But, in truth, the Wolf responds well to rider input. Think of it as a Wolf in sheep's clothing, and the end result is a predictable ride that gets you from Point A to Point B in true custom-bike style. Who says that a long custom bike must handle like a drunken sailor on Saturday night?

 S&S Cycle developed the X-Wedge engine to accept large displacements of up to 150 cubic inches.

 One of the first bikes to be powered by S&S Cycle's X-Wedge engine.

 Take the Wolf to Yellowstone National Park where you can hang out with the real wolves.

 ★ ★ ★
My, what big buttons and zippers you have.

Engine: Air-cooled, 1,976cc (121-cubic-inch), four-stroke, 56-degree V-twin
Horsepower: n/a
Top Speed: n/a
Weight: 770 pounds
Value Now: $$

# BMW

## R32

### Building a better "stupid conveyance"

What's an airplane engine designer to do when his company has been banned from building airplane engines by the Versailles Treaty? Well, if you're Max Friz, chief design engineer of *Bayerische Moteren Werke GmbH*, otherwise known as *BMW*, you tell the allies to piss off and keep on designing airplane engines illegally. At least until the Allied Control Commission confiscates all of your plans and blueprints. Then you'd better find something else to build. In the case of BMW, which already owned the struggling Otto motorcycle company, builder of a lousy little two-stroke called the *Flink*, you build a motorcycle, even though Friz considered the motorcycle a "stupid conveyance."

 Max Friz used the famous blue-and-white "spinning propeller" BMW badge as a token act of defiance.

 Turned the then-common longitudinal opposed-twin engine design on its head (or at least sideways).

 Somewhere without traffic, given the token stopping power of the crude braking system.

 ★ ★ Other than the rebellious BMW propeller emblem, the first Beemer is about as rebellious as a bowtie.

Engine: Air-cooled, side valve, horizontally opposed twin
Horsepower: 8.5 at 3,300 rpm
Top Speed: 55 miles per hour
Weight: 264 pounds
Value Now: $$$$$

John Penton (of soon-to-come Penton motorcycles fame) rode an R69S to set a new record time for New York to Los Angeles, 77 hours and 53 minutes.

 The R69S' entire reason for being was to provide a sporty alternative to BMW's less-than-glamorous touring models.

 As long as the road's paved, the R69S isn't especially picky, particularly if it's one of the Earles-fork versions.

 ★★ These bikes were intentionally conservative, with the R69S made to stand slightly apart because of its lightly hot-rodded engine.

Engine: Air-cooled, pushrod-operated, OHV, four-valve, horizontally opposed twin
Horsepower: 42 at 7,000 rpm

Top Speed: 109 miles per hour (claimed)
Weight: 450 pounds (claimed, wet)
Value Now: $$$$

**"Only touring bikes? Nein, that is not all we make. Look at this! 42 horsepower!"**

Believe it or not, even 40 years ago BMW was looking for a way to escape the perception that it was solely a purveyor of dull, slow, who-cares touring bikes. And, as always, the answer was the same: offer a breathed-on model with extra performance, and *shazam!* job done. The R69S lump had bigger carbs, a hotter cam, and a significantly higher compression ratio (9.5:1 versus 7.5:1) than its predecessor, the R68. The R69S also benefited from a leading-link, Earles-type fork—which was actually a leftover from the previous model that was geared toward sidecar use but was superior to the telescopic forks of the era. Result: a reliable, superbly finished, gentleman's express motorcycle that could cruise effortlessly at 100 miles per hour.

# BMW

## R90S

### Teutonic touring luxury

At a price of $3,430, BMW's R90S rocked the motorcycling world back on its heels when it was introduced in 1974. That price might not seem that high now, but it surely was 36 years ago, when a Ducati 750 Sport retailed for $2,250, Moto Guzzi's V7 Sport cost $2,490, and a Kawasaki Z1 went for $1,995. Was the R90S worth its princely tariff? That depends on your point of view. If you were looking for a piece of hardcore sporting tackle, then, no. If, however, your sights were set on the ultimate grand touring machine, with near-perfect ergonomics and a grunty engine that could dust a Z1 in top-gear roll-ons, allied with supersoft, long-travel suspension that smothered bumps with Teutonic efficiency, then the answer was a loud, unqualified, yes.

 In 1976, a factory-backed team not only won the very first AMA Superbike race at Daytona but went on to take the first AMA Superbike Championship as well.

 Primarily, it's famous for its gold-plated price, but it's also known for embodying grand touring perfection—in the German idiom, that is.

 The autobahn, pure and simple, with a destination suitably far away.

 ★ ★ ★ ★
Yes, four, largely because of the bike's price but also because it flew in the face of then-contemporary high-performance motorcycles.

Engine: Air-cooled, pushrod-
   operated, four-valve,
   horizontally opposed twin
Horsepower: n/a

Top Speed: 126 miles per hour
Weight: 498 pounds
Value Now: $$$$

**I'm a space cowboy—bet you weren't ready for that**

Just as its elder stablemate, the R90S, did two years prior, BMW's 1976 R100RS burst onto the scene and immediately forced us all to recalibrate what we thought BMWs were capable of doing—mechanically, dynamically, and esthetically. In the engine department, a model-wide field trip to the boring bar yielded 980cc displacement. Various other fettles and mods all seem to come under the heading: "Make fitter for a purpose." Most visible, of course, both to the eye and to the R100RS' reason for being, is that magnificent fairing—21 pounds of it, relatively easily removed, wind-tunnel-tested for stability, and with such superb weather protection that one can only imagine any improvement would come from a fully sealed egg.

 The wind-tunnel-tested full fairing was claimed to lower drag by a whopping 17.4 percent compared to the quarter fairing on the R90S.

 After the acclaimed R90S, the R100RS represented another leap forward for two-wheel sophistication.

 Er, the autobahn, of course, but one magically connected to California Highway 1, and also to a deep-rural, desert, two-lane road during a low full moon.

 ★ ★ ★ ★ ★
Yes, five, simply because nothing else in motorcycling looked—or worked—like that.

Engine: Air-cooled, pushrod-
   operated, four-valve,
   horizontally opposed twin
Horsepower: 70 at 7,250 rpm
   (claimed)

Top Speed: 124 miles per hour
   (claimed)
Weight: 535 pounds (claimed)
Value Now: $$$$

# BMW

## R80 G/S

### Of bumblebees and Boxers

Just as a bumblebee supposedly shouldn't be able to fly, it seems equally unlikely a BMW Boxer twin should not make a decent off-road bike. And yet both actions have occurred, with no visible legerdemain or wire fu. For BMW, it started with the 1980 R80 G/S, essentially an R80/7 engine in a modified R65 frame but with a crucial difference: the Monolever rear suspension with single-side swingarm. The R80 G/S was the first production motorcycle to use such a device. The motorcycle also introduced a new class, which at that time went by many names: the big trailie and the adventure-tourer, to name two. To that, the German firm added *reiseenduro*, or touring enduro, perhaps the most apt but least used. A hit with the public, modified versions of the R80 G/S also manhandled the rough-and-ready Paris–Dakar Rally, winning it four times, in 1981, 1983, 1984, and 1985.

 The G/S at the end of the bike's name/model designation stands for *gelände/strasse*, or, in English, off-road/street, tipping its hand as to its intentions.

 All by itself, the R80 G/S not only created the adventure-tourer/big trailie class but has owned it ever since.

 'Round the block or 'round the world, pavement or not, BMW's R80 G/S is there, up on its toes and ready to take you the full distance.

 ★ ★ ★ ★
It didn't happen overnight, but the engineers of BMW's R80 G/S ultimately changed the face of motorcycling in one of the least likely ways imaginable: by making a successful off-road racer out of a BMW flat twin streetbike.

Engine: Air-cooled, pushrod-operated, four-valve, horizontally opposed twin
Horsepower: 50 at 6,500 rpm

Top Speed: 104 miles per hour
Weight: 410 pounds (wet)
Value Now: $$$

At the U.S. K1 introduction, someone from BMW thought it would be a good idea to wipe the tires down with Armor All. Several members of the press didn't even make it out of the parking lot.

BMW intended the K1 to be the firm's answer to the Japanese hegemony in the superbike class—but not necessarily a sportbike.

If not fun, fun, fun, at least fahr'n, fahr'n, fahr'n, on the autobahn, of course.

★ ★ ★ ★
In one respect, the K1 showed the German firm at its quirky and fearless best: it was prepared to go to almost any length to create something *different* yet something that was still very much a BMW motorcycle.

Engine: Liquid-cooled, DOHC, 16-valve, longitudinal, inline four
Horsepower: 100 at 8,000 rpm
Top Speed: 149 miles per hour (claimed)
Weight: 515 pounds (claimed, wet)
Value Now: $$$

## BMW tries to knock one out of the park

By the end of the 1980s, BMW once again had to overcome the prejudice that it made "old men's bikes," fit for little more than chasing horizons at suitably decreased speeds and equipped with dull flat twins whose vibration could massage their ancient riders' prostates long enough to get to their destination. So BMW picked up its bat, pointed at the bleachers, and swung—coming up with the K1, BMW's interpretation of a superbike, and not exactly a home run. Certainly, the K1 was a remarkable motorcycle—for BMW. It had a hot-rodded K100 motor pumping out a claimed 100 horsepower (yet it wasn't as quick as some 600s); extensive, radically styled, and extremely aerodynamic bodywork; a single-side Paralever swingarm; and, of course, more. But it was by no means a real superbike. Still, it's satisfying in its own way and needs to be ridden to experience its stalwart Teutonic-ness.

# BMW

## R1200GS Adventure

**When you're bound to wander way out yonder**

Apparently the Marlboro Man myth lives. It seems red-blooded men everywhere fantasize about riding off into the sunset, taking on whatever terrain terra can throw at them, and—maybe—finding that perfect romance, either in a Romanian gypsy encampment or perhaps even farther off the trail, in a tiny African village. For them, BMW offers its R1200GS Adventure, the most qualified traveling companion for such a trek. (That is, as long as you're a few inches taller than the 5 foot 6 inches of the average human; otherwise, the 36-inch saddle height could be forbidding.) As it is, the GS is certainly up to the task, but various aftermarket companies can make the bike even more adventure-worthy. Of course, most of these motorcycles are used as city or touring bikes. But that's okay—your secret is safe with us.

 Some of the finest aftermarket accessories for the world-traveling R1200GS Adventure can be found from Touratech, at www.touratech.de.

 For the rider with far, distant horizons on the brain, there is no better motorcycle. After all, it worked for Ewan and Charley in the *Long Way Round*, didn't it? What more could you want?

 In your dreams? La Ruta Maya or the Dakar Rally, or anywhere off the beaten path, off the grid. In reality? Route 66, or maybe the Route Napoleon. Or Wall Street.

 ★ ★ ★ ★
An easy four, just for its mind- and route-expanding capabilities.

Engine: Air- and oil-cooled, DOHC, eight-valve, horizontally opposed twin
Horsepower: 110 at 7,750 rpm (claimed)
Weight: n/a
Top Speed: 120-plus miles per hour (claimed)
Value Now: $$$$

# BMW

At BMW's request, Ricardo plc (founded by Sir Harry Ricardo, one of the greatest engine development specialists ever) reconfigured the K1200R's combustion chambers, spec'd new cams, and flowed the head to get a substantial performance boost for the K1300R.

Oh, nothing special: just being the most potent, quickest, and fastest hyper-naked bike available on the planet.

Oh, somewhere very, very fast, please. Maybe South Africa, which has the required ultrafast roads but with an almost nonexistent traffic cop presence.

★ ★ ★ ★ ★

It's impossible to argue with the results the K1300R generates: hair-levitating performance, a metaphorical raised middle finger to speed limit and nanny states everywhere.

Engine: Liquid-cooled, DOHC, 16-valve, inline four
Horsepower: 173 at 9,500 rpm (claimed)

Top Speed: 155 miles per hour
Weight: 536 pounds (claimed)
Value Now: $$$

**Dinner with Mr. Jason Voorhees, anyone?**

BMW is one of the few manufacturers that can pull it off, "it" being the near-perfect union of bull-goose-loony hyper-naked bike attitude and a heaping measure of all-around usefulness. A ride on the K1200R/1300R is like going to the house of *Friday the 13th*'s Jason Voorhees for dinner, only to find out that, while he still has designs on sticking you, he's also learned to make an incredible risotto and displays impeccable table manners. It's the four-cylinder engine that displays the K-R's hotcha side, with 173 (claimed) peak horsepower (K1300R) making sub-3-second 0 to 60 mile-per-hour times possible. The chassis' stability (courtesy of a lengthy wheelbase), BMW's Duolever front end, plus its 535-pound wet weight provide a measure of calmness without blunting the bike's exuberance. A lengthy list of worthwhile options—ABS, ESA II electronic suspension adjustment, and ASC (automatic stability control)—add character and expand the K1300R's dynamic range even further.

# BMW

## C1

**BMW makes a scooter, as only BMW can**

It's hardly an original notion—nor does it amount to unassailable evidence—but certain motorcycles emanating from BMW suggest the firm's water coolers just might be spiked with an unspecified psychotropic substance. Take, for instance, BMW's curious C1, which might be viewed as a combination of car and scooter. BMW worked overtime to provide the odd little device with carlike safety via crumple zones and an aluminum roll cage. According to BMW, the C1 was sufficiently safe so that the operator didn't need a helmet. And while several countries waived their helmet-law requirements, the United Kingdom and Sweden did not, essentially rendering what was perhaps the C1's central appeal to buyers null and void. It sold only for two years: 2001–2002.

 BMW is attempting to revive the C1, but with a zero-emissions electric motor, with its C1-E concept vehicle.

 BMW claimed the C1 offered safety equal to a Euro compact car in a head-on collision.

 Urban, urban, urban.

 ★ ★ ★
An interesting, if misguided, attempt to sidestep Euro traffic laws.

Engine: Liquid-cooled, SOHC, four-valve single
Horsepower: 18 at 9,000 rpm

Top Speed: 70 miles per hour
Weight: 408 pounds (claimed, dry)
Value Now: $$$

## F800S/ST

Mechanically the two F-bikes are all but identical, but there are a few differences. The ST has a taller, wider, conventional handlebar in place of the S bike's clip-on; a full fairing with taller screen; differently styled wheels; and saddlebag mounts.

BMW's F twins are the first bikes targeted at entry or re-entry riders for some time. To its credit, though, both bikes punch well above their weight so that they're amply entertaining, even to those with decades of riding under their belts.

For the sportier S, twisty, medium-speed back roads. For the ST, similar roads but perhaps more open, more flowing—more in tune with its sport-touring nature.

★ ★
Rebellion? Hardly—unless you mean against type.

| | |
|---|---|
| Engine: Liquid-cooled, DOHC, eight-valve, parallel twin | Weight: n/a |
| Horsepower: 81.6 at 8,000 rpm | Top Speed: 135 miles per hour |
| | Value Now: $$$ |

### Two of a kind

During BMW's last self-reinvention in the previous decade, the mavens in Munich mulled over the matter of making a middleweight motorcycle for entry-level and re-entry riders. Such a bike should be welcoming and secure but with a level of performance sufficient to grow as riders' confidence did likewise; and it should ensure they wanted to remain part of BMW's tribe. *Und voila*: the F800S (sporty) and F800ST (sport-touring). Virtually identical, the two BMWs fulfill their marching orders with ease and skill, and their acceleration and road manners belie their seemingly ordinary station in life as mere learners' bikes. As a result, the F800S/ST should satisfy riders across a broad range of experience, from novice to talented.

## R1200ST

The R1200S claimed a number of records for the venerable Boxer motor: fastest, most powerful, and highest compression ratio.

The R1200S was the closest thing to a true sportbike BMW had ever produced—that is, until the HP2 Sport appeared.

Mile upon mile of fast, smooth, twisting road, possibly with a destination some distance away—or not.

★ ★ ★
The R1200S made for a strong undercurrent to BMW's typically staid reputation (at the time), but not quite strong enough. This was no sportbike—yet.

| | |
|---|---|
| Engine: Air- and oil-cooled, high-cam, eight-valve, horizontally opposed twin | Weight: n/a |
| | Top Speed: n/a |
| | Price New: $14,725 |
| Horsepower: 122 at 8,250 rpm (claimed) | Value Now: $$$$ |

### Decidedly not your father's BMW . . . unless your father's Helmut Dahne

Every now and then, BMW's reputation descends to that of a manufacturer of efficient and comfy—but slow and somewhat dull—touring bikes. The R1200ST, over its short, two-year life, was built to dispel that notion. And, boy, did it ever. This is a Boxer with some 'tude, backed up by a claimed 122 horsepower at 8,250 rpm and 89 percent of its peak torque (83 lbs-ft.) from 3,500 rpm to redline, 8,800 rpm. Telelever front suspension (especially with optional Öhlins units) does a fine job of separating steering and braking forces, while the Paralever rear end masks over the shaft drive's peccadilloes. Not quite a full-on sportbike—BMW says it's a Character-Sport motorcycle, whatever that is—the R1200ST comes tantalizingly close.

# BMW

## HP2 Sport

 Each cam opens one intake and one exhaust valve, rather than pairs. What's more, the radial-valve arrangement means the cams are conically ground rather than the conventional flat lobe faces.

 The fastest, sportiest Boxer twin yet—no mean feat for an engine design that sprang from an inline six that powered Fokker D VIIs in World War I.

 Oh, fast and twisty, please. And preferably without too many current Japanese liter-size sportbikes, *nicht wahr?*

 ★ ★ ★ ★
In truth, remarkable only for BMW, and hardly a trendsetter (or a pacesetter).

Engine: Air-/oil-cooled, DOHC, eight-valve, horizontally opposed twin
Horsepower: 130 at 8,750 rpm (claimed)

Top Speed: 124 miles per hour (claimed)
Weight: 392 pounds (claimed, dry)
Value Now: $$$$

### The Boxer finally learns to really fly

If you're really a neophyte to motorcycling—and to cars as well—you might not know BMW made its bones building aircraft engines, courtesy of engine designer Max Friz. Or that homeboy Max also designed the first BMW, the R32, with its horizontally opposed Boxermotor in 1923. To see that same basic configuration now in BMW's HP2 Sport, with four-valve DOHC heads and pumping out a claimed 130 bhp, almost strains credibility. Then, you find out it's attached to every high-tech piece BMW can throw at it, including a self-supporting carbon-fiber cowl and subframe, BMW's Telelever front and Paralever rear suspensions, 2D Systems instruments, and much, much more. It's simply stunning to see such an engine dragged forward through almost a century of technology. Nice work, Max.

# BMW

Despite other R-models getting the R1200GS' engine upgrades (double overhead cams and four-valve heads from BMW's HP2 super-sporter), it looks like the R1200R will have to wait one more year—if not longer.

The latest—so far—normal/naked/standard flat-twin-powered bike gets fresh dollops of technology to make the R1200R the most sophisticated Boxer bike yet.

Almost any paved road—be it urban, freeway, or country—at a friendly, spirited pace.

★ ★ ★

Three, because of the R1200R's combination of utter conventionality and cutting-edge options, such as electronic suspension adjustment and automatic stability control.

Engine: Air- and oil-cooled, SIHC, eight-valve, horizontally opposed twin
Horsepower: 109 at 7,500 rpm (claimed)
Top Speed: 120-plus miles per hour (estimated)
Weight: n/a
Value Now: $$$$

## A higher standard

Virtually every year since 1923, which saw the introduction of BMW's first motorcycle (the R32), the German manufacturer has kept in its lineup a naked, standard motorcycle, powered by a Boxer twin engine. These days, however, anthropomorphically speaking, it's possible the R32 and the current 2010 R1200R might not even recognize each other as having the same ancestors, except for the BMW roundel on the tank. For instance, the R1200R's Telelever front and Paralever rear suspensions bear little to no resemblance to the R32's twin-cantilever, trailing-axle design and rigid rear end. Likewise, despite their similar configuration, the R1200R's Boxer motor could have come from another planet compared to the R32's. Add in options like ESA, ASC, ABS, and more, and it's easy to see just how far the Boxer bikes have come—and why BMW has kept a standard flat twin in its lineup since day one.

# BMW

## S1000RR

**BMW points to the bleachers and knocks one clean out of the park**

There's some debate as to when—if ever—BMW made a *real* sportbike. But there's no such argument about when the German firm built its first *superbike*. That would be 2009, with the introduction of the startlingly capable (and most un-BMW-like) S1000RR. However, as a sportbike, the S1000RR excels, with more than 160 horsepower at the rear wheels and (among other things) the most prescient traction-control software yet, with four discrete settings. And, as a superbike, the BMW acquitted itself more than honorably in its first season. Lead rider and two-time superbike world champion Troy Corser scored 12 top-10 placings in BMW's first season (2009), set the fastest lap in the first race at Australia's Philip Island, and scored BMW's first podium at Monza in May, 2010. You can be assured there's much more to come.

 The S1000RR's traction-control system offers four settings: Rain, Sport, Race, and Slick. Slick is accessible only by inserting a key in an under-seat slot.

 This is the first BMW built to be a superbike from the get-go, not merely intended to be hot-rodded into one.

 Well, pretty much every paved twisty road on the planet. Or, every road-race circuit.

 ★ ★ ★
Why only three? Because it's so conventional, lacking any of the typical BMW earmarks, such as Duolever or Paralever, to name but two.

Engine: Liquid-cooled, DOHC, 16-valve, inline four
Horsepower: 193 at 13,000 rpm (claimed)
Top Speed: 180 miles per hour (claimed)
Weight: n/a
Value Now: $$$$

The cast aluminum wheels were one of the bike's few innovations that would eventually become popular among motorcyclists.

 The first (and last) motorcycle ever to use this frame configuration.

 To a romantic bed and breakfast in Krasna Lipa.

 ★ ★ ★ ★ ★
Because it's so far out there that the word *conventional* has a court order to maintain at least five hundred yards of distance between it and the Bohmerland.

Engine: Air-cooled, pushrod, two-valve, single
Horsepower: 16 at 3,000 rpm (claimed)
Top Speed: 60 miles per hour (claimed)
Weight: n/a
Value Now: $$$$$

**When no one knows better, the sky's the limit**

In the early years of motorcycling, the basic design of the machine had yet to be set in stone. Thus, designers were willing to try any idea, regardless of how far-fetched it might seem today. This is how we ended up with most of the technical advances that make today's motorcycles as good as they are. But on occasion early designers went too far. Such was the case in 1924, when one Albin Liebisch began manufacturing motorcycles in Krasna Lipa, a village in what was then northern Bohemia. While Liebisch used a fairly conventional engine (albeit one with hemispherical heads), his chassis, a long, low affair constructed of steel tubing, was anything but conventional. To emphasize the unusual nature of his frame, Liebisch painted it bright yellow. In spite of being relatively fast and stable, the Bohmerland was too unconventional for most buyers, and Liebisch sold fewer than 1000 units over the machine's fifteen-year production run.

# Boss Hoss

## Boss Hoss

**So what'd they do with the other two wheels and tires? And where's the steering wheel?**

No, it's not a rolling engine stand for a hot rod V-8. This is a motorcycle, one you ride on the streets and byways of America. And, as you can see, the Boss Hoss is as American a bike as you're going to find, matching two-wheel basics with Chevrolet pedigree. Despite its weight, girth, and, well, intimidating presence, the Hoss isn't all that difficult to maneuver or command in traffic. And when you want to accelerate quickly, all you need to do is dig your spurs into its haunches and then hold on!

 Originally, the company was going to be called "Boss Hog," but Harley objected.

 Riding the Boss Hoss means you never have to say, "Wow, I could have had a V-8!"

 Nevada's Highway 50, termed the "Loneliest Road."

 ★ ★ ★ ★ ★ Make sure the jackets aren't made of horsehide—that could offend other Hoss owners.

Engine: Liquid-cooled, 376-cubic-inch, four-stroke V-8
Horsepower: 445 at 5,750 rpm

Top Speed: Would *you* ride this bike WFO?
Weight: 1,065 pounds
Value Now: $$$$

According to more than one source, Honda applied pressure on Bridgestone to cease building bikes and concentrate on the tire business—which it did.

The first motorcycle from Japan capable of giving a Triumph Bonneville a run for its money through the gears.

Anyplace that has a succession of stop signs or traffic lights that allow you to accelerate through the first few gears.

★ ★
Real rebels don't quit just because Honda says so.

| Engine: Air-cooled, 345cc, two-stroke, vertical twin | Top Speed: 95 miles per hour |
|---|---|
| Horsepower: 37 at 7,500 rpm | Weight: 354 pounds |
| | Value Now: $$ |

**A quick bike that, as you might guess, rolled on Bridgestone tires**

By 1967, the age of the two-stroke motorcycle had reached its zenith, and among the quickest of those oil-burners was Bridgestone's 350 GTO. Conceived by the same company that supplied tires to the Japanese motorcycle industry, the GTO was considered to be a handful during acceleration. *Cycle World*'s editors flatly stated, "Further, it's, as we've said before, a full-size motorcycle, as big and as fast as any 500—and considerably faster than most." But speed wasn't enough to keep Bridgestone in the business of building motorcycles, and production of all models—the 90, 175, and 350—was suspended in 1971.

# Britten

## V1000

**A friend of John Britten's once said, "John did not just want to win; he wanted to dazzle." That he did.**
Every now and then, a frighteningly talented individual comes along and, almost at a stroke, forces everyone to reevaluate their most cherished beliefs and conventions. Motorcycling had New Zealander John Britten as one such individual, and his V1000 race bike, which he essentially hand-built in a space the size (and general sophistication) of a garden shed. There, he and a hearty band of Kiwis cast engine crankcases and heads to build a 985cc, fuel-injected, 165-horsepower V-twin of Britten's own design, then wrapped layer after resin-dipped layer of carbon fiber to create a girder front fork and a swingarm, both of which attached to that thunderous V-twin without a conventional frame. As Tim Hanna wrote in his book, *John Britten*, "Even though the bikes are now more than a decade old, they remain exotic, and staggeringly fast."

 John Britten himself felt his creation might be *too* over the top, saying one time, "The power can be a bit unsettling. I'm frightened by it."

 The V1000 earns its place in moto-history because it succeeded as the pure, innovative expression of one man, John Britten.

 Daytona, circa 1992, where Britten rider Andrew Stroud shamed the factory Ducatis by wheelie-ing up to them, then passing them on the back wheel as well.

 ★ ★ ★ ★ ★
Britten's utter lack of constraints resulted in a ground-breaking motorcycle that owed little to what came before it and is still considered ferociously fast.

Engine: Liquid-cooled, DOHC, eight-valve, 60-degree V-twin
Horsepower: 166 at 11,800 rpm (claimed)
Top Speed: 188 miles per hour (claimed)
Weight: n/a
Value Now: $$$$$

T. E. Lawrence was a personal friend of George Brough and named each of his motorcycles in succession *George I*, *George II*, and so on up to *George VII*.

The SS100 embodied the "superior" part of the bike's name in every way—Brough stood for superior parts and materials, build quality, fit and finish, performance, and speed.

Endless B roads, as the British call them, in their singularly green and pleasant land.

★ ★ ★ ★ ★
Simply put, nothing like Brough's bikes—each one handcrafted and custom-built—had been offered before or has been offered since.

| | |
|---|---|
| Engine: Air-cooled, four-valve, OHV, 50-degree V-twin | Top Speed: 100-plus miles per hour |
| Horsepower: 52 at 5,000 rpm | Weight: 400 pounds |
| | Value Now: $$$$$ |

### "Atmosphere disturbers" of the absolute first order

T. E. Lawrence, a.k.a. Lawrence of Arabia, wrote, "A skittish motor-bike with a touch of blood in it is better than all of the riding animals on earth." He was speaking of one of history's most admired and sought-after motorcycles, then as now: the Brough Superior SS100. The motorcycles that bore George Brough's name were built to the highest possible standards, as well as being custom-made to the whims of each owner. Perhaps the most commonly used powerplant for the SS100 (Super Sports, and 100 stood for the top speed in miles per hour it could easily achieve) was a 976cc V-twin from well-known U.K. engine builder J. A. Prestwich. Modified engines ensured Broughs were as well-regarded for the dozens of speed records they earned as they were for build quality. George Brough wrote all the ad copy himself and referred to the machines as "atmosphere disturbers."

# BSA

## 441 Victor

The 441cc Victor engine was based on the C15, which was a 250cc single-cylinder engine.

Back-to-back 500cc motocross world championships.

Cruise New York's Finger Lakes District before jogging east for a stop at Unadilla Valley Sports Center for a tribute lap on one of the best natural-turf motocross courses in America.

★ ★ ★
You can work up a sweat kick-starting this high-compression single, so dress lightly at first.

Engine: Air-cooled, 441cc, four-stroke single-cylinder
Horsepower: 30 at 6,000 rpm

Top Speed: 93 miles per hour
Weight: 305 pounds
Value Now: $$$

### Hard to start, cantankerous to keep running, a pure delight to ride

By the mid-1960s, motorcycle manufacturers rarely considered single-cylinder motors as candidates for their large-bore models. Instead, twins (and, later, triples and fours) studded the field. Even so, it was in 1966 that BSA introduced the thumper known as the 441 Victor to the lineup. The overhead-valve engine, with a bore and stroke of 79x90mm, was originally developed for 500cc motocross racing, and the 441 propelled Englishman Jeff Smith to world titles in 1964 and 1965. Buoyed by that success, a production version hit the streets for 1966, and for the next few years the swinging single set the bar for its class.

## A65LC Lightning Clubman

**Bonnie beater**

In production for barely a year, real Lightning Clubmans are extremely rare. So you're probably riding an imposter. Does it have a shiny, chrome, two-into-one exhaust? Rearsets, a cool solo seat with a racing hump, and clubman bars? Twin carbs and a close-ratio gearbox? It's still probably just a tarted-up Lightning, but ride it anyway; you'll enjoy yourself. Mike Hailwood did. He used a Lightning to beat the Bonnevilles at Silverstone in 1965. Well, his was a real Clubman, right down to the gold paint and optional 190mm front brake. And, since he was Mike the Bike, he got the optional fiberglass fairing too.

**?** James Bond Girl Fiona Volpe rode a Lightning in *Thunderball*. Hers wasn't a real Clubman either, but it did have the optional missile launchers.

★ Ridden by Mike the Bike.

Silverstone Circuit, Towcester, Northhamptonshire, United Kingdom.

★ ★ ★ ★ Everybody likes a good David-versus-Goliath story.

Engine: Air-cooled, 654cc, OHV, two-valve-per-cylinder, four-stroke, inline twin

Horsepower: 51 at 6,750 rpm
Top Speed: 108 miles per hour
Weight: n/a
Value Now: $$$

# BSA

## DBD34 Gold Star Clubman

### A real dynamo

Want a bike that defines "high-strung"? Whose engine, after 19 years of development, was built by one set of hands from meticulously chosen components (one of which was called a dynamo), then was bench-tested by those same caring hands before it ever saw a frame? Take a few laps around the Mountain Circuit on a DBD34 Gold Star Clubman. The DBD34 came with clip-ons and a detachable electrical system, so you could ride to the Isle of Man, ditch your lights and battery, go out and win your Clubman's race, come back in, put the lights back on, and ride home. Which isn't exactly how Bernard Codd did it in 1956, but you get the idea. Just the sort of performance you'd expect from a bike with a dynamo in it.

 With roots going back to 1937, the DBD34's engine was pretty well tricked out. Learn to love the high-revving melodrama. You'd be on edge if you were worked over that long too.

 BSA's 350 and 500 Gold Stars dominated just about every Isle of Man Clubman's TT race, climaxing in 1956 when Bernard Codd won both the Junior and Senior classes. He also had a little dynamo in him.

 Mountain Circuit, Isle of Man.

 ★ ★ ★ ★ ★
A single built in 1956 that revs to 8,000 rpm and propels a motorcycle a tenth again past a ton. You'd better have five pairs of matching leather pants. And boots. And gloves. And an open-face helmet and goggles. It's that cool.

Engine: Air-cooled, 400cc, OHV,
two-valve-per-cylinder,
four-stroke, inline twin
Horsepower: 42 at 7,000 rpm

Top Speed: 110 miles per hour
Weight: n/a
Value Now: $$$$

If Edward Turner hadn't been so cantankerous, the Rocket 3 and the Trident might have been released several years before the CB750 instead of several weeks before, thus preserving the British motorcycle industry.

That awesome sound only a triple can make.

North Circular Road past the Ace Café, London, United Kingdom.

★ ★ ★ ★
Too darn late to a party that was just getting started.

Engine: Air-cooled, OHV, two-valve-per-cylinder, four-stroke, inline triple
Horsepower: 58 at 5.000

Top Speed: 115 miles per hour
Weight: n/a
Value Now: $$$

## Four weeks of world domination

For a bike made by a company called Birmingham Small Arms, the Rocket 3 seems oddly misplaced. It's more of a cannon than a pistol. Officially put into prototype development the moment Edward Turner retired in 1964, it was the last spasm of BSA's last climax. Maybe if Honda hadn't introduced the CB750 a month later. . . . Some say minor differences like the frame distinguished a Rocket 3 from a Triumph Trident. Minor differences like the frame! As if the twin-cradle Beezer design was just an exercise in style and had nothing to do with how much more planted it felt than the Trumpet in a fast sweeper! The Power Egg timing covers? Okay, they were for looks, but, c'mon, brand identity is important too.

# Buell

## S1 Lightning

**Thunderbolts and lightnings, very, very frightening!**
The Buell S1 Lightning struck a nerve in the American motorcycle market that brought out, well, the worst in our behavior. The S1's stubby wheelbase and steep steering head angle—55 inches and 25 degrees, respectively—encouraged rowdy conduct. You know, wheelies, stoppies, and burn-outs, those sorts of things. In 1998 Buell followed the S1 with the S1 White Lightning, a similar model with 101 horsepower. Oh, behave.

 The first motorcycle to wear the Buell name badge was actually a road racer powered by an Armstrong, a square-four, two-stroke engine that originated in England.

 This was Buell Motorcycles' first "civilized" hot rod model.

 In a 1995 article, *Cycle World* magazine described the S1 Lightning as "king of the truly demented road." You get the picture.

 ★ ★ ★
You'll feel like Thor riding this bike, and after a few miles, your theat will be thore too, thanks to that thin theat.

Engine: Air-cooled, 1,203cc, four-stroke, 45-degree V-twin
Horsepower: 91 at 5,800 rpm
Top Speed: 124 miles per hour
Weight: 425 pounds
Value Now: $

# Buell

## Ulysses XB12X

**Going where no Buell has gone before**
Pick a spot on a map, and if a motorcycle can roll to it and over it, chances are you can do so on a Buell Ulysses XB12X, a bike that's just as home off-road as it is on pavement. Credit that to ample suspension travel: 6.5 inches in the fork and 6.4 inches in the rear shock, 7 inches of ground clearance, and ergonomics that would satisfy a motocross racer.

 The Ulysses' final-drive belt was developed by Goodyear to hold up under the rigors of off-road riding.

 The first Buell engineered specifically for on- and off-road use. All other Buells that went off the road only did so because of rider error.

 Explore the San Bernardino Mountains in Southern California, where the paved roads offer inviting twists and turns.

 ★ ★
One jacket for highway use, the other jacket for off-highway riding.

Engine: Air-cooled, 1,203cc, four-stroke, 45-degree V-twin
Horsepower: 103 at 6,800 rpm
Top Speed: 131 miles per hour
Weight: 471 pounds
Value Now: $$

The 1125R Helicon engine was developed jointly by Buell and Rotax. By the way: Buell Motorcycles is no longer in business.

This was the first, and only, liquid-cooled Buell engine.

A nice place to enjoy the 1125R is in Buell's home state of Wisconsin.

★ ★ ★
The 1125R's refined chassis takes a lot of the work out of the ride.

| | |
|---|---|
| Engine: Liquid-cooled, 1,125cc, four-stroke, 72-degree V-twin | Top Speed: 161 miles per hour |
| Horsepower: 146 at 9,800 rpm | Weight: 375 pounds |
| | Value Now: $$ |

**The final, and fastest, bike Buell ever made for the street**

*Cycle World* staffers deemed the 1125R the best-handling Buell the magazine ever tested. That fact alone warrants must-ride status for the 1125R, the first Buell to utilize liquid cooling for its engine (which is supplied by Rotax of Austria). And with 146 horsepower on tap, the 1125R ranks as the fastest streetbike the Troy, Wisconsin, company ever served up. The engine was packaged in a compact chassis—what Erik Buell described as *mass centralization*—allowing for ideal sportbike ergonomics. And when you tuck in behind the fairing's abbreviated windscreen, you can lose yourself in a world of speed because the 1125R tops out at over 160 miles per hour. To be sure, there are faster bikes on the road, but few offer the user-friendly powerband provided by this 1,125cc V-twin.

# Bultaco

## Metralla Mk2

### Quick, good-handling, and eternally cool

Quarter-liter road-burners never really caught on in this country of wide-open yet speed-limited highways and byways. Spain, however, has long felt such tiny tearabouts are just the ticket, and has seemed to have a direct line on building the rortiest ones—such as Bultaco's 1960s-era Metralla. The quintessential model was the 1966 Mk2, once believed to be the fastest two-stroke street bike available. Of course, it wasn't—but with the optional Kit America (fiberglass tank and seat, plus rearsets, expansion chamber, and more), it certainly looked and *sounded* as if it were. Even without the optional 'glass, the Metralla, in its classy and classic black and silver with white stripes, was absolutely drop-dead gorgeous.

 Bultaco came up with its own ingenious oil injection for the Metralla, with a separate oil tank and a small plunger/syringe plumbed into the gas tank. After filling the tank with straight petrol, a fixed amount of oil was added to get the ratio correct.

 Just being one of the coolest little 250 pocket-rockets Europe ever produced.

 What remains of the Montjuic Circuit in Barcelona, Spain.

★ ★ ★ ★
Look at it this way: If James Dean had been Spanish, he'd have ridden a Metralla, okay?

Engine: Two-stroke, air-cooled, piston-port single
Horsepower: 28 at 7,500 rpm
Top Speed: 101 miles per hour
Weight: 220 pounds (claimed)
Value Now: $$$$

## Pursang 240 Mk7 Pomeroy Replica

According to an interview with Pomeroy, at the first race of the 1974 Trans-AMA Series at Road Atlanta, his race bike didn't clear customs in time. So, he borrowed a spectator's Pursang (360 version) and with only minor changes took third, first, and second in the three motos and the overall.

Supposedly a faithful replica of what Bimbo rode to win his first—and America's first—motocross GP.

Pure, outdoor motocross tracks, the more European—fast and rough—the better.

The Pomeroy Rep differed little from Bultacos that came before it, except for minor details; nor did it advance the state of the motocross art. It was, at heart, utterly conventional.

| | |
|---|---|
| Engine: Two-stroke, air-cooled, piston-port single-cylinder | Top Speed: 77 miles per hour |
| | Weight: n/a |
| Horsepower: 24 at 8,000 rpm | Value Now: $$$ |

### A Spanish bike named for an American hero

When Jim Pomeroy won the 1973 Spanish 250 Motocross Grand Prix—the first time an American had ever won a motocross GP—it was as if he'd strapped a lit Saturn V to the fortunes of Bultaco, the Spanish bike he rode to victory. The very next year (1974), Bultaco unleashed the Pursang 250 Mk7 Pomeroy Replica, a bit of a mouthful, really, but the bike was more than up to the task. Liveried in a stunning sky blue and white, it evoked the look of the U.S. team's ISDT helmets. What's more, the quarter-liter Bul' featured light, conical hubs; a new pipe with a mellower bark than its strident, chrome-pickle-silencer-equipped predecessor; plus a touch more reliability than previous 'Sangs. For a few years, then, the 250 Pursang rode high at the top of every MXer's wish list.

# Bultaco

## Model 92 Sherpa T 350

Sete Gibernau's grandpa founded Bultaco. Probably why Valentino Rossi won't ride 'em.

With Sammy Miller's victory in 1965 on the original Sherpa T, Bultaco became the first non-British marque to win the Scottish Six Days Trials. Many more victories were to come.

Wherever you want to go.

★ ★ ★ ★ ★
It was an actual paradigm changer.

Engine: Air-cooled, 326cc, piston-port, two-stroke single
Horsepower: 21 at 5,000 rpm
Top Speed: n/a
Weight: n/a
Value Now: $$

### Rock crawler

In 1965, Sammy Miller went to the bigwigs who paid him to ride for Ariel and suggested they build an entirely new kind of trials bike, one that was lightweight and powered by a 250cc two-stroke motor. The bigwigs at Ariel said no. So he went to Bultaco. They said yes, and he not only won the Scottish Six Days Trials that year, he and Bultaco changed the face of trials competition forever. A direct descendant of that first Sherpa T, the Model 92 became the bike of choice for crossing the uncrossable and climbing the unclimbable back when the New York Dolls were paving the way for punks and "discotheque" hadn't yet shed its last six letters.

The Cagiva name comes from CAstiglioni GIovanni VArese. Castiglioni Giovanni formed the company as a parts supplier in 1950 in the town of Varese, Italy.

 An affordable mid-weight Ducati—sort of.

 The parking lot.

 *
After you get over the thrill of the engine, the ride is essentially over.

Engine: Air-cooled, 650cc,
  four-stroke, 90-degree V-twin
Horsepower: n/a

Top Speed: 113 miles per hour
Weight: 432 pounds
Value Now: $$

**If it sounds like a Duck and performs like a Duck, is it really a Duck?**

The Cagiva Alazzurra's heartbeat is its engine, based on a 650 V-twin originally found in the Ducati Pantah. As you'd expect, the familiar 90-degree V-twin delivers a broad, usable powerband that's normally associated with Ducati-powered motorcycles. There's no mistaking the exhaust note, either—pure Duck. What you don't expect to find in the Alazzurra package is stiff suspension that responds poorly to pavement irregularities. Adding to the Alazzurra's woes are high-effort hand controls. The combination makes for a painful ride under normal sport-riding conditions. In the end, the Alazzurra just isn't alluring. But, hey, its sexy styling makes us want to ride it—one last time.

# Confederate

## P120 Fighter

### Apocolypse redux

This is a remarkable bike in many ways. It makes its older brother, the Confederate Wraith, look downright normal. Eschewing the Wraith's use of mundane materials like carbon fiber, the Fighter is all aluminum. All angular, blocky, looks-like-it-was-born-in-a-metal-storm aluminum. If the Wraith looks like something you'd see on Judgment Day, the Fighter is definitely post-apocalyptic. And, with more than 160 horsepower, riding one might cause a few moments of reckoning too. There are those who say the bike handles quite well, citing taut suspension, good ground clearance, and excellent brakes. But, as with every sequel except *Godfather II*, most think it falls short of the original.

 The P120 Fighter design is based on a right triangle.

 Launched at the Quail Motorsports Gathering during the 2009 Pebble Beach Concours D'Elegance. Elegance, you say?

 The set of the *Transformers* movie.

 ★ ★ ★ ★ ★
Just because the Confederate Motorcycle Company credo has something to do with celebrating the art of rebellion.

Engine: Air-cooled, 1,967cc, OHV, four-stroke V-twin
Horsepower: 166 at 5,500 rpm
Top Speed: 190 miles per hour
Weight: n/a
Value Now: $$$$$

# Confederate

## B120 Wraith

 Confederate Motorcycles are manufactured on site at Barber Motorsports Park in Alabama, the company's original N'awlins facilities having been destroyed by Hurricane Katrina in 2005.

 Designed by J. T. Nesbitt, the Wraith prototype took second place in the 2004 Motorcycle Design Association Concept Bike category. Honda's Griffon took first place. The Griffon is nothing but a memory now, while people are doing double takes when they see production Wraiths in the real world.

 Any well-populated boulevard will do.

 ★ ★ ★ ★ ★
C'mon, just look at it.

Engine: Air-cooled, 1,967cc, OHV,
four-stroke V-twin
Horsepower: 125 at 5,500 rpm
Top Speed: 166 miles per hour
Weight: n/a
Value Now: $$$$$

**WTF?**

Pull up on one of these, and you're gonna have some 'splainin' to do. Even folks who couldn't care less about motorcycles will start asking some variation of "What the hell is that?" If great design inspires love in some and hate in others, then this is great design. But love it or hate it, the Wraith turns heads. Sometimes it jerks them. There are many who quite like the bike—lots of torque, adequate handling, unique styling in every sense of the word, good ergonomics despite the aforementioned unique styling—and there are a few who don't. The latter group cites reliability problems.

# Curtiss

## V-8 Custom

### Fastest bike on Earth

On Thursday, January 24, 1907, Glenn Hammond Curtiss covered a mile in 26.4 seconds on this motorcycle, garnering him the moniker "The Fastest Man on Earth." It took 11 years for a car to top his speed and 23 for another bike to do it. Curtiss simply wanted to demonstrate a lightweight V-8 engine he had designed for aircraft use, so he stuffed it into a beefed-up bicycle frame and hit the four-mile, salt-sprayed beach. Two miles in he hit top speed, held it for a mile, slowed over the last mile, turned around, and did it again. And that was pretty much it for Glenn Curtiss and motorcycles. He would make many more marks on society, but all would be in the burgeoning field of aviation.

 A universal joint in the driveshaft broke on Curtiss' return run, preventing him from making a second set of passes under official observation. Thus his record was never certified.

 Propelled the Fastest Man on Earth.

 Ormond Beach, Florida. On the actual beach.

 ★ ★ ★ ★ ★
It held the motorcycle land speed record for 23 years, besting Harley-Davidsons, Indians, Excelsiors, Hendersons, and everything else.

Engine: Air-cooled, 4,000cc, four-stroke, 90-degree V-8
Horsepower: 40 at 3,500 rpm
Top Speed: 136.3 miles per hour
Weight: n/a
Value Now: $$$$$

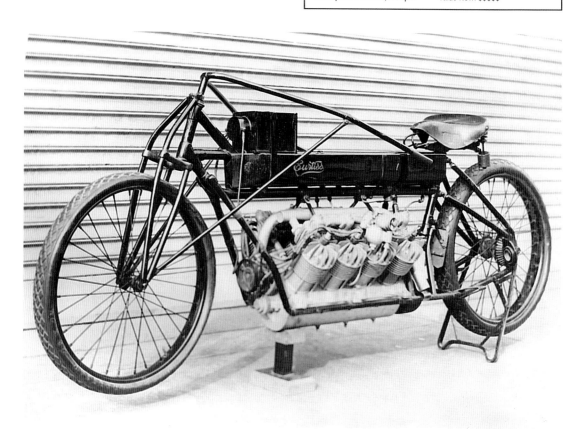

**Motocross' 500 class sees a changing of the guard**

Up until 1966, big, heavy four-strokes ruled motocross' World Championship 500 class, ridden by men equal to their motorcycles in stature and strength, and doubtless possessed of near-toxic testosterone levels. In 1966, though, East German Paul Friedrichs (perhaps slightly less fierce-looking than the four-stroke pilots but no less flint-hard) took the 500-class title on a two-stroke ČZ 360 Twin Pipe, distinguished by its two down-swept, chromed expansion chambers. Friedrichs went on to win a hat trick of titles (from 1966 through 1968) on his Czechoslovakian-built *shay-zed*, a near-identical replica of which got sold to consumers in this country. The Czech chargers were the equal of other European machinery and became legendary for the immense quality and near-unburstability of their two-stroke engines.

 ČZs were made in the town of Strakonice in what is now known as the Czech Republic, a town that is also famous for its bagpipe players.

 Apart from the ČZ's sheer strength, it was also known for precise handling, rider-friendly powerband, and the phenomenal spares kit that came with each bike. Less popular were the Pal spark plugs and the despised Jikov carb.

 A 1960s-era motocross track—fast and rough but with no straightaway-long whoop or rhythm sections, and definitely no stadium jumps, please.

 ★ ★ ★ ★
Four, yes, for helping bring about the new two-stroke world order in motocross.

Engine: Two-stroke, air-cooled, piston-port single-cylinder
Horsepower: 30 at 6,000 rpm (claimed)

Top Speed: 79 miles per hour
Weight: n/a
Value Now: $$$$

# ČZ

## 250 Falta Republic

This bike featured the best factory ČZ kit, including a Spanish Motoplat electronic ignition in place of the stocker's points and a Japanese Mikuni carb instead of the much-maligned Jikov.

This was the closest thing to what the factory riders used since the old chrome-twin-pipers. Yet it still embodied all the best traits of past ČZs.

Motocross tracks, of course, from Glen Helen to Unadilla and all points in between.

★ ★ ★
For all the chutzpah of its aluminum coffin tank and alloy-body air shocks, the Falta Replica still came with some traditional lowball ČZ components, such as the steel rear fender, fiberglass airbox, and pleated paper filter.

Engine: Air-cooled, two-stroke, piston-port single-cylinder
Horsepower: 26.8 at 7,000 rpm

Top Speed: approximately 60 miles per hour
Weight: n/a
Value Now: $$$

### Czech-ered past

Czech ČZ rider Jaroslav Falta won the 1974 250-class Motocross World Championship, at least until the sanctioning body, the F.I.M., vigorously screwed him out of the title at the behest of the Russian team. Fortunately, the obvious perfidy created a groundswell of enthusiasm both for Falta and ČZ. ČZ responded with the 250 Falta Replica, a near-as-dammit version of the young Czech's works racer. From the aluminum coffin-shaped tank, to the four-fin cylinder with radial head, to the skinny fork sliders, to the Load-Leveler-look-alike air shocks, the Falta rep meant serious business. The typical near-bombproof engine and precise steering were merely icing on the cake for this *Ceske Zavodny* weapon.

Essentially, the Reitwagen was a test bed for Daimler's first automobile.

 Being the first accepted true (because of its four-stroke Otto-cycle engine) motorcycle on the planet.

 A very, very smooth road. As in concrete, with an extremely thick layer of tarmac over the top. Preferably laid down that very day.

 ★ ★ ★ ★ ★ +
How could it be anything else? It was the first, the motorcycle that paved the way (so to speak) for MotoGP, the Hells Angels, Marlon Brando, Lee Marvin, Tom Cruise, Don Vesco, Kenny Roberts, Gary Busey . . .

Engine: Air-cooled single-cylinder with slide valve(s)
Horsepower: 0.5 at 700 rpm

Top Speed: 7 miles per hour
Weight: n/a
Value Now: Priceless

### Motorcycle Number One

Any jaded motorcyclist should take a close look at this and see what it was like to ride way back in "the day." For instance, Daimler's Reitwagen ("Riding Car") had less than a single horsepower to provide forward motion, and it had no suspension—hence its nickname the "Bone Crusher." That diamond-stitched leather pad is starting to look good to you, isn't it? The Otto-cycle (four-stroke) engine pumped out its 0.5 horsepower at 700 rpm. (Honda's 50cc RC166 road-racer spun up to 22,500 rpm—32 times faster!) Daimler's partner, Wilhelm Maybach, rode the beast less than 2 miles along the Neckar River in Germany at a top speed of (maybe) 7 miles per hour. It was registered with the local patent office in August 1885.

# Derbi

## 50cc Grand Prix

**The Spanish acquisition of the 50cc world title**

When the F.I.M. instituted the 50cc Grand Prix class for 1962, Derbi jumped in with a bike powered by a liquid-cooled single. However, the little Spanish bike was outclassed by its Japanese competition from Suzuki, Honda, and Yamaha, prompting the team to switch to an air-cooled engine. Each season, the team from the Iberian Peninsula found more and more speed from its air-cooled 50cc engine. By 1969, however, Derbi had returned to liquid cooling, and with the new single-cylinder rule instituted, the Spanish marque found itself in a competitive role. By the end of the season, a young Spaniard named Angel Nieto would claim the company's first Grand Prix World Championship. Nieto went on to establish himself as one of the top riders throughout the 1970s.

 There's an Angel Nieto Museum in Madrid, Spain, that contains many of the Spaniard's trophies and motorcycle memorabilia.

 The first Derbi 50cc Grand Prix engine was liquid cooled, but engineers felt air cooling would be better, so for several seasons the engine relied on fins to control engine heat.

 The best place to ride the Derbi 50 is at the site of Nieto's final win aboard the bike—fittingly, in Spain at the Montjuïc Circuit, which was a street circuit located on Montjuïc Mountain in Barcelona, Catalonia.

 ★ ★ ★
Despite its diminutive size, riding a 50cc GP bike requires a deft throttle hand because the engine's powerband is so narrow.

| | |
|---|---|
| Engine: Liquid-cooled, 50cc, two-stroke single | Top Speed: 100-plus miles per hour |
| Horsepower: 15.5 at 14,500 rpm | Weight: n/a |
| | Value Now: $$$$ |

50 CC DERBI PRODUCTION ROAD RACER
11 H.P. 12000 R.P.M.
5 SPEED GEAR BOX    WT. 88 LBS.

## 125 Gran Sport Marianna

 Fabio Taglioni was an engineer at Mondial when he was hired by Ducati in 1954.

 This bike saved Ducati from economic ruin.

 SR435 West from Montecatini.

 ★ ★ ★ ★ ★
It was the first Taglioni-penned bike to save Ducati from financial ruin.

| Engine: Air-cooled, 124cc, helical-gear-driven DOHC, four-stroke single. Horsepower: n/a | Top Speed: n/a Weight: n/a Value Now: $$$ |
| --- | --- |

### The bike that saved Ducati, take one

Sabotage by a nefarious "private mechanic" affiliated with Mondial rider Paolo Maranghi almost derailed Ducati forever. Riding a 125 Gran Sport in the 1956 Motociclistico Giro d'Italia, official Ducati team rider Giuliano Maoggi was about to start the final stage from Montecatini when he noticed his rear tire had mysteriously gone flat. Spanning the Italian peninsula, the Motogiro was pivotal to an Italian marque's commercial success in those days. In fact, the only reason the Ducati managing director, Giuseppe Montano, had hired future Ducati icon Fabio Taglioni a couple of years earlier was to build a bike that would save the company by winning that race. Fortunately, Maoggi noticed the subterfuge in time, fixed the flat, caught Maranghi, and won the race. And the Ducatisti lived happily ever after.

## 250 Scrambler

 Scramblers quickly became Ducati's best-selling line. They were to Ducati then what the Monster is now.

 This bike was the key to solidifying Ducati's place in the American market.

 Anyplace you can smell surf.

 ★ ★ ★
By definition, something can't be overly rebellious if was built specifically to be rebellious.

| Engine: Air-cooled, 249cc, helical-gear-driven SOHC, four-stroke single | Horsepower: 27 at 4,500 rpm Top Speed: 64 miles per hour Value Now: $$ |
| --- | --- |

### As American as Ducati and apple pie

Sometimes you don't want to be crouched behind a fairing on a long, lefthand sweeper at speed. Sometimes you just want to sit up and cruise to the beach and wave at girls. Or guys. But you still want to be on a Ducati. Thanks to Ducati importer Joe Berliner, you can. He convinced Ducati to build the Scrambler.

## 1260 Apollo

**The god of too much too soon**

Ducati has made three four-cylinder motorcycles over the years. Two were race bikes, separated by almost half a decade. And then there was the Apollo, meant to displace the Harley-Davidson as America's police bike of choice. Joe Berliner was so convinced this could happen that his Berliner Motor Corporation underwrote the costs of designing and building a prototype. The resulting Apollo was 50 pounds lighter than the Harley and almost twice as powerful. But 100 horsepower proved far too much for any 16-inch motorcycle tire of the day. Detuning the engine to 65 horsepower kept the tires from spontaneously disintegrating but not the project. Politics became its undoing, but not the politics you might think. It was Italian bureaucrats who killed the god.

 The Apollo was powered by the first 90-degree V engine Ducati ever made.

 But for a set of tires, it could have been king. Joe Berliner would later sell Moto Guzzis to the LAPD, making them the first American law enforcement agency to use European bikes.

 Escorting a motorcade.

 ★ ★ ★
Yet another stillborn legend.

Engine: Air-cooled, 1,257cc, OHV, 90-degree, four-stroke V-4
Horsepower: 100 at 7,000 rpm

Top Speed: 120-plus miles per hour
Weight: n/a
Value Now: $$$$$

**Italian sixties child**

*Cycle World* described the Mark 3 as "enchanting." Many a racer was victorious on one; many a tourer thought it was a pain in the ass. It was quirky (read: Italian), it was peppy (it taught you the meaning of "on the cam"), it was needy (it taught you the meaning of "*keeping it* on the cam"), and it was designed by Fabio Taglioni (no parenthetical reference needed). It would get three different types of engines (narrow-case bevel-drive SOHC, wide-case bevel-drive SOHC, and wide-case desmodromic-drive SOHC) in three different displacements (250, 350, and 450) before its run ended in 1976, but the one with the 250cc, narrow-case engine mated to the five-speed transmission will always have a special place in history's garage.

 In 1968, Mark 3 buyers were offered a new engine option, making them the first to agonize over the potential pros and cons of production desmo Ducatis.

 Ran the fastest quarter-mile by a 250 at the time.

 Through the streets of Bologna at midnight. During the work week. At 8,500 rpm. With the optional—and supplied—megaphone exhaust.

 ★ ★ ★ ★
It was the fastest production 250 you could buy in the world. In the *world!*

Engine: Air-cooled, 249cc, helical-gear-driven SOHC, four-stroke single
Horsepower: 30 at 8,000 rpm

Top Speed: 109 miles per hour
Weight: n/a
Value Now: $$$

# Ducati

## 450 Desmo

### Paradigm of the sublime

You get more grunt from the trusty internal-combustion engine at low rpm, but higher revs get you more speed. So, how high can you go? Answering that question provides pretty much every engine builder's introduction to valve float. The solution? There are two: better springs or a different paradigm. While most of the motoring universe pursued the first option, Fabio Taglioni pursued the second, and we have a better world because of it. But that's only partly why the Desmo 450 is so sublime. The rest is down to Franco Farne, under whose development as a test rider pretty much every Ducati chassis became the finest in the world. This one is no exception.

 In 1896, German Gustav Mees got the first patent involving desmodromically driven valves.

 While you could already get a Mark 3 with an optional "D" at the end of the model name, this was the first Ducati to be so openly Desmodromic.

 The Marche Mountains west of Bologna, where Franco Farne test-flogged prototype and production Ducatis.

 ★ ★ ★ ★ ★
Desmo and proud of it.

Engine: Air-cooled, 436cc, helical-gear-driven SOHC, desmodromic-valve, four-stroke single

Horsepower: n/a
Top Speed: n/a
Weight: n/a
Value Now: $$

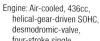

Ducati's commercial foray into big bikes began on March 20, 1970—the last day of winter—when Fabio Taglioni drew a sketch of what would become the first production 750 GT.

 This was the first production Ducati with a 90-degree V-twin.

 Highway 9 through the Santa Cruz Mountains of California.

 ★ ★ ★
Sure, it was Ducati's first big production bike, but its valves were closed by springs.

Engine: Air-cooled, 748cc, helical-gear-driven SOHC, four-stroke V-twin
Horsepower: 60 at 7,800 rpm

Top Speed: 110 miles per hour
Weight: n/a
Value Now: $$$

## Big Pump

There are people who think this bike has the finest engine Ducati ever made. Whole online communities of Bevelheads will call you dirty names in capital letters if you dare malign one of their beloved "Pompones" ("Big Pumps"). For example, by saying the engine looks like two singles grafted onto the same crankcase. Or by saying it's funny that a bike with such a long wheelbase should weave so much at high speeds. Or by implying that "high speed" on a 750 GT might be classified as "loping along" on other big bikes of the era. So, let's just say the GT was a superb start to a line of big bikes to which almost every rider now aspires in his heart of hearts.

# Ducati

## 750 Imola Desmo

### The fantastic ride

Imola, 1972. It was the first time Ducati's first big race bike saw competition. It was also the first 200-mile F750 race, the first 200-miler that wasn't at Daytona, and the beginning of what would turn into decades of Ducati world domination in big-bike races. And it was the first time Ducati had officially sponsored a race team since Giuliano Maoggi won the Giromoto d'Italia in 1956. As you might have guessed by now, it was a successful debut, with Paul Smart winning and Bruno Spaggiari coming in second. The bike was raced three more times but never duplicated what became known as the "fantastic ride" at Imola. Still, it kick-started a racing legacy back to life.

 Fabio Taglioni was experimenting with four valves per cylinder at the time this bike was created but wasn't yet getting enough extra power to justify the added expense.

 The 750 Desmo beat world champion Giacomo Agostini on his MV Agusta at Imola.

 Autodromo Imola, Italy.

 ★ ★ ★ ★ ★
Love 'em or hate 'em, the racing legacy of Ducati motorcycles has been unmatched since this bike appeared in the paddock.

Engine: Air-cooled, 748cc, helical-gear-driven SOHC, desmodromic-valve, four-stroke V-twin

Horsepower: 84 at 8,800 rpm
Top Speed: 155 miles per hour
Weight: n/a
Value Now: $$$$$

# Ducati

## 750 SS

### Screamer

You don't just own a Ducati desmo; you live with it. We've all heard about the pitfalls of riding race bikes for daily transport and bringing supermodels home to meet mothers. But there's a reason one chooses to share one's life with the high-strung and beautiful. While there are those who say they don't want to deal with the neediness, what they really mean is they're not capable of living up to expectations. They can make neither bike nor model scream with delight. So, living with a bike bred directly from a racer sounds scary to some—and downright blissful to others. For the latter is the Ducati 750 SS, a direct descendent of the bike Paul Smart rode to victories at Imola and Brand's Hatch in 1972. It's a keeper.

 Even though it's a desmo, tiny hairpin valve springs were used to make sure the valves were completely closed when starting the engine.

 Arguably the second bike to save Ducati from economic ruin.

 Any track holding an AHRMA road race.

 ★ ★ ★ ★
We might never have seen this bike had it not been for homologation rules in the F750 class. Wait, we're talking about Ducati here. Sure we would have.

Engine: Air-cooled, 748cc, helical-gear-driven SOHC, desmodromic-valve, four-stroke V-twin

Horsepower: 72 at 9,500 rpm
Top Speed: 137 miles per hour
Weight: n/a
Value Now: $$$$$

# Ducati

## 900 SS

 Hailwood wanted to race under a pseudonym at the Isle of Man in 1978 because he wasn't sure he or the 900 SS would stand up to the test.

 Mike Hailwood rode a 900 SS to victory in the 1978 Formula 1 TT race at the Isle of Man, beating the multi-cylinder Hondas and solidifying Ducati's official return to racing.

 Road America, Elkhart Lake, Wisconsin.

 ★ ★ ★ ★
Mike the Bike rode one on the Isle of Man in his triumphant return to motorcycle racing. That's cool enough to mention twice.

| | |
|---|---|
| Engine: Air-cooled, 864cc, helical-gear-driven SOHC, desmodromic-valve, four-stroke V-twin | Horsepower: 70 at 7,000 rpm Top Speed: 132 miles per hour Weight: n/a Value Now: $$$$ |

### The last real motorbike

Kawasaki's GPz1100 cost 20 percent less. Suzuki's GS1100 had 10 percent more power. Both Japanese bikes went faster, and both combined required less service in a year than the 900 SS did in a month. But comparing motorcycles on paper is a fool's errand. Motorcycles are best examined on tarmac, and this is a motorcycle born and bred for that, with a frame that begs for fast, sweeping corners, an engine that defines performance not in numbers but in usability, and a service regimen that requires a small army of mechanics to fulfill. All of which adds up to what motojournalist Michael Scott determined in 1981 to be "the last real motorbike." Or maybe that was because it still had a kick-starter.

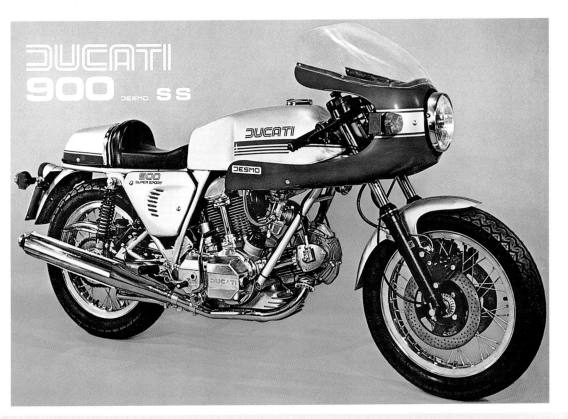

# Ducati

## 900 Mike Hailwood Replica

### Be like Mike

While visiting British Ducati dealer Steve Wynne's paddock at the 1977 Silverstone F1 race, Mike Hailwood sat on a 900 SS and joked that it might be fun to race one at the Isle of Man next year. A deal was struck over a handshake a few weeks later, and another chapter of motorcycle racing history began. According to Wynne, Mike the Bike wasn't much for giving feedback during tests. While sorting the gearbox at Mallory for the Post TT, Wynne asked Hailwood what gear he was in at a certain part of the track. "How many gears does it have?" was the reply. Still, he was helpful. "Though he didn't want to pick up the spanners and work on the bike, he'd bring us a pie and a pint from the hotel," said Wynne.

 Hailwood's actual race bike blew an engine (the bevel-drive gears stripped) as he crossed the finish line at the 1978 Isle of Man Formula 1 TT.

 Based on the bike with which Hailwood triumphantly returned to motorcycle racing after an 11-year absence.

 Mountain Course, Isle of Man.

 ★ ★ ★
It looks better than a standard 900 SS, it's faster, and it has a solo seat. But it's still just a replica.

Engine: Air-cooled, 864cc, helical-gear-driven SOHC, desmodromic-valve, four-stroke V-twin

Horsepower: 72 at 7,000 rpm
Top Speed: 137 miles per hour
Weight: n/a
Value Now: $$$$

Taglioni's trellis frame evolved out of a Colin Seeley design for Ducati race bikes.

 Motorbooks publisher Zack Miller, a man widely known for his exquisite style and taste, rides one.

 SP27 from Tempio Pausania to Aggius, Sardinia, Italy.

 ★ ★ ★ ★
Taglioni stuck to his "light is right" guns no matter what the competition did.

Engine: Air-cooled, 499cc, belt-driven SOHC, desmodromic-valve, four-stroke V-twin
Horsepower: 50 at 8,500 rpm

Top Speed: 124 miles per hour
Weight: n/a
Value Now: $$$

### Taglioni's last stand

This is where it all began: belt-driven camshafts for desmodromic valvetrains, trellis frames, shorter wheelbases, and steeper rakes. In short, the Pantah is the prototype for today's modern Ducati superbikes. How ironic that it should be the last major contribution by Fabio Taglioni, arguably the single most influential personality in Ducati's heritage. But what a contribution it was. True to form, he kept Ducati on the light and narrow path, proving again that a pick is more accurate than a sledgehammer. It was because of Taglioni and his Pantah that even today Ducati eschews multiple cylinders and overwhelming muscle in favor of mechanical efficiency and usable power.

# Ducati

## 750 F1

### Change is gonna come

Just another Ducati whose parents were racers, this bike is a direct descendent of the TT1 and TT2 race bikes. Among the innovations for a Ducati production bike were the monoshock rear suspension, fully floating front and rear disc brakes, and two-into-one exhaust system. The first new bike produced by Ducati under the Castiglioni brothers' reign, it was a no-holds-barred racer with lights. It was also the last Ducati with exhaust outlets at the front of both cylinders. A seemingly trivial point, but a harbinger of major engine revisions to come at the hands of Taglioni successor Massimo Bordi.

 Ironically, the 750 F1 was more successful in Battle of the Twins races than it was in Formula 1.

 Marco "Lucky" Luchinelli won the 1986 Battle of the Twins race at Laguna Seca on a 750 F1, prompting Ducati to produce a commemorative 200-unit special edition.

 Montjuich Park, Barcelona, Spain.

 ★ ★ ★ ★
Fabio Taglioni was coaxed out of retirement to help design this bike.

Engine: Air-cooled, 748cc, belt-drive SOHC, desmodromic-valve, four-stroke V-twin
Horsepower: 76 at 9,000 rpm

Top Speed: 162 miles per hour
Weight: n/a
Value Now: $$$$

The right fork leg controls all the rebound damping, and the left fork leg controls all the compression damping.

 This was the first Ducati designed by Massimo Tamburini.

 Across the Italian countryside on a secondary road.

 ✷ ✷ ✷
It was new, it was beautiful, and it had chronic fuel and electrical gremlins.

Engine: Air-cooled, 748cc, belt-driven SOHC, desmodromic-valve, four-stroke V-twin
Horsepower: 73 at 7,900 rpm

Top Speed: 123 miles per hour
Weight: n/a
Value Now: $$

**Beautiful new world**

Although there were fully faired sportbikes on the market already, the Paso was the first to use its bodywork to fully enclose everything. Well, you could say the same about Honda Hurricanes, but who cares about them (and anyway, they came along after the Paso). Job one for the bodywork was to cover the radiator and its unsightly plumbing. In other words, the idea was born of laziness. But when you saw a Paso on the street, you watched it go by, every time. You might have lamented not being able to see the new(ish) belt-drive desmo engine or the trellis frame, but you ogled at the unique beauty of such a complete design. Later you realized why: it was the first step into a beautiful new world of motorcycle aesthetics.

# Ducati

## 851 Strada

### The past has always been the future

As soon as he was out from under Fabio Taglioni's giant thumb, Massimo Bordi set about making his own mark on Ducati. First, he turned around the desmo's rear cylinder head so that the exhaust came out the back. Then he fully enclosed the Paso. Finally, it was time to really do something, so the 851 got a new trellis frame, liquid cooling, four valves per cylinder, electronic fuel injection, and a dry clutch. It took a few years, but in 1991 these changes brought Ducati its first World Superbike Championship, in the hands of Raymond Roche. Then, in 1991 and 1992, the bike won its second and third with Doug Polen. Like Taglioni before him, Massimo Bordi started his reign at Ducati with a slew of world championships. History never changes.

 Massimo Bordi designed a four-valve desmo head for his thesis at the University of Bologna in 1973.

 This bike won the very first World Superbike race, then brought Ducati its first World Superbike Championship three years later.

 Where the highway patrol isn't.

 ★ ★ ★
Cool new engine, but the bike wouldn't handle until it got a 17-inch front wheel after its first year of production.

Engine: Water-cooled, 851cc, belt-driven DOHC, desmodromic-valve, four-stroke V-twin
Horsepower: 109 at 10,000 rpm
Top Speed: 174 miles per hour
Weight: n/a
Value Now: $$

# Ducati

 The 888 won 43 of 52 World Superbike races in 1991 and 1992.

 The bike that brought Ducati its second and third World Superbike championships.

 Pick a track. Any track.

 ★ ★ ★
It won multiple world championships. There just aren't many bikes that can say the same.

Engine: Water-cooled, 888cc, belt-driven DOHC, desmodromic-valve, four-stroke V-twin
Horsepower: 134 at 12,000 rpm

Top Speed: 180 miles per hour
Weight: n/a
Value Now: $$$

**"Ever-so-much-more-so"**

Fabio Taglioni loved to grow orchids, and that's a perfect metaphor. You can't grow a completely new orchid. All you can do is continually refine and improve existing orchids. Which is exactly what Taglioni did at Ducati. All right, in a godlike act of inspiration he created a completely new Ducati orchid when he first got there in 1954, but that just makes the metaphor ever so much more poignant. From then on, everything Ducati did followed a persistent path of refinement and improvement. A tradition left intact by Massimo Bordi. Maybe he likes to grow orchids too. In any case, the 888 is everything the 851 (pictured here) was and then some. Quite a lot of some, actually; 25 horsepower's worth of some. It has, in a word coined by children's book character Homer Price, "ever-so-much-more-so."

# Ducati

## Supermono

### Lucky bastard

Supermono. Just hearing the name makes any real racer's face soften as he imagines throwing around something so light and agile. Then his face hardens again because his imagination is the only place he's likely to ride one. Maybe 70 were made, each with 75 horsepower and weighing in at only 269 pounds. It's a Ducati, so it's for neither the timid nor the destitute. But if you have balls and a wallet, you can rev one of these singles that thinks it's a double to 10,500 rpm as many times as whatever straight you're on will allow; you can use brake markers way past any you've ever used before; you can carry more corner speed than you thought possible; and you can do all of this over and over and over again. You lucky bastard.

 The Supermono sprang from Pierre Terblanche's pen, who later designed the 999. Who'da thunk it?

 This bike won just about every Sound of Singles race it entered.

 TT Circuit, Assen, Netherlands.

 ★ ★ ★ ★ ★
Needs no justification.

Engine: Water-cooled, 550cc, belt-driven DOHC, desmodromic-valve, four-stroke, double-connecting-rod single

Horsepower: 75 at 10,000 rpm
Top Speed: 137 miles per hour
Weight: n/a
Value Now: $$$$$

# Ducati

## M900 Monster

Over 130,000 Monsters have rolled off the Borgo Panigale production line, and around half of all Ducatis sold now are Monsters.

Ironically, after starting the trend of completely shrouded bikes with the Paso, Ducati started the next trend of completely naked motorcycles with the Monster.

Boulevards. Racetracks. It doesn't matter.

★ ★ ★ ★ ★
Creators of (successful) new categories get five leather jackets.

Engine: Air-cooled, 904cc, belt-driven SOHC, desmodromic-valve, four-stroke V-twin
Horsepower: 80 at 7,200 rpm

Top Speed: 120 miles per hour
Weight: n/a
Value Now: $$

### The bike that saved Ducati, take three

The wolves were at the door again. Domination in the racing world wasn't leading to sales in the real world. Ducati badly needed a hit. What the company got from Miguel Galuzzi when he designed the Monster was an icon. Those wolves? The Monster drove them all away, and they haven't been back since.

# Ducati

## Monster S4Rs

The very first Monster—*Il Mostro* in Italian—was designated the M900. The bike was designed by Miguel Galuzzi, and it made its debut on dealers' floors in 1993. It's long been said the sales success of the various iterations of the Monster is what makes Ducati's racing programs possible.

Being the quickest, fastest, stompingest Monster yet.

Try an exotic urban locale, such as Milan, Paris, New York, and the like.

★ ★ ★
For Ducati, for Monster, and for naked bikes in general, the S4Rs hoes a familiar row.

Engine: Liquid-cooled, DOHC, eight-valve, 90-degree V-twin
Horsepower: 117 at 9,750 rpm

Top Speed: n/a
Weight: n/a
Value Now: $$$$

### Think of it as a 999 that's been given a Treblanchectomy

To say Ducati's Pierre Treblanche–styled 999 got a cool reception from those in love with the previous-generation 916's looks is an understatement of Olympic size and quality. Yet it was true—the 999 was a love-it-or-hate-it kind of bike, with most people falling into the latter category. So, what were lads (or lasses) to do when they wanted 999 performance in a package that didn't make them gag? Enter, stage right, Ducati's Monster S4Rs. With nearly 120 horsepower (thanks to a 999S-spec powerplant), premium Öhlins suspension, and radial-mount, four-piston Brembo calipers mated to 320mm discs, the S4Rs was astonishingly fast and more than capable of ruining a conventional-sportbike rider's day.

# Ducati

## 916

Massimo Bordi's first desmoquattro head was designed for a Ford Cosworth V-8.

Carl Fogarty won 13 of 24 World Superbike races on a 916 en route to the 1995 championship. And other Ducati WSB riders took 7 more wins that year.

Ulster Grand Prix, Dunrod Circuit, Belfast, Northern Ireland.

★ ★ ★
Face the facts: it's a bike built when Ducati was owned by a computer company. Patently uncool.

Engine: Water-cooled, 916cc, belt-driven DOHC, desmodromic-valve, four-stroke V-twin
Horsepower: 104 at 9,000 rpm

Top Speed: 162 miles per hour
Weight: n/a
Value Now: $$$

### Dog stupid

The bike that made Carl Fogarty a household name in the civilized world. The first Pierre Terblanche–penned machine to be displayed at the Guggenheim. True Ducatisti are drawn to this bike the way dogs are drawn to anti-freeze. Everything about it is so sweet, yet it's really bad for you. A 916 can kill you. More likely, though, it'll just get you a lot of speeding tickets. And you'll spend thousands on valve adjustments, and maybe you'll even need a set of camshafts or two, depending on how many times they delaminate. But still, you'll lap it up, happy as a dog.

All 1,000 bikes offered were sold within an hour of being posted.

First bike to be sold exclusively over the Internet.

Information Highway, cyberspace.

★ ★ ★
A first, but not the right kind.

Engine: Air-cooled, 904cc, belt-driven SOHC, desmodromic-valve, four-stroke V-twin
Horsepower: 75 at 8,000 rpm

Top Speed: 130 miles per hour
Weight: n/a
Value Now: $$$$

### Cybernetic milestone

Yes, the MH900e was designed by Pierre Terblanche as a testament to Mike Hailwood's triumphant return to motorcycle racing at the Isle of Man in 1978, and, yes, it's one of the most striking Ducatis ever sold. But the story here isn't *what* was sold, but *how*. In an interesting juxtaposition of old and new, this retro-styled bike was sold exclusively over the newfangled Interweb. Some say it was brilliant; others think it was far too much money for tarted-up, outdated technology. Either way, the Mike Hailwood evoluzione is going down in history as the first bike ever to be sold new only in binary code.

# Ducati

## 999

**Did Ducati step in it with the 999? Or did the Borgo Panigale firm actually step it up?**

Ducati's 999 has long been considered just shy of Medusa-quality ugly, at least when compared to the aesthetic perfection of its 916 predecessor. Such a myopic view misses the 999's virtues entirely. With more than 130 horsepower available at your right wrist (and extraordinarily high-quality acceleration from 6,000 to 10,000 rpm) allied to a stable, precise-steering chassis, the 999 makes for an exceptional tool with which to dismantle twisty backgrounds—or to whisper past other, lesser vehicles that clog the nation's transport arteries. Riding Ducati's 999 almost makes you feel sorry for the proles, because, as befits such a thoroughbred, it operates on a higher, more sophisticated reality they'll never know. Almost.

 The 999 uses some 230 fewer pieces than its 916/998 predecessor. In 2005, the 999 got a host of changes, including a swingarm patterned after the piece used by Ducati's World Superbike team.

 Simply by being a motorcycle superior to its 916/998 forbears, the 999 destroyed the argument of those who claimed it was ugly as sin—at least, it did with those who thought with their big heads. . . .

 If a road has curves in it, the 999 belongs on it; and you should take it to track days too.

 ★ ★ ★ ★
Pierre Treblanche's styling, clearly and sharply different from that of the previous 916/998 series, badly divided opinion and so upset Ducatisti smitten with the earlier design that they called for his head.

Engine: Liquid-cooled, DOHC, eight-valve, 90-degree V-twin
Horsepower: 131 at 10,000 rpm
Top Speed: 168 miles per hour
Weight: n/a
Value Now: $$$

This bike is a direct descendent of the Cagiva Gran Canyon.

 Supermoto on steroids.

 Hounding an R6.

 ★ ★ ★
A blatant attempt by Ducati to start yet another motorcycle category.

Engine: Air-cooled, 992cc, belt-driven SOHC, desmodromic-valve, four-stroke V-twin
Horsepower: 83 at 7,750 rpm

Top Speed: n/a
Weight: n/a
Value Now: $$$

**Every mother's nightmare**

In 1961, Ducati introduced the Scrambler. The bike was a dual-sport before there were dual-sports, and Ducati's success in America, a crucial market for anyone selling anything, hinged on it. In 2003, Ducati finally deemed a twenty-first-century Scrambler, the Multistrada, ready for the public. At last, a comfortable bike for long-legged Ducatisti. Well, comfortable insofar as ergonomics were concerned. Mothers of long-legged Ducatisti lost much sleep over their Multistrada-riding progeny on edge, probably because they saw a motorcycle that went like a bat out of hell. Or maybe it's because they agreed with the motojournalist who suggested the bike looked like a wet cat with a big forehead. Who really knows what mothers think? What we do know is that the original Multistrada wasn't a sales success and forced Ducati to go back to the drawing board.

# Ducati

## 749R

### Homologation special

When Ducati plops an "R" into the name of a bike, you know the Italian company means business. The R means that the bike's primary purpose is racing, and as often as not R models are built solely to satisfy the homologation requirements of various production-based racing series' around the world, which usually require a manufacturer to build a certain number of road-going machines before that motorcycle is allowed to compete. This in turn means that the R models get all the top-shelf parts, which the 749R has in spades, from its carbon-fiber bodywork to its titanium fasteners to its Öhlins suspension.

 The 749R was only available as in monoposto (single-seat) form? There are no passengers on the racetrack.

 Built to homologate Ducati's 749 model for World Supersport racing.

 Any racetrack in the world.

 ★ ★ ★ ★ ★
Like most of Ducati's homologation specials, the 749 was never legally imported into many countries, making its very existence illegal.

Engine: Liquid-cooled, eight-valve, 749cc V-twin
Horsepower: 121 at 10,500
Top Speed: NA
Weight: 405 pounds
Value Now: $$$

## Desmosedici RR

 The bike comes with a race exhaust system and corresponding ECU that bump the V-4's output to 200 horsepower.

 What else? Being the only street-legal MotoGP replica bike offered for sale. Is that enough?

 Fast—*really* fast—back roads. Or Spa in Belgium, or Eastern Creek in Australia, or maybe Laguna Seca (excuse me, *Mazda Raceway*).

 ★ ★ ★ ★ ★ ★ ★ ★ ★

Nothing else comes close to this level of rebellion.

Engine: Liquid-cooled, DOHC, Desmodromic, 16-valve, 90-degree V-4
Horsepower: 188 at 13,800 rpm (claimed)

Top Speed: 198 miles per hour
Weight: n/a
Value Now: $$$$$

**This really is a race bike with lights**

Simply put, no other manufacturer has had the *cojones* (or ovaries, if you prefer) to put its MotoGP bike on the street. But that's precisely what Ducati did to create the Desmosedici RR: the closest possible thing to a MotoGP bike (from the 990 era!) with as few exceptions as possible to allow it to have a three-year warranty and meet Euro 3 emissions standards. That's astonishing enough, but the D16RR's performance is something else yet again. Every control response is sharp, immediate. Yet life with such a motorcycle does have a downside: Your riding ability is unlikely to match its potential. If you're cool with that, then happy trails. If not, your money can't buy what you need.

# Ducati

## 1098

### The ultimate(um) bike

Don't like your sanctioning body's rules? Get them to write new ones. Tell them you're going to quit if they don't. Say it like you mean it, and they'll cave. Especially if you've won more championships than everyone else combined. Go ahead and build a bike around that new engine you've been designing. So what if it's 198cc bigger than it should be? Just tell them your engine's at the end of its lifespan, that you've refined and improved it as much as you can. Wait a minute, isn't that exactly what you're so proud of, that your bike is a direct descendent of the first 125 desmo you raced 50-some years ago?

The 1098's 90.4 lbs-ft. of torque and 380-pound curb weight give it the highest torque-to-weight ratio of any production sportbike on the market.

Won political *and* racing championships.

To the library to pick up a copy of *Robert's Rules of Order.*

★ ★
Acting as if rules will be changed isn't rebellious. Acting as if rules don't exist is rebellious.

Engine: Water-cooled, 1,099cc, belt-driven DOHC, desmodromic-valve, four-stroke V-twin

Horsepower: 160 at 9,750 rpm
Top Speed: 180 miles per hour
Weight: n/a
Value Now: $$$

*Old Blue* made 90.4 horsepower and got 11 miles per gallon.

*Old Blue* gave Ducati its first Daytona 200 victory in 1977.

Through a wormhole back to the 1977 Daytona 200.

★ ★

Rebels don't cost more than a decent year's salary.

| Engine: Air-cooled, 992cc, belt-driven SOHC, desmodromic-valve, four-stroke V-twin | Top Speed: 135 miles per hour |
| --- | --- |
| | Weight: n/a |
| | Value Now: $$$ |
| Horsepower: 116 at 8,450 rpm | |

### History repeats itself, again

NCR, Ducati, and motorcycle racing: three inseparable entities. In 1967, three guys in Borgo Panigale (Giorgio **N**epoti, Rino **C**aracchi, and Luigo **R**izzi) started a race shop. They worked closely with Ducati icon Fabio Taglioni and Ducati legend Franco Farne, and NCR became the de facto Ducati race team. Their methodology fit Ducati's perfectly—both were always refining, always improving. Ten years later, Cook Nielsen won the Daytona 200 on an NCR Ducati 750 SS nicknamed *Old Blue* by ace mechanic Phil Shilling. A few decades after that, and we have yet another Ducati commemorative bike, nicknamed *New Blue* by some marketing exec. It's basically a 2008 Ducati SportClassic Sport 1000 S that was sent to NCR for 30 more horsepower and 80 fewer pounds. And carbon-fiber brake lines. Yay.

The 1198 has so much torque, it doesn't propel the bike forward. It spins the earth backward.

Less than half the price of a Desmosedici.

To the bank.

★ ★ ★ ★

Yeah, it's outrageously expensive, but you sure get what you pay for.

| Engine: Liquid-cooled, 1,198cc, belt-driven DOHC, desmodromic-valve, four-stroke V-twin | Horsepower: 180 at 9,750 rpm |
| --- | --- |
| | Top Speed: 192 miles per hour |
| | Weight: n/a |
| | Value Now: $$$$ |

### Wow

Ducati, your 999 fiasco was, shall we say, a rough patch. You took some hits, didn't you? But that's all history. Time to get back to building kick-ass bikes. You did? It's called the 1198R? That's it? Wow! With 99.1 lbs-ft. of torque, a 364-pound curb weight, top-shelf Öhlins suspension, traction control, data acquisition, lots of carbon-fiber and unobtainium bits, all that and good ol' Ducati handling too? Good freakin' job! It costs how much? Oh, wow. Good freakin' job. What's the S model cost?

# Ducati

## Hypermotard 1100 EVO SP

**Send out the clowns**

ABC once had a show called *Wide World of Sports*. And a wide world it showed, airing events from lacrosse to surfing, but not in a look-at-what-these-clowns-are-up-to-now sort of way. In 1979, *WWoS* and race promoter Gavin Trippe hosted a motorcycle event that actually created a fork in the racetrack. One path led to superbikes. The other went toward something that didn't get a name until it hit France: supermotard. Serious supermotard racers use big dirt bikes with 17-inch road wheels because you just can't ride a humongous road bike on one peg without looking like a clown. Until you try it on an 1100 EVO SP. Then you'll get gawkers but in more of a holy-crap-did-you-see-that sort of way. As long as you do it right.

 The high-beam switch also triggers a lap timer.

 The SP version has 10 more horsepower and weighs 19 pounds less than a standard 1100 EVO.

 Arizona Highway 88 through the Superstition Mountains.

 ★ ★ ★ ★
If you can ride a 1,000cc bike on tarmac with your foot out instead of your knee, you are a rebel.

Engine: Air-cooled, 1,078cc, belt-driven SOHC, desmodromic-valve, four-stroke V-twin
Horsepower: 95 at 7,500 rpm
Top Speed: 135 miles per hour
Weight: n/a
Value Now: $$$

This bike's 95 lbs-ft. of torque and 383-pound curb weight led one motojournalist to say riding it like "pissing Mike Tyson off and taking him to your local bar."

The Streetfighter is the first naked sportbike with traction control.

Anyplace you can go really, really fast without being seen.

★ ★
Superbike performance; ugly bike appearance.

| Engine: Liquid-cooled, | Horsepower: 155 at 9,500 rpm |
| 1,099cc, belt-driven DOHC, | Top Speed: 175 miles per hour |
| desmodromic-valve, | Weight: n/a |
| four-stroke V-twin | Value Now: $$$$ |

### Reconstructing Harry

First Ducati deconstructed the motorcycle with the Monster. Now they've gone and started reconstructing the motorcycle. The Streetfighter might still be a naked bike, but it's starting to get dressed. And not in the elegant Italian couture one might expect from Ducati. No, this is more angular; from the headlight and instrument cluster back across the tank and through the tail, it's high-tech industrial at its best. But, still, its roots are in the 1098, so you forgive its aesthetic shortcomings for the combination of superbike-like performance and actual comfort. Remembering, of course, that comfort is in the seat of the beholder. You always have to trade away something for the opportunity to feel a 150-mile-per-hour breeze on your chest.

# Ducati

## Multistrada

**Jack—and master—of all trades . . . on paved roads, at least**

Just as with Ducati's 999, the European press was merciless toward the Multistrada (another Pierre Treblanche design). Special scorn was heaped upon this bike, with some calling it the ugliest motorcycle ever. Fortunately, clearer heads understood the Multistrada's potential as a versatile platform, which was developed on the Futa Pass, a bumpy, goat-track-like road near the Ducati factory. Excellence there meant an upright riding position, a tractable, torquey engine, and softish, longer-travel suspension. Such elements created a satisfying, accommodating, broad-band bike that could challenge sporting tackle yet still take on commuting and even light touring. It's that versatility that makes the Multistrada (to borrow a phrase from David E. Davis) more fun than a bathtub full of otters.

 The 2005 and later models are your best bet. If your budget will stretch, go for the S-model, which benefits from Öhlins suspension and a few carbon-fiber bits.

 From day one, the Multistrada was developed to live up to its name, which means, roughly, "many roads." Insert the word "paved" between those two, and the bike's intention becomes clear.

 The Futa Pass, where it was developed, of course.

 ★ ★ ★ ★
With its trailie looks, combined with its lusty liter-size V-twin and competent chassis, the Multistrada just goes against the grain—there's nothing else quite like it. But it works.

Engine: Air-cooled, SOHC, four-valve, 90-degree V-twin
Horsepower: 76.7 at 7,500 rpm
Top Speed: 131 miles per hour
Weight: n/a
Value Now: $$$

## Vincent

In 1966, Fritz Egli built his first Vincent-powered bike to use for hillclimb competition.

Our spiritual link to the original Vincent.

Enter the Knox Mountain Hillclimb, held in Kelowna, British Columbia, Canada.

★ ★ ★ ★
Hey, it's a Vincent!

Engine: Air-cooled, 1,000cc, four-stroke, 50-degree V-twin
Horsepower: 66 at 6,200 rpm
Top Speed: 130 miles per hour
Weight: 398 pounds
Value Now: $$$$$

### A new twist on an old design

The Egli name is to Switzerland what Bimota is to Italians. As a company formed by Fritz Egli back in the 1960s, the Egli name has also migrated to England, where John Mossey assembles bikes under that banner—in this case, the Egli Vincent. The engine is a reproduction of the legendary Black Shadow and, when shoehorned into an Egli reproduction frame, makes for an interesting retro-style café racer. The backbone to the Egli Vincent is a spine frame that has a 4.5-inch-diameter tube that doubles as an oil tank, resulting in a stable ride to yesteryear.

# Egli

## Supercharged V-Max

Fritz Egli has four dogs and four cats that he picked up as strays while in Italy, Greece, and Egypt.

Yet another bike in a long line of Egli-inspired motorcycles.

Ride the Maxton's Magic Mile in North Carolina, where you can uncork all that V-Max power.

★ ★ ★ ★
Riding this V-Max is one thing; riding it wide open is another matter entirely.

Engine: Liquid-cooled, 1,500cc, four-stroke V-4
Horsepower: 204 at 9,000 rpm
Top Speed: n/a
Weight: n/a
Value Now: $$

### Overkill to the Max

Fritz Egli has always been known for his eccentric motorcycle designs that produce record-breaking results. Case in point? In 1986, a surpercharged Egli set a world speed record in its class from a standing start to 10 kilometers at nearly 210 miles per hour. Indeed, over the years Egli bikes have produced stellar results, and one of the more interesting design exercises was supercharging a Yamaha V-Max. The package includes 44mm Weber carburetors, a SuperTrapp exhaust, and Cosworth pistons atop Carrillo rods, all compressed into an Egli chassis riding on 17-inch wheels and tires. You can only surmise what the adrenaline rush is like when you thwack the throttle.

# Fischer

## MRX

### Your choice

We've always had small, independent motorcycle manufacturers. Some grow to become market behemoths; others fall by the wayside. It's hard to sell a niche product in a niche market. So why try? Because you have a passion for what you're doing. For Fischer Motor Company, that means you build an $8,000, 357-pound, handmade, 650 V-twin. With Öhlins suspension, no less. And no high-falutin' electronic fuel injection; it's carbs all the way, baby. If they're good enough for NASCAR, they're good enough for a bike from NASCAR's home country. And, really, who wouldn't rather fiddle with jets and screws than a laptop? That's what manly men and women do. Will the Fischer MRX succeed where others have failed? It's entirely up to you.

 It has a leather seat cover.

 World's first single-piece chassis.

 Entrepreneur Lane, Palm Desert, California.

 ★ ★
We just don't know yet.

Engine: Liquid-cooled, 647cc, DOHC, four-stroke V-twin
Horsepower: 80 at 9,400 rpm
Top Speed: n/a
Weight: n/a
Value Now: $$

That thing had a Hemi.

 This bike gave Italy a source of national pride, as per Mussolini's divine will.

 Via Messina Marine south from Palermo, Italy.

 ★ ★ ★ ★
Built at the suggestion of a historic rebel, albeit not the cuddly, James Dean kind.

| | |
|---|---|
| Engine: Air-cooled, 498cc, OHV, four-stroke single | Top Speed: 130 miles per hour (with dustbin fairing) |
| Horsepower: 42 at 6,500 rpm | Weight: n/a |
| | Value Now: $$$$ |

## The bike Benito built

Benito Mussolini was a bad, bad man. But he wasn't all bad, especially if you're a fan of Italian motorcycle racing. Mussolini is responsible for all Italian motorcycle racing success, since he decreed that Italian manufacturers had to produce winning race machines. So Giuseppe Gilera went to work, and in 1940 the first Gilera Saturno won its first race, the Targa Florio. It kept winning until the multicylinder Gileras took over in the mid-1950s and was particularly successful as a sidehack. Gilera would influence the sport in other ways too. The company made the transverse four a motorcycle-racing staple, and in 1956, Gilera engineer Franco Passoni created the dustbin fairing. The latter worked so well it was immediately banned by the F.I.M. An ironically Benito-like move.

GILERA 500 4C.

336

# Gilera

## 500cc World Grand Prix Champion

### Swan song

Giuseppe Gilera's son, Ferruccio, had a heart attack and died as the 1957 racing season began. Gilera was at the peak of its success in motorcycle competition, but Giuseppe lost interest in everything after his son's death. Thus Gilera coasted to its final manufacturer's title that year. The new dustbin fairing required changes in the motorcycle's frame, but those changes never came. Primary rider Geoff Duke injured his shoulder in a fall at the first race in Imola and missed the next three races. Bob McIntyre broke the ton mark at the Isle of Man Senior TT on the Gilera multi, and Gilera riders finished 1–2–3 in the world championship, but in 1958, Giuseppe Gilera pulled the plug, and Gilera would race no more.

 In addition to Gilera's 44 international Grand Prix titles, the company also won numerous ISDT medals.

 This was the first bike to break the ton at the Isle of Man.

 Via Ferruccio Gilera northeast out of Arcore, Italy.

 ★ ★ ★ ★
Props for winning six of eight world titles before being retired.

Engine: Air-cooled, 499cc, DOHC, four-stroke, inline four-cylinder
Horsepower: 70 at 10,500 rpm
Top Speed: 155 miles per hour
Weight: n/a
Value Now: $$$$

# Gurney

## Alligator

### Only in America

What the hell is this? It's gotta be designed by a car guy—look how you sit *in* it. If leaning back with your feet stuck out in front of you is trademark chopper design, and if choppers are wildly popular, then this thing should be wildly popular, right? It's simple logic. But maybe design by committee isn't so bad, if the Alligator is what one man's vision can give us. Everything about it does make sense: the aforementioned exercise in aesthetic logic; the straight-up physical facts concerning gravity centers; and the sublime beauty of a single-cylinder engine. But moving one's weight about is a crucial part of riding. Keeping one's body fixed in place is a crucial part of driving. You do the math.

 You can have a lot of fun with an Alligator. Just don't try to make it do stuff it doesn't want to do.

 The Alligator's creator motorized the recumbent bicycle.

 Eyre Highway, Nullarbor Plain, Australia.

 ★ ★ ★ ★ ★
Think what you want, the Alligator defines rebelliousness.

Engine: Air-cooled, 670cc, SOHC, four-stroke single
Horsepower: Not enough
Top Speed: Too high
Weight: n/a
Value Now: $$$

# Harley-Davidson

## Model 1

**Proof that William Harley and Arthur Davidson's big bang theory worked**

Historians concur that this is indeed the bike that William Harley, with the help of the Davidson brothers (Arthur, Walter, and William) built in the legendary wooden shed back in aught-three. Those historians base their conclusions on evidence that the number *1* was found stamped on various components, among them the engine's flywheel and carburetor, and the frame's fork stem. Sure, much has changed on the bike since then because the bike served as a rolling test bed, but think about it in terms of the family hammer: the handle has been changed three times, and the head was replaced once, but it's still the same hammer that Grandpa handed down to my dad who passed it on to me.

 William Harley and Arthur Davidson originally considered a liquid-cooled engine but decided an air-cooled design would be less complex and cheaper to build.

 The first Harley-Davidson—ever.

 Start your ride at the Harley-Davidson Museum in Milwaukee, Wisconsin, and finish it there, because that's the only place this priceless motorcycle is going.

 ★ ★ ★ ★ ★
This is the leader of the pack.

Engine: Air-cooled, 25-cubic-inch, four-stroke single-cylinder
Horsepower: 3 at 1,000 rpm
Top Speed: n/a
Weight: 180 pounds
Value Now: You'll have to buy the company if you want to buy the bike.

## Model X-8-A Silent Gray Fellow

 Early Harley-Davidsons, such as the X-8-A, had a belt final-drive. Those belts were made of leather, not a rubber composite like that used for belt construction today.

 The X-8-A represented a fresh approach for Harley-Davidson in terms of frame design.

 Any road that has a posted speed limit under 35 miles per hour.

 How cool is it to ride a century-old motorcycle?

Engine: Air-cooled, 30-cubic-inch, four-stroke single cylinder
Horsepower: A couple—maybe
Top Speed: n/a
Weight: n/a
Value Now: $$$$$

**State-of-the-art riding comfort, thanks to an innovative system known as a Ful-Floteing Seat**

Before there were Hogs, there were Silent Gray Fellows, a moniker that Harley-Davidson motorcycles earned back in the day. Two features accounted for the name: the early Harley engines were relatively quiet, and the motorcycles they powered were, well, gray in color. But the Model X-8-A was more—it also offered, for the era, a rather comfortable ride, thanks to a feature known as a Ful-Floteing Seat. The odd name was a marketing description for a frame that included a spring in the seat post. Harley eventually eliminated the standard gray color, and the bikes got louder, but the sprung center post remained until 1958 when somebody in Milwaukee finally realized that shock absorbers would work on Big Twin bikes as well as on Sportsters.

# Harley-Davidson

## Model S Peashooter

**No transmission, no exhaust pipes, no suspension, no brakes. No kidding.**

Imagine, if you will, swinging a leg over the Peashooter's token rear fender, placing your most cherished anatomical parts onto its sliver of a saddle, gripping the low-slung handlebars, and then heading onto the racetrack where you'll be sliding through the turns with about a dozen other crazy riders to see who's fastest. Oh, yeah, and your bike has no brakes and no suspension. And we mustn't forget that the tires are about the size of those on a bicycle. Sound exciting? That's what some of America's top racers had to look forward to back in the 1920s and early '30s with Harley-Davidson's Model S Peashooter. Finally, about the name, Peashooter: according to legend it came from the *pop-pop-pop* sound from the open exhaust.

 The Peashooter dominated its class until the British-built J.A.P. entered the racing scene a few years later.

 Among the riders to race a Peashooter was a young man named Joe Petrali, who became one of America's most successful racers of his time.

 A smooth, hard-pack, half-mile (or shorter) oval dirt track.

 ★ ★ ★ ★ ★
Despite its corny name and diminutive engine size, the Peashooter earns all five leather jackets.

Engine: Air-cooled, 346cc, four-stroke single cylinder
Horsepower: 12 at 3,500 rpm

Top Speed: n/a
Weight: 240 pounds
Value Now: $$$$$

# Harley-Davidson

## Model EL Knucklehead

The 61-inch engine remained in the lineup until 1953, coincidently, the same year that Indian went out of business.

The overhead-valve EL's debut in 1936 accelerated the coming demise of the Indian Motorcycle Company, which floundered with its antiquated flathead and inline four engines.

A lazy, meandering country road during a warm, sunny autumn day. Destination: yesterday.

★ ★ ★ ★
The Knucklehead was among the bikes present at Hollister in 1947.

Engine: Air-cooled, four-stroke, 45-degree V-twin
Horsepower: 40 at 4,500 rpm
Top Speed: 100 miles per hour
Weight: 515 pounds
Value Now: $$$$$

**Every overhead-valve Big Twin from Milwaukee traces its DNA to the 1936 E and EL**

What is it about the number *1* that's so special? We covet first-print editions of classic novels, and there's something unique about owning a No. 1 limited-run lithograph. Even gearheads enjoy taking delivery of a vehicle—be it car, truck, or motorcycle—with a 001 serial number. And so it is with the 1936 Harley-Davidson Model E or EL, the first overhead-valve Big Twin from America's iconic motorcycle company: this is the touchstone model among Harley enthusiasts today. In truth, there's nothing special or exciting about riding the EL; it's slow, cumbersome, and bouncy. But, dang it, this was the first of a breed that now numbers in the millions. That big Electra Glide or chrome-laden Softail that you ride today owes its heritage to the 1936 EL. That's rather special.

# Harley-Davidson

## Model EL Land Speed Record Bike

### How you break wind determines how you set a land speed record

Before this EL could break the American land speed record, it needed a few modifications, among them performance parts for the engine and a streamlined body to cut through the air more efficiently. Some Harley engineers answered the call, corralling 65 horsepower into the 61-cubic-inch engine and wrapping the package with what they felt was slippery sheet metal. The engine worked, but the aerodynamic body didn't; those special body panels and fairing created handling problems when crosswinds blew. Turns out that rider Joe Petrali set the record with most of the speed armor removed. Petrali's first run copped the record at 134.830 miles per hour, and he followed that with a 136.183-mile-per-hour pass. That same day, Petrali also broke the Class C speed record, riding a Model WL to 102.047 miles per hour.

 After retiring from racing, Joe Petrali worked for Hughes Aircraft, serving as flight engineer on the Spruce Goose.

 This bike broke the American land speed record of 132 miles per hour.

 Ride on Daytona Beach, Florida's hard-packed beach, where it set the record back in 1937.

 ★ ★ ★ ★ ★
Joe Petrali was fearless.

Engine: Air-cooled, 61-cubic-inch, 45-degree V-twin
Horsepower: 65 at 5,700 rpm

Top Speed: 136 miles per hour
Weight: n/a
Value Now: $$$$$

Harley-Davidson introduced a KR race version of its new Model K in 1952, eventually relegating the WR to field-filler status.

 Jack Dale set a Class C land speed record for 45-inchers at the Bonneville Salt Flats in 1951, registering a top speed of 123.521 miles per hour through the lights.

 Slip on a steel shoe and take a ride at the annual AMCA meet at Davenport, Iowa, and take on the Indian Scout 101s.

 ★ ★ ★ ★ ★
Remember, the WR doesn't have brakes.

Engine: Air-cooled, 45-cubic-inch, four-stroke V-twin
Horsepower: 38 at 5,000 rpm
Top Speed: 110 miles per hour
Weight: 300 pounds
Value Now: $$$$$

**A Class C racer that was a class A act**

Ever since Walter Davidson earned a Diamond Medal in the 1908 National Endurance Run, the Harley-Davidson Motor Company has been synonymous with motorcycle racing. Among the bikes that carried the Bar and Shield logo onto the racetrack was the Model WR. The WR was based on the WL, which was powered by a rugged 45-cubic-inch, flathead engine. By stripping the WL to the bare essentials—it helped that early Class C rules disallowed brakes—a race-ready WR could check in at the start line weighing about 300 pounds. Add a set of aluminum high-compression heads, some performance camshafts (Tom Sifton cut his teeth with that formula), and a set of straight pipes, and a WR was good for more than 110 miles per hour on a mile-long oval dirt track.

# Harley-Davidson

## Model WLA

 For many years after World War II ended, surplus WLAs were available in the crate for less than $500.

 This is the bike that helped win the war.

 The Normandy beaches are a good place to start.

 If leather ain't your style, try a flak jacket.

Engine: Air-cooled, 45-cubic-inch V-twin,
Horsepower: Enough to kick Hitler's butt

Top Speed: 65 miles per hour
Weight: 576 pounds
Value Now: $$$$$

### At ease, men, we're only going for a brief ride this morning

Motorcycles proved their worth for messenger and escort duty during World War I, so when the United States entered World War II, the armed forces turned to Harley-Davidson and Indian to supply the military with newer, more modern motorcycles for that conflict. The bikes had to withstand abuse and rugged terrain, and the best choice turned out to be a modified version of Harley-Davidson's WL. The WL's low-compression, L-head engine could run all day on low-grade gasoline; the bike's basic platform was rugged and time-tested; and the Motor Company was already geared to produce the WLA in mass numbers. Which it did, producing more than 90,000 units by the war's end.

The XA was based on Germany's BMW motorcycles.

 The XA was the first Harley-Davidson to utilize a foot-shift transmission, an active rear suspension, and a wet-sump lubrication system.

 A lap around the Pentagon might earn a salute or two.

 ★ ★ ★ ★ ★
We give the XA five jackets because Harley-Davidson set aside its jingoistic pride and copied the enemy's design to beat them at their own game.

| | |
|---|---|
| Engine: Air-cooled, 45-cubic-inch, horizontally opposed twin | Top Speed: 65 miles per hour |
| Horsepower: 23 at 4,600 rpm | Weight: 538 pounds |
| | Value Now: $$$$$ |

**An opposed twin to oppose the enemy in Europe**
In 1939, the smashing success that Hitler's army enjoyed using *blitzkrieg* tactics sent this chilling message to Allied forces: if your army isn't mobile, then you stand a chance of losing big time. The top brass calling the shots for the U.S. military realized that, and part of their solution was to modernize the army with motorcycles, which offered fast-action response under varied conditions. Harley-Davidson answered the call with two basic candidates, the WLA and the XA. In the end, the WLA was chosen, primarily due to its low cost and high reliability. Even though the XA met all of the military's requirements in the field, the bike's complexity and high cost played against it.

# Harley-Davidson

## Model K

### An American-made bike with a British accent

By the early 1950s, the British bike invasion was in full swing. Bikes with nameplates like Norton, Triumph, BSA, Royal Enfield, Ariel, and AJS were eroding sales from Harley-Davidson's and Indian's markets. Something had to be done, and the K model was Harley-Davidson's first retaliatory shot across the bow of the Queen's invading armada. Even though the Model K's performance was inferior to that of the Brit bikes, the shot ultimately proved effective; by 1984 all of the British brands had sunk into oblivion. Oh, Triumph resurfaced in the 1990s, and most recently Norton has made a minor comeback, but both revived companies are stuck in the wake left by the Harley-Davidson juggernaut that gained so much momentum during the past three decades.

 With its foot-shift transmission, hand clutch, and integral four-speed transmission, the K represented the most technologically advanced model in Harley-Davidson's lineup for 1952.

 This is the bike that eventually led to the creation of a much faster Sportster.

 A short hop to the local watering hole. Just hope that a 1952 Triumph doesn't show up at the same traffic light as you.

 ★ ★
By 1952, Harley's 45-cubic-inch, side-valve engine was getting long in the tooth.

Engine: Air-cooled, 45-cubic-inch V-twin
Horsepower: 30 at 4,500 rpm

Top Speed: 80 miles per hour
Weight: 400 pounds
Value Now: $$$$

Even though Harley-Davidson replaced its side-valve K model with the overhead-valve Sportster in 1957, it wasn't until 1970 that the first XR750—a race version of the Sportster—appeared on the racing scene.

 The last Harley to win the Daytona 200 was the KRTT ridden by the late, great Cal Rayborn in 1969.

 While any oval dirt track will suffice, the top choice is the Springfield Mile.

 ★ ★ ★ ★ ★
American heroes with names like Resweber, Markel, Roeder, Reiman, Lawwill, and Rayborn rode KRs.

| | |
|---|---|
| Engine: Air-cooled, 750cc, four-stroke V-twin | Top Speed: 125 miles per hour |
| Horsepower: 50 at 7,000 rpm | Weight: 320 pounds |
| | Value Now: $$$$$ |

**This old side-valver just refused to lose**

From 1955 through 1969, Harley-Davidson's KR750 was winner of all but three AMA Grand National Championships, making it the most successful race bike of its time. The side-valve engine produced what Mert Lawwill, the last rider to win a race and a championship aboard the KR, described as "a soft kind of power. You could really control it on the dirt." Fittingly, the KR's success and longevity were surpassed by its replacement, the XR750, an overhead-valve model that bowed in 1970.

# Harley-Davidson

## Model B Hummer

### A smokin' good time!

What is it about little bikes that fascinates us so much? Maybe the tiny tiddlers remind us of our formative years as motorcycle riders. Or, simply, the teapot engines aren't threatening pieces of hardware. Macho experience doesn't account for much when there's only about 3 horsepower beneath you in the first place. And so it is that Harley-Davidson's Model S—offered in various engine displacements and chassis configurations through the years—has become so popular among collectors today. We've selected the 1955 Hummer for our ride, basing it on the model's original intent of swaying first-time buyers into the Bar and Shield fold.

 The Model S bowed in 1948, but it wasn't until 1955 that Harley applied the moniker "Hummer" in honor of Dean Hummer, a dealer in Omaha, Nebraska, who sold more Model S motorcycles than any other H-D franchise owner.

 The original Model S was based on blueprints for the German-built DKW. As part of the war reparations, patent rights were shared by America (Harley-Davidson), England (BSA Bantam), and the Soviet Union (Mockba M1A).

 Any New England township that is situated on level ground and has a town square to cruise around.

 * No doubt it's a cute little bike, but come on, it's a 125 that can barely keep up with its own shadow!

Engine: Air-cooled, 125cc, two-stroke single
Horsepower: 3.5 at 3,000 rpm

Top Speed: n/a
Weight: 178 pounds
Value Now: $$

Cook Neilson, former editor for *Cycle* magazine and winner of the 1977 Daytona Superbike race, owned a 1964 XLCH.

In 1957, California Harley dealers supposedly asked the Motor Company for a Sportster that would convert easily for competition, requesting that its engine have high compression. Thus was born the XLCH.

Just getting that magneto-fired engine started was worthy of being called a perfect ride!

★ ★ ★ ★ ★
Starting the XLCH's engine was half the fun; riding the bike constituted the other half of the excitement.

| | |
|---|---|
| Engine: Air-cooled, 883cc, four-stroke V-twin | Top Speed: 122 miles per hour |
| | Weight: 480 pounds |
| Horsepower: 55 at 5,000 rpm | Value Now: $$$$ |

**You might say that Harley-Davidson built this bike just for kicks**

Today, macho Harley riders are quick to label the Sportster a "girl's bike." Not so back in 1958 when the XLCH rolled into the limelight. This was the king-daddy of Sportsters, the hairy-chested equivalent of today's GSX-R1000. The potent XLCH engine sported competition cams and high-compression pistons and heads. The 883cc mill also used a magneto ignition, and there was no battery, which meant that you kick-started the engine. And that was the rub, because the XLCH answered the call when it was damn well ready, and no sooner. As Allan Girdler wrote in his book *Harley-Davidson Sportster*: "Tests of the day always said you had to learn the drill and then it was easy (and former XLCH owners always said they had it down pat)." Girdler's key phrase: *former* XLCH owners.

# Harley-Davidson

## Model C Sprint

### An American bike with Italian spirit

No doubt, when the first Sprint was uncrated by a Harley-Davidson dealer in 1961, there must have been a sense of curiosity and concern among the tattooed brethren who were used to more manly bikes occupying the dealership's showroom floor. The Italian-made bike looked a little odd—the 250cc engine had its cylinder horizontally positioned, and the frame was a mix of round tubing and pressed-steel sections. The tank and seat favored aesthetics associated with European bikes—certainly not American—and there was little chrome to accent the red-and-white paint. Yet the bike was, well, cool-looking in an odd sort of way. It helped, too, that a sexy CRTT road-race model soon followed, and that a few years later the Motor Company built a Sprint-powered streamliner that went 177 miles per hour.

 George Roeder rode a Sprint-powered streamliner to a 250cc land speed record at the Bonneville Salt Flats in 1965. He went 176.817 miles per hour.

 The Sprint was the first model that Harley-Davidson imported after acquiring the Italian-based Aermacchi company.

 Threading through New York City traffic to fulfill a dinner engagement with actress Carla Gugino at Da Nico Ristorante in Little Italy.

 Remember, there's no replacement for displacement.

Engine: Air-cooled, 250cc, four-stroke single
Horsepower: 18 at 5,500 rpm
Top Speed: 90 miles per hour
Weight: 280 pounds
Value Now: $$

Even the three-wheeled Servi-Car, first introduced in 1931, was given electric starting one year before the Big Twin.

Made for a much cooler movie title than *Duo-Glide in Blue* would have.

Daytona Beach, Americade, and any other event where regal-legal eagles soar.

★ ★
How tough can it be? You've got the electric leg to help you start the engine now.

| | |
|---|---|
| Engine: Air-cooled, 74-cubic-inch, four-stroke V-twin | Top Speed: 98 miles per hour |
| Horsepower: 60 at 5,400 rpm | Weight: 783 pounds |
| | Value Now: $$$$ |

**The electric leg joins the FL line to produce the Electra Glide**

When Harley-Davidson debuted its EL engine in 1936, the overhead-valve Big Twin was hailed as a milestone design. Its advanced technology clearly placed the Motor Company at the forefront of American motorcycle design and innovation. And then, with glacial speed, Harley's engineers set about finding ways to adapt an electric starter to their new engine. Finally, 29 years later, their epic quest came to an end, and thus was born the Electra Glide. With the simple push of a plastic button, the 74-cubic-inch engine could be fired to life.

# Harley-Davidson

## Captain America

**When somebody says the word *chopper*, this is the bike that comes to mind**

Forget about performance, and don't even think about comfort or a smooth ride. The Captain America bike isn't about any of that. In fact, like *Easy Rider*, the film that it starred in, this Panhead chopper flips the finger to all that's right and wrong about the world as it was in 1969, as it is today, and as it will be tomorrow. Even so, when you settle your American fanny onto that wafer-thin banana seat and reach for the ape-hanger handlebars, you're going to feel cool and hip.

 Dennis Hopper, Peter Fonda's *Easy Rider* co-star, wasn't an accomplished rider, so his bike lacked the radical raked front end found on the Captain America bike.

 This was the bike that pretty much launched the chopper craze that swept over America during the 1970s.

 Anywhere but a Louisiana swamp during duck-hunting season.

 ★ ★ ★ ★ ★
What is it rebelling against? What have you got?

Engine: Air-cooled, 74-cubic-inch, four-stroke V-twin
Horsepower: 60 at 4,500 rpm

Top Speed: Depends on your drug of choice
Weight: n/a
Value Now: $$$$$

The FX Super Glide wasn't equipped with an electric starter until 1974. That model was known as the FXE.

 The FX created a new market niche—the factory custom.

 The next Harley-Davidson Homecoming. And when you see Willie G. Davidson, have him autograph the gas tank.

 ★★
Hey, it's a factory custom, so everybody knows that *you* didn't build it.

Engine: Air-cooled, 74-cubic-inch, four-stroke V-twin
Horsepower: 65 at 5,400 rpm
Top Speed: 108 miles per hour
Weight: 559 pounds
Value Now: $$$$

**A bike with a parts manifest that was shaken, not stirred**

When Willie G. Davidson stripped the FL Electra Glide of its bulbous components, plucked a few odds and ends out of the Sportster bin, and then combined it all to create the 1971 FX Super Glide, he changed the way Harley-Davidson markets its bikes to this day. The concept is simple, when you think about it—take the smallest number of parts, spend as little money as you can, and blend it all together to produce a whole new motorcycle. In the process, the company saves money on the design and developmental stages of various models. The net result: more profits for future company growth. How simple can it be?

# Harley-Davidson

## XR-750

### Milwaukee's finest

Ever since its introduction in 1972, Harley-Davidson's XR-750 dirt-track weapon has had but one mission: chew bubblegum and kick ass from Indianapolis to Sacramento. And it was always out of bubblegum. Result? The winningest race bike—ever. Not only did the XR-750 take the AMA Grand National Championship in its debut year, up until 2008 it swept 29 out of 37 such AMA titles, and it still wins races today. Not too shabby for a motorcycle Harley stopped selling as a complete bike in 1980. Even Evel Knievel, the most famous motorcyclist in the world, used the XR-750 for many of his airborne exploits.

 The first XR-750s, with iron cylinders and heads, were introduced in 1970, but their distinctly average performance—and distinctly below average reliability—meant the 1972 XR with its alloy parts was a welcome change.

 Most successful race bike of all time—even with a low-tech, air-cooled, pushrod V-twin.

 Flat out, left foot down, ass hanging out, around the classic AMA Mile tracks: Indy, Springfield, or Sacramento.

 ★★ H-Ds have always been the go-to motorcycle for rebels and easy riders. In this country, though, the XR-750 has represented the status quo in dirt-track racing for most of a generation.

Engine: Air-cooled, 45-degree, OHV V-twin
Horsepower: 90 at 9,000 rpm
Top Speed: 130 miles per hour
Weight: n/a
Value Now: approximately $$$$$

The Shortster's 65cc, two-stroke engine was originally used in the Aermacchi Legero.

 Who knows how many of today's mondo-macho Big Twin riders got their start on the Shortster?

 Zipping through the pits at the Indy Mile on your way to the riders' meeting.

 ✳ Too many jackets will weigh this bike down. After all, it's a mini.

Engine: Air-cooled, 65cc, two-stroke single
Horsepower: n/a

Top Speed: n/a
Weight: 126 pounds
Value Now: $$

**Make no mistake, this mini isn't short on fun**

What's in a name? A lot, really. For instance, take the Shortster. Without looking at the picture, what's the first thing that comes to mind when you hear the name Shortster? That's right, a short bike. Harleyites will be even more specific and tout the word to describe "a short Harley" because Shortster sounds so much like Sportster. And they would be right because the Shortster was Harley's venture into the mini-bike market that was so popular at the time. Truth be told, the Shortster was probably one of the hippest minis of its time. Its styling favored that of an off-road bike, which was appealing to the youth market, and chromed fenders gave the mini a somewhat sophisticated look. The Shortster may have been diminutive in size, but it wasn't short on character.

# Harley-Davidson

## Model OHC-1100 Experimental

**Had somebody in Harley-Davidson management given the nod, this could have been the Evolution engine**

Ever since the days of Adam and Eve, the appeal of consuming the forbidden fruit has challenged man's discipline and self-control. Who among us can resist taking a swipe of frosting off a freshly baked cake, or dipping into the cookie batter for a quick taste? The same holds true about our motorcycles, and we'd love to ride this prototype that Harley-Davidson toyed with during the mid-1970s. The 1,100cc V-twin engine had overhead cams, and its cylinders were offset and splayed more than the customary 45 degrees. Each cylinder also had its own carburetor, and the engine was rubber-mounted. The OHC-1100's frame favored that of imports, and no production Harley had yet utilized triple disc brakes and cast-aluminum wheels. Nobody knows the impact the OHC-1100 would have had on the industry, but wouldn't it be grand to ride this bike today?

 The surviving OHC-1100 prototype isn't a runner, but several engines were tested on dyno stands.

 This bike shows how ominously close Harley-Davidson came to mimicking the rest of the industry during the AMF years.

 Any roadhouse or hangout frequented by the Harley brethren.

 ★ ★ ★ ★
You just know some of the Harley faithful are going to question if this is a *gen-u-ine* Hog.

Engine: Air-cooled, 1,100cc, OHC, four-stroke V-twin
Horsepower: n/a
Top Speed: n/a
Weight: n/a
Value Now: $$$$$

Enzo Ferrari, the patriarch of the automobile company that bore his name, described Walter Villa as "the Nicki Lauda of the bike world—a thinking racer."

Italy's Walter Villa rode the RR-250 to three straight Grand Prix World Championships (1974–1976). He also won the 350cc world championship in 1976 aboard a similar model, the RR-350.

Mugello, Imola, or Monza racetracks, with thousands of screaming Italians cheering you on.

★ ★ ★ ★ ★
Make those five fine, handcrafted, Italian-leather jackets.

| | |
|---|---|
| Engine: Liquid-cooled, 246cc, two-stroke twin | Top Speed: 140 miles per hour |
| Horsepower: 53 at 11,000 rpm | Weight: 240 pounds |
| | Value Now: $$$$ |

**When two strokes will get you four . . . world championships**

Why, oh why would Harley-Davidson ever want to take its orange, white, and black colors onto the road-race courses of Europe? The whole idea is—please excuse the pun—**foreign** to any red-blooded Harley rider's way of thinking. Yet the company did just that during the mid-1970s with a motorcycle powered by a twin-cylinder, two-stroke engine. In truth, about the only two things American about that road-race venture were that the bike carried the name AMF/Harley-Davidson on the fairing and that it required American greenbacks to underwrite the program. The net result: Walter Villa and company scored gold in the 250cc world championships (three times) and struck it rich a single time in the 350cc class for the American capitalists.

# Harley-Davidson

## SX-250

**¡Gringos en Motocicletas Invaden Baja California!**
Sometimes heroes are born overnight. Case in point: this motorcycle. Before 1975, few people took Harley-Davidson's Aermacchi-built 250cc off-road model seriously. But two young men familiar with desert and off-road racing in Southern California saw things differently, and with the help of a local dealership, they began to transform a rather sedentary SX-250 into a contender to win the 1975 Baja 500 in Mexico. Larry Roeseler and the late Bruce Ogilvie gave their two-stroke Harley more than a few modifications, and in the end, their work—not to mention their hard riding—paid off. They won the Baja 500 motorcycle class on June 13, 1975.

 Ogilvie and Roeseler won the Baja 500 aboard their modified SX-250 on Friday the 13th. They completed the race in 8 minutes, 16.53 seconds.

 The only Harley to win the Baja 500.

 The Baja California peninsula, of course.

 ★★★★★
Larry Roeseler is known as the ironman of off-road racing, and the late Bruce Ogilvie was no slouch in the saddle, either.

Engine: Air-cooled, 250cc, two-stroke single
Horsepower: n/a
Top Speed: n/a
Weight: n/a
Value Now: $$$$

Some of the XLCR's key components—chief among them the triangulated frame, Siamese exhaust system, and seven-spoke cast-aluminum wheels—were used on future Sportster models.

Café racers were popular during the 1970s, prompting Harley-Davidson to join the pack in 1977.

A smooth mountain road with long, gentle curves.

✷✷
The XLCR looks cool, but if you're looking for snappy performance, it ain't a fun ride.

| | |
|---|---|
| Engine: Air-cooled, 1,000cc, four-stroke V-twin<br>Horsepower: n/a | Top Speed: 105 miles per hour<br>Weight: 470 pounds<br>Value Now: $$$$$ |

**A café racer or a decaf racer?**

Harley-Davidson's XLCR is a model that you either love to hate or hate to love. In step with the café racer trend that prevailed in Europe, Willie G. Davidson penned an all-new bike for Harley customers in 1977 with the XLCR. Even to this day, enthusiasts comment about the CR's classic styling, but clearer heads prevail when discussing the bike's lethargic performance in terms of handling, speed, and braking. As the lads at *Hot Bike* magazine wrote in their December 1977 issue, "It is a motorcycle that, no matter what its performance figures indicate, will be the focal point for riders to swarm around and ask the proverbial question, 'How do you like it?'"

## XR1000

### An oh-so-sexy engine cradled in an oh-so-plain chassis

Harley's XR1000 is a classic example of a good idea gone bad. The original concept was to offer a Sportster-based bike that shared much of its DNA with the Motor Company's legendary XR750 flat track racer. For the most part, the XR1000's engine lived up to its billing, boasting high-flow heads, shark-tooth cams, twin carbs, and upswept exhausts similar to those of the XR750. Sadly, this jewel of

 Despite their intimidating appearance, the XR's upswept mufflers aren't as loud as you might suspect.

 The XR1000 lacks a lot of the race-bred refinement of the XR750, but it's as close as Harley-Davidson has ever come for such a street model.

 Head to the Bonneville Salt Flats so that you can enjoy the unadulterated racket presented by that air-cooled engine's high-lift cams, dual Dell'Orto carbs, and upswept exhaust pipes.

 ★ ★ ★
Had Harley's stylists given the XR1000 a seat and gas tank combo similar to what's on the XR750 racer, and had they laced a set of 18-inch wheels front and rear, this bike would warrant the full five-jacket wardrobe.

| | |
|---|---|
| Engine: Air-cooled, 1,000cc, four-stroke V-twin | Top Speed: 120 miles per hour |
| Horsepower: 70 at 7,000 rpm | Weight: 470 pounds |
| | Value Now: $$$ |

an engine was nestled into a rather plain and agrarian XLX chassis. And the XLX was the company's low-line model in 1983. Add in the fact that Harley lacked the funds to properly develop the engine for street use, and you have a bike that makes a better museum piece than a motorcycle.

## Lucifer's Hammer

### Nailing the competition to the cross because the devil made them do it

Back in the early 1980s, the AMA instituted a new road-race class called Battle of the Twins (BOTT). The BOTT was enough reason for Harley-Davidson's race team manager, Dick O'Brien, to build a bike for the series' first race, the 1983 Daytona BOTT. Jay Springsteen was the rider, and he effectively told all the other racers where to go, easily winning aboard his Harley-Davidson. Subsequently, O'Brien dubbed the bike *Lucifer's Hammer*, which ultimately found its way into the hands of seasoned tuner Don Tilley, who also happened to own a Harley dealership in North Carolina. Tilley gained sponsorship from HOG (Harley Owner's Group), hired Gene Church to swing the *Hammer* on the track, and proceeded to win three BOTT championships in a row.

 The *Hammer*'s frame originated from the twisted pile of tubing that once was Mark Brelsford's ride—an XRTT—when he had his infamous ball-of-flames crash at Daytona in 1973.

 Carroll Resweber, the AMA's first four-time Grand National Champion (1960–1964), helped H-D race team manager Dick O'Brien resurrect the bike for its first race in 1983.

 Daytona International Speedway, the same place where Jay Springsteen, and later Gene Church, won.

 ★ ★ ★ ★ ★
Thanks to an enormously wide powerband, you can ride the *Hammer* with a devil-may-care attitude.

| | |
|---|---|
| Engine: Air-cooled, 1,000cc, four-stroke, 45-degree V-twin | Weight: 385 pounds (estimated) |
| Horsepower: 115 (estimated) at 7,500 rpm | Value Now: There's only one *Lucifer's Hammer*, owned by Don Tilley, and it'll be a cold day in hell before he sells it! |
| Top Speed: 165 miles per hour | |

The Nova engine was designed as a modular motor. The concept allowed for V-twin, V-4, and even V-6 versions.

 Porsche's engine specialists helped develop the Nova's powerplant.

 A trip to the Ronald Reagan Presidential Library in California to salute the man who supported import tariffs for motorcycles with engines larger than 700cc.

 ★ ★ ★
Two things to keep in mind about the Nova: it was a masterful stroke by Harley to develop it, and it proved an even more masterful stroke that the company decided not to market it.

Engine: Air-cooled, 1,000cc, four-stroke V-4
Horsepower: 90 at 8,000 rpm
Top Speed: n/a
Weight: n/a
Value Now: Tens of millions of dollars would probably make it yours

## Back to the future that never was

In 1976, the Harley-Davidson Motor Company was struggling with quality and reliability issues. Subsequently, during an executive meeting that addressed the company's future, management settled on two programs that would influence upcoming designs. First, they decided to follow through on updating the Shovelhead engine, the result being the Evolution project. Second, they set in motion an all-new program for a touring machine with a liquid-cooled V-4 engine, a project that became known as the Nova. While much of the Nova was based on technologically sound ideas, history tells us today that the multi-cylinder engine probably would have been the wrong path for America's premier motorcycle company to follow.

## FXRS Low Rider Sport Edition

**A Harley that's cool on the boulevard yet agile in the turns**
There's something unsettling about combining the words
*Low Rider* and *Sport Edition* in a motorcycle's name. But that's
exactly what Harley-Davidson did in 1986 to produce the
FXRS Low Rider Sport Edition. (FXLR custom edition shown
below.) Despite the supposed oxymoron, the FXRS provided
a rather balanced package for someone seeking to have
the boulevard cool of a Harley cruiser without sacrificing
ride and handling. The FXRS's suspension was compliant
over stretches of mundane road, yet when curves presented
themselves, the bike lived up to its sport billing. Perhaps the
editors of *Cycle Guide* magazine stated it best when, in their
December 1985 issue, they stated that the FXRS "flies in
the face of the notion that cruisers need be narrow-focus,
single-purpose motorcycles."

 The FXR and FXRS joined the Harley-Davidson lineup in 1982, and from the beginning they received favorable reports from various enthusiast magazines.

 By shuffling a few parts among the various models, each FXR platform could be tailored for different target groups.

 Sepulveda Boulevard, which, at 42.8 miles long, is the longest street in Los Angeles.

 ★ ★
The Low Rider's rather mundane styling (by Harley standards) belies its predictable handling manners.

Engine: Air-cooled, 80-cubic-inch, four-stroke V-twin
Horsepower: 69 at 5,500 rpm
Top Speed: 115 miles per hour
Weight: 592 pounds
Value Now: $$$

## *Terminator* **Fat Boy**

Rumor has it that the name *Fat Boy* was picked by combining *Fat Man* and *Little Boy*, the code names for the atomic bombs dropped on Hiroshima and Nagasaki.

The Fat Boy ranks as one of the longest-running models in Harley-Davidson's storied history.

The streets of Los Angeles, including a stint in the city's cement river.

★ ★
Fat Boys are cool, but in truth, this bike didn't make this movie any cooler than it already was.

Engine: Air-cooled, 80-cubic-inch, four-stroke V-twin
Horsepower: 72 at 5,000 rpm

Top Speed: 112 miles per hour
Weight: 633 pounds
Value Now: $$$

### Hasta la vista, baby!

You don't need to be the governor of California or a muscle-bound former Mr. Universe to ride a Fat Boy—the motorcycle that Arnold Alois Schwarzenegger's character rode in the movie *Terminator 2: Judgment Day*. Harley's familiar Softail model has been available since 1990, making it plentiful in today's motorcycle market. But riding it wildly through the streets of Los Angeles, shotgun in hand while eluding termination by a killer robot that's been transported from the future? Well, now that's a different story altogether. Should you find yourself in that situation aboard a Fat Boy, not to worry—just remind yourself, that's Hollywood.

# Harley-Davidson

## FXDB Sturgis

### An American cruiser worthy of its name

The 1991 Sturgis ushered in an updated chassis for the FX family. The new, stiffer frame required only two rubber engine mounts; the previous FXR design used three. Other improvements included changing the FXDB's primary case casting to alter the mounting angle of the motor by 4 degrees, allowing the assembly to be moved closer to the front of the frame. This, coupled with a 32-degree steering head angle, helped give the Sturgis its longer, lower look.

 The FXDB Sturgis was the first model to use the new Dyna Glide chassis.

 The town of Sturgis, South Dakota, founded in 1878, was named after Colonel Samuel D. Sturgis, commander of nearby Fort Meade.

 The Black Hills Motorcycle Rally in August.

 ★ ★
It seems that every Tom, Dick, and Harry makes it to the Sturgis rally these days.

Engine: Air-cooled, 80-cubic-inch, four-stroke V-twin
Horsepower: 69 at 5000 rpm
Top Speed: 115 miles per hour
Weight: 598 pounds
Value Now: $$$

---

# Harley-Davidson

## FXDWG Dyna Wide Glide

### Since this was a limited-edition model, Harley-Davidson made only 1,993 Wide Glides

Forget the long FXDWG Dyna Wide Glide nomenclature. Hardcore Harleyites refer to this all-American cruiser simply as the Wide Glide. It was first offered during one of the Motor Company's landmark years—feeding off the longevity and heritage factor, Harley-Davidson enthusiasts celebrate the company's anniversary every five years. To commemorate the 90th anniversary in 1993, the factory in York, Pennsylvania, cranked out 1,993 Wide Glides.

 Being an all-new model, the Wide Glide was Harley-Davidson's poster bike for 1993.

 The iconic FXR chassis was still produced in 1993. Production overlap of the Dyna and FXR platforms continued until 1995.

 Take this bike to the next Homecoming, as the celebration ride is called. Every five years, Harley-Davidson hosts a huge party in Milwaukee.

 ★ ★ ★
While the Wide Glide doesn't necessarily have leader-of-the-pack qualities, it's still considered a cool ride when you're hitting the road with the bros.

Engine: Air-cooled, 80-cubic-inch, four-stroke V-twin
Horsepower: 69 at 5,000 rpm
Top Speed: 110 miles per hour
Weight: 598 pounds
Value Now: $$$

## FLSTS Heritage Springer Softail

When Harley-Davidson launched its 1997 new-model line, the company did so with a nationwide open house program that included hundreds of dealers. The event was called OGLEFEST '96. True story.

The FLSTS Heritage Softail was among the Honorable Mentions in *Cycle World* magazine's annual Top 10 Motorcycles.

Cruise past Iowa's cornfields on your way to Anamosa for a visit to the National Motorcycle Museum. Careful where you park—somebody might think your FLSTS belongs to the museum.

★ ★ ★

How many times must we fall back on the nostalgia theme, anyway?

Engine: Air-cooled, 80-cubic-inch, four-stroke V-twin
Horsepower: 69 at 5,000 rpm

Top Speed: miles per hour
Weight: 690 pounds
Value Now: $$$$

**"It's a dramatic motorcycle. It's not for everybody. It's not supposed to be."—Willie G. Davidson**

Most people are familiar with Harley-Davidson playing the heritage trump card when marketing new models based on old designs. But when the Heritage Softail bowed in 1997, Willie G. and company might as well have played the ace of spades, for no other model has dripped and oozed as much nostalgia as the FLSTS. Indeed, Harley-Davidson made no bones about it—the FLSTS took many of its styling cues from the 1948 FL, the last Big Twin to sport a springer fork. "Our history is an important part of our future," stated Willie G. at the bike's unveiling. "It all led to this bike." As the saying goes, to know your future, you need to understand your past.

# Harley-Davidson

## VR-1000 Road Racer

**The most famous superbike never to win a race**
**The last significant Harley-Davidson to race in the prestigious Dayt**ona 200 had been the KR750 that the late Cal Rayborn rode to victory in 1969. In subsequent years, Harley fielded XR750 entries, but they never achieved winning results. Then, in 1994, the orange, white, and black returned with a contender, the VR-1000. The bike showed promise, but with each incremental improvement, the competition found even more speed and reliability from their bikes. As time progressed, the VR-1000 didn't, until the Motor Company threw in the towel in 2001. The VR-1000 never won a race, but it certainly garnered a lot of publicity for the folks in Milwaukee, who hadn't enjoyed this much attention at Daytona's superspeedway since 1969.

 To comply with international World Superbike homologation rules, the base bike must be street legal. The first VR-1000 was registered in Poland.

 Much of the technology from the VR-1000's engine was later applied to the VSRC V-Rod.

 Talladega International Speedway, where the bike never raced. And after you ride the high-banked turns, you can honestly say, "I gave the bike its best finish there."

 ★ ★ ★ ★
Had the VR-1000 won a race, we'd have you don a fifth jacket.

| | |
|---|---|
| Engine: Liquid-cooled, 1,000cc, four-stroke V-twin | Top Speed: 170 miles per hour Weight: n/a |
| Horsepower: 135 at 12,000 rpm | Value Now: $$$$$ |

Pros could turn 9.4-second quarter-mile ET's with the Destroyer.

 The Destroyer represented Harley-Davidson's official return to pro drag racing at the grassroots level.

 Pomona Drag Strip for the Winternationals, where you'll compete in front of 50,000 rabid race fans.

 ★ ★ ★ ★ ★
Our fear-factor rating only goes to five . . .

Engine: Liquid-cooled, 130cc, four-stroke V-twin
Horsepower: 165 at 12,000 rpm
Top Speed: 134 miles per hour (*Cycle World*)
Weight: n/a
Value Now: $$$$$

**How good are you _really_ with the clutch and throttle?**
"It is like walking on tiptoes to the brink of Armageddon. It's louder than hell, you're not sure what's in your near future, you're wondering about your past, and nothing happens until everything happens and you are hurled into the abyss at nearly 2 g's." So wrote *Cycle World*'s Mark Hoyer after riding the V-Rod Destroyer through the quarter-mile. The Destroyer represented Harley-Davidson's contribution to grassroots racing, and the program delivered outstanding results as H-D dealers flocked to the Custom Vehicles Operations' order desk to sign up. But not just anybody was eligible; only qualified racers were allowed in the saddle. That, or you had to be a motojournalist like Hoyer.

# Harley-Davidson

## XL1200N Nightster

**A Dark Custom that brightened up sales for the Motor Company**

It's no secret that the average Harley-Davidson customer today is close to 50 years old. That's half a century old (350 in dog years)! So in its quest to recruit new, younger customers, Harley-Davidson launched what it calls its Dark Customs. Several attempts were made using Big Twins as the styling canvas, but art fully imitated life when in 2007 the XL1200N Nightster saw the light of day. Looking more like a rat bike that a pimply faced hooligan hot-rodder threw together so he could make the Wednesday night grudge drags, the Nightster all but thumbs its nose at vehicle codes across the country. Your 10 grand gets you all sorts of custom features, like a swingarm-mounted license plate, but you'll have to supply the badass attitude yourself.

 The Nightster was designed by 27-year-old Richard Christoph and vice president of Styling Willie G. Davidson. For comparison, Willie G. was 37 when he penned the FX Super Glide.

 Even though several Big Twin models were given the same dark, sinister styling treatment, it was the Nightster that was most responsible for Harley-Davidson's Dark Customs concept catching on.

 Daytona Beach, Florida, during Bike Week, where you can hook up with the cool cats from the Limpnicke Lot. If you don't know who they are, you don't understand what the Nightster is about.

 ★ ★ ★ ★
A bike designed for rebels that costs less than 10 grand? How cool is that?

Engine: Air-cooled, 1,200cc, four-stroke V-twin
Horsepower: 62 at 5,000 rpm
Top Speed: 115 miles per hour
Weight: 545 pounds
Value Now: $$$

The Rocker was the first Harley to be equipped with a 240mm-wide rear tire.

 Harley stylists gave customers what they wanted—or at least what the stylists thought customers wanted.

 Sunset Strip in Hollywood. Ride safe.

 * By 2008, when Harley finally got into the game, the chopper craze had once again subsided.

Engine: Air-cooled, 96-cubic-inch, four-stroke, 45-degree V-twin
Horsepower: 63 at 5,025 rpm
Top Speed: 114 miles per hour
Weight: 686 pounds
Value Now: $$$

### Rock on—with or without a passenger

The fat tire craze among custom bike builders reached its zenith in 2008, the same year that Harley-Davidson joined the party with its Rocker. The Rocker gets its name from the rear fender/tire/swingarm design that enables a fat 240mm Dunlop tire to fit snug under the reinforced rear fender that moves up and down—it "rocks"—with the tire. The complete system was supposed to place the Rocker smack dab in the middle of the custom bike world. The fly in the ointment was that the fold-up rear seat—accomplished by stashing it under and in the rider's seat—consumed valuable space for padding. Result: a rock-hard ride for the biker's fanny. Oh, and also the fact that the whole assembly looked like something pilfered from a personal watercraft.

# Hesketh

## V1000

### The Lord works in mysterious ways

Lord Alexander Hesketh was responsible for the bike that bears his name—the Hesketh V1000. The Hesketh sported an engine developed by Weslake Engineering (the same folks responsible for the V-12 engine used by Dan Gurney's Eagle Formula 1 car in 1967). It was less than spectacular in performance yet breathtaking in appearance and mechanical beauty.

 The good Lord's motorcycle company was in business less than a year. The engine's downfall was poor cooling for the rear cylinder.

 Prior to dabbling in the business of building motorcycles, Lord Alexander Hesketh fielded his own Formula 1 race team with James Hunt as his driver.

 The North Circular Road—officially designated A406—that crosses North London. A stop at the legendary Ace Café to lord that bright red bike over the commoners' pedestrian rides should be on the agenda too.

 **★ ★**
(Tweed) A top-heavy, overweight chassis resulted in a less-than-stellar ride.

Engine: Air-cooled, 992cc, four-stroke V-twin
Horsepower: n/a

Top Speed: 130 miles per hour
Weight: 551 pounds
Value Now: $$$$

# Hesketh

## Vampire

### This Hesketh almost didn't see the light of day

The history of Hesketh Motorcycles reads like a Harlequin romance novel. The incestuous story begins with Lord Hesketh, who formed the company, and weaves its way to include Triumph (that rejuvenated company considered buying Hesketh MC and puting the famous Triumph badge on a Hesketh tank to see if it was a match—it wasn't) before bankruptcy put Hesketh MC out of business. That led to the formation of Hesleydon Ltd., which produced a revamped Hesketh V1000 in the guise of the Vampire. The story doesn't end there; eventually Hesleydon morphed into Broom Development Engineering, which, if we can keep up with the twisting plot, experienced a theft of its key parts inventory during a move to its current digs near the old Silverstone Circuit in England. Yet through all these machinations, Broom et al. managed to build about 50 Vampires. A stake has yet to find its mark, and rumor has it that more Vampires might be on the way.

 The Hesketh was the first British motorcycle engine to use four valves per cylinder and double overhead cams.

 The Vampire was the touring version of the groundbreaking Hesketh V1000.

 As far away from the bankruptcy courts and lawyers as possible.

 **★**
For some reason, it seems more appropriate that a bike called Vampire should have a batwing fairing.

Engine: Air-cooled, 993cc, four-stroke, 90-degree V-twin
Horsepower: n/a

Top Speed: 110 miles per hour
Weight: 538 pounds
Value Now: $$$

## Wombat 125

Hodaka officially went by the company name PABATCO, standing for Pacific Basin Trading Company, with headquarters in Athena, Oregon.

A lightweight, dual-purpose bike that lived up to its name.

A ride down Mexico's Baja Peninsula, where Hodaka established its reputation for speed and reliability nearly 50 years ago.

*
It may not be an exciting ride, but it certainly is a rewarding time in the saddle.

Engine: Air-cooled, 123cc,
    two-stroke single-cylinder
Horsepower: n/a

Top Speed: n/a
Weight: 208 pounds
Value Now: $

### A little bike with big-bike styling

In 1964, most small-displacement motorcycle engines were mounted in pressed-steel frames that looked like they were developed for, well, small-displacement engines. A small company in Oregon changed that by introducing a bike with a 90cc engine cradled in a tube-steel frame that looked as though it were developed for a much larger engine. Hodaka quickly gained a faithful following by offering many successful small-bore designs, among them the Wombat 125, a model that saw both trail and street duty.

## Super Combat 125

Among motocross racers sponsored by Hodaka were Tommy Croft (who later rode for American Honda) and Jody Weisel (now editor for *Motocross Action* magazine).

Considered to be one of the fastest Hodaka motocross models built between 1964 and 1978.

Take it to the annual Hodaka homecoming, Hodaka Days, near Athena, Oregon.

* * *
Though the bike was competitive, it's real rebellion was in its attempt to stop the Japanese from dominating motocross racing.

Engine: Air-cooled, 125cc,
    two-stroke single-cylinder
Horsepower: n/a

Top Speed: n/a
Weight: n/a
Value Now: $$

### A small bike with a big heart

Hodaka motorcycles first appeared in 1964 as small street/trail bikes powered by 90cc Yamaguchi engines. Within 10 years, the company had grown large enough to be a thorn in the sides of the Big Four from Japan. In order to keep up with its Japanese counterparts, Hodaka produced bikes with larger engines, among them the Super Combat 125 that proved to be rather competitive in the aspiring 125cc motocross class. But even the Super Combat wasn't enough to save Hodaka, which went out of business in 1978.

# Honda

## Model D Dream

**The first real Honda motorcycle**

If you put any stock in legend, here's how it went down: after the first Model D came off the line, Honda employees stayed late to drink homebrewed sake, eat pickled fish, and admire their handiwork. One, perhaps rendered effervescent by the sake, exclaimed, "It's like a dream!" Right on cue, Soichiro Honda himself said, "That's it! We'll call it the Dream!" With a 98cc, two-stroke engine, the D pumped out an uninspiring 3 horsepower via a clutchless, two-speed transmission. The chassis comprised a stamped channel-steel frame with a front fork. A sizable rear rack touted the machine's ability as a utility bike, something desperately needed in postwar Japan.

 The Model D was the first complete two-stroke-powered motorcycle Honda made—and the last, for a very long time. *Oyagi* (old man) Honda's distaste for stinkwheels was legendary.

 This was the first true motorcycle Honda made, albeit one with a two-stroke engine, a type Soichiro Honda came to despise for its smell and smoke.

 Short distances, smooth roads—say, Japanese or even English country lanes—and at an extremely relaxed pace. It's only fair.

 ★ ★ ★ ★ ★
As Honda's first genuine motorbike, the Dream D's legend looms large over the history of Honda.

Engine: Air-cooled, two-stroke single
Horsepower: 3 at 5,000 rpm
Top Speed: 37 miles per hour
Weight: 176 pounds
Value Now: $$$$$-plus

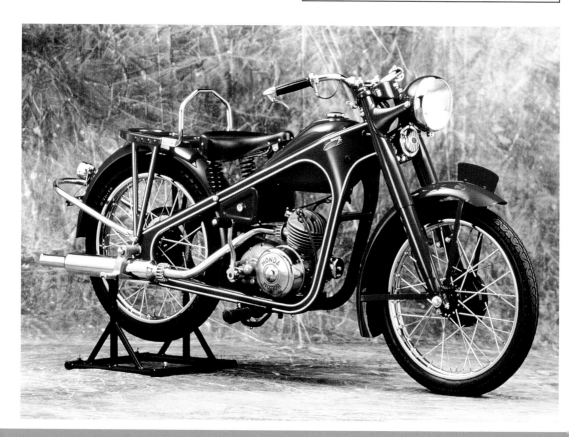

## C100 Super Cub

Erik Buell has identified the Honda Cub as the most technologically important motorcycle ever built just because of its brilliant simplicity.

The little Super Cub was the basis for Honda's groundbreaking "You meet the nicest people on a Honda" ad campaign.

Dense urban centers in Third World countries.

★ ★ ★ ★ ★ ✦
It's safe to say this little mechanical wonder changed the face of human transportation forever, and for the better too.

Engine: Air-cooled, pushrod-operated, two-valve single
Horsepower: 4 at 7,000 rpm
Top Speed: 40 miles per hour (claimed)

Weight: 165 pounds (claimed)
Value Now: $$$ (original 1958 model, not the current version)

### Changing the face of human transport, one Super Cub at a time

Sixty million. That's how many Super Cubs Honda says it has sold. And that makes it the best-selling motor vehicle in history. One of the most important needs of modern humanity is inexpensive individual mobility. Performance isn't a consideration; trouble-free mobility is. And at that, the C100 Super Cub has excelled for more than half a century.

## Benly CB92 Super Sport

The 92 came in almost as many flavors and varieties as Baskin Robbins.

This was the first time Honda engineers decided to flex their developing muscles and show just what they really could build when they felt like it.

The Mount Asama Clubman Race, but remember: you've only got 15 (claimed) horsepower.

★ ★
Aside from expending considerable company resources to make a little 125 road scorcher as perfect as a sphere—not so much.

Engine: Air-cooled, SOHC, four-valve, parallel twin
Horsepower: 15 at 10,500 rpm (claimed)

Top Speed: 81 miles per hour (claimed)
Weight: 243 pounds (claimed, dry)
Value Now: $$$

### Honda's earliest example of corporate jewelry: a bauble for the brain, not the brawn

Mr. Honda had gone to Europe in 1954 to see what the state of motorcycling was like away from insular Japan. It shook him badly to witness how far behind his company was, and the CB92 was one direct result of that realization. From its efficient stamped-steel frame, to its lightweight magnesium hubs, to its punchy 125cc twin with 360-degree crank, the Benly Super Sport eloquently said that Honda had indeed arrived.

# Honda

## CB77 305 Super Hawk

### What it means to be a Honda motorcycle

If there's one motorcycle that best illustrates Honda's success, top votes have to go to the CB77 305 Super Hawk, produced from 1961 through 1967. Anyone old enough to remember the Bad Old Days, especially those associated with certain motorcycles from perfidious Albion, will know what a watershed Japanese bikes represented in general, and Honda in particular. After years of referring to their bikes as altars (because riders were often seen kneeling next to them at the roadside), riders were stunned by Honda's reliable electrics, ignitions, and—oh, blessing be—electric starters. Hondas also did not mark their territory with oil leaks, another revelation. What sealed the deal, though, was the 305 Super Hawk, then a "big bike" for the Japanese and one that simply kicked sand into the headlights of many larger-displacement motorcycles. Honda had arrived and was on the move.

 Author Robert Pirsig rode a Super Hawk on the trip chronicled in his book *Zen and the Art of Motorcycle Maintenance*.

 Ridden by rock legend Elvis Presley in *Roustabout* and acting legend Al Pacino in *Serpico*.

 From Minneapolis to Montana, via Highway 212.

 ★ ★ ★ ★
As the biggest Honda yet, the Super Hawk humbled bigger bikes.

Engine: Air-cooled, SOHC, four-valve, parallel twin
Horsepower: 28 at 9,000 rpm (claimed)

Top Speed: 96 miles per hour (claimed)
Weight: 351 lb. (claimed)
Value Now: $$$

With only 60 horsepower—at 18,000 rpm!—the 249cc RC166 had a top speed of 149 miles per hour.

Simply the most complex and incredible four-stroke powerplant of its time. Just as important, though, was its success: two 250 GP world titles and a win at the Isle of Man TT.

A Grand Prix road-race track. There's really no other place it could work, or even survive.

★ ★ ★ ★ ★
It has to be five, you know. The RC166 is simply epic in the way it extended Honda's knowledge of four-stroke engines— and what the rest of us even imagined was possible.

Engine: Air-cooled, DOHC, 24-valve, inline six
Horsepower: 60 at 18,000 rpm (claimed)
Top Speed: 149 miles per hour (claimed)
Weight: 247 pounds (claimed)
Value Now: Priceless

## Pure Honda magic

In the 1960s, Honda doubled down on the engineering principle that increasing rpm was a sure and certain route to horsepower. Cylinder multiplication was the way to make it work, which led to perhaps Honda's most famous race bike: the six-cylinder RC166. Mike Hailwood won the 250 title in 1966 and 1967 with it, scoring a perfect 10 out of 10 victories in 1966.

The RC174 engine was based on the RC166, a 250cc, six-cylinder engine.

A replica of the top GP bike of the 1960s.

Any of Europe's remaining classic road courses.

★ ★ ★ ★ ★
Wear good earplugs when you reach the 17,000-rpm redline.

Engine: Air-cooled, 297cc, four-stroke, inline six
Horsepower: n/a
Top Speed: n/a
Weight: n/a
Value Now: $$$$$

## A classic six-pack to go

When Honda built a bike to compete in the 350cc class, it didn't need to start from scratch. Instead, the engineers in Honda's racing department simply bored out the wildly successful RC166 and increased the stroke to achieve a capacity of 297cc. Even with 50cc less displacement than most competitors, Hailwood sewed up the championship halfway through the 1967 season.

# Honda

## CT-90 Trail 90

**You can meet the nicest people off-road too**

With all the varied types of two-wheel machines Honda offers—from Gold Wing to Silver Wing, and Rebel to Ruckus—it's easy to forget the company once prized utility and ability to create innovative new bikes that, in turn, launched new classes of motorcycles. The CT-90 Trail 90 is a perfect example. Starting production for sale in 1966, the Trail 90 was obviously meant for off-road use—but not exclusively, since it was street-legal. Yet it also wasn't a serious, European dirt bike. No, it was meant as a low-key, nonthreatening camp bike, if you will. With its Super Cub–style step-through frame, auto clutch, and thoroughly mellow 89cc OHC motor, the Trail 90 provided a low-stress, inexpensive, and reliable avenue to off-road riding, something no other manufacturer offered, for sure.

 Trail 90s, depending on their model year, had two different kinds of dual-range transmissions.

 Like a Super Cub for the dirt, the Trail 90 allowed novices to easily break their duck learning to ride off-road.

 Almost anywhere the spirit moves you.

 ★ ★ ★
Yep, just three for the Trail 90. It borrowed much from the Super Cub. Too much, some might say.

Engine: Air-cooled, SOHC, two-valve single
Horsepower: 7 at 8,500 rpm
Top Speed: 55 miles per hour
Weight: 179 pounds
Value Now: $$

A *Cycle* magazine test criticized the Black Bomber's vibration, saying, "The thing shook in an exotic new way previously unexperienced in all of motorcycling."

 Honda's first so-called "big bike."

 It might not exist, given the four less than wonderfully chosen gearbox ratios and epic vibration.

 ★ ★ ★ ★
Four for sure because, as flawed as it was, the CB450 showed everyone that the Japanese had the technology, the will, and the backbone to make big bikes.

Engine: Air-cooled, DOHC, four-valve twin
Horsepower: 43 at 8,500 rpm (claimed)

Top Speed: 102 miles per hour
Weight: 430 pounds (claimed, wet)
Value Now: $$$

### Honda proves them all wrong

You'd have thought Honda's 305 Super Hawk would have silenced them—"them" being the nattering numpties of negativity, the ones who kept parroting the same tired claim that the Japanese weren't capable of producing a big bike. Apparently the 305 Super Hawk wasn't big enough. Then came the Black Bomber, Honda's CB450. Technically, it was a knockout, largely because of its double-overhead-cam architecture. No other production motorcycle had such a thing; only dedicated race hardware sported this exotic technology at the time. And with that came the elaborate cylinder head, a masterpiece of the casting art, and near miraculous for a die-cast production part. Functionally, though, the Bomber was more of a dud, not quite as quick as was hoped and with otherworldly vibration. But the fact the CB450 existed was enough—imperfect though it was, it signaled the start of the British bike industry's long, slow demise.

# Honda

## CB750

**The bike that forever changed motorcycling, and motorcycles**

No one was really prepared for Honda's CB750K0 when it first burst onto the scene. Here was a motorcycle that had it all . . . and so much more: an inline-four based on Honda's legendary GP road racers, electric starting, a hydraulic front disc brake; the list goes on. And the engine came with a Nancy Grace guarantee it would be reliable and never leak oil, just like so many other Hondas. What about power? And smoothness? Oh, my, yes, it had those in spades. In short, the CB750 shifted the motorcycle world off its axis. Before it arrived, the ignorant had said such a motorcycle was too complex, too expensive to mass-produce. Afterward, everybody wanted one, and every other manufacturer wished they had built one.

 According to legend, Honda wasn't sure the CB750 would be a big enough hit, so the company built 4,714 bikes with sand-cast engine cases before dropping big money into die-casting molds.

 First modern production motorcycle with an inline-four engine and hydraulic disc front brake. The CB750 also provided a direct link to Honda's then glory days in GP road racing and the firm's many multi-cylinder race bikes.

 Anywhere you'd like to go, really. Route 66? Laguna Beach? The Rocky Mountains? Anyplace will do just fine.

 ★ ★ ★ ★ ★
Five, because the big Honda changed motorcycling overnight. What had seemed impossible to some, a flight of fancy, Honda made come true—just like that.

Engine: Air-cooled, SOHC, eight-valve inline-four
Horsepower: 67 at 8,000 rpm
Top Speed: 131 miles per hour
Weight: n/a
Value Now: $$$

The SL's 325cc vertical-twin engine is all but identical to the engines powering Honda's CB and CL350 streetbikes; no changes were made to suit its new role.

 The SL350 was little more than an early element of resistance to Yamaha's phenomenal DT-1 dual-purpose bike.

 Pavement mostly, please. This really is not a dirt bike, you know.

 ✶ It's difficult to envision what the SL350 could be rebelling against.

Engine: Air-cooled, SOHC, four-valve twin
Horsepower: 33 at 9,500 rpm (claimed)
Top Speed: 86 miles per hour
Weight: 366 pounds (claimed; with half-tank of gas)
Value Now: $$

## How Honda learned to build dirt bikes: one step at a time

To understand the SL350, you need to understand that Honda didn't really have a clear concept of what a genuinely competent off-road motorcycle should be. Such is the nature of an island nation with severely limited available space, which is one of the most basic requirements for off-road riding. With such limitations in mind, you can see how progress in building "real" dirt bikes might be slow for any of the Japanese manufacturers. What it took was real-world testing in the market where the bikes would be sold, such as the United States, an expensive and time-consuming undertaking. But once this testing began, genuine progress could be made. Yamaha moved swiftest, debuting its DT-1 in 1968, while Honda moved more slowly and perhaps more cautiously, resulting in the SL350. It would be another year or so before Honda came up with a real competitor—the XL250.

# Honda

## XL250 Motorsport

**Honda finally gets serious about dual-purpose bikes—five years after Yamaha's DT-1 hit the scene**

It's unlikely that you, gentle reader, will ever know the hostility with which Soichiro Honda viewed two-strokes. Let us simply say he had issues with them. So, Honda's first real dual-purpose bike *had* to be a four-stroke. And what a four-stroke it was: extremely over-square, with a bore/stroke ratio of 1.28:1, resulting in a short engine height. It also allowed the use of a four-valve head, a first for modern motorcycling. Power was an unremarkable 24 brake horsepower but was spread evenly from tick-over to 8,000 rpm. A fine powerplant, to be sure, but it was mated to an underachiever of a chassis, resulting in a package that was just too heavy for serious dirt work. Still, the XL no doubt made an excellent learning experience for engineers developing Honda's CR250R Elsinore, released the following year. Yes, it was a two-stroke. Oh, how Mr. Honda must have howled!

 Before the XL250 was released, rumors flew hither and yon about its possible displacement, with the most popular notion being 500cc, with pushrod-operated valves.

 Not only was the XL250 Honda's first real dirt bike, it was also the first real four-stroke dirt bike of its day.

 These days? Easy trails, nothing too fast, too bumpy, or too challenging. That is, unless you want to wear your XL like an ill-fitting cravat.

 ★★
Honda's XL250 only rates two jackets, mostly for being stubborn, though, rather than rebellious, for steadfastly keeping its faith in four-strokes.

Engine: Air-cooled, SOHC, four-valve single
Horsepower: 24 at 8,000 rpm
Top Speed: 80 miles per hour

Weight: 287 pounds (claimed; with a half-tank of gas)
Value Now: $$

## CR125M/CR250M Elsinores

The CR125M was the first production 125 motocrosser from Japan to have a six-speed gearbox.

The 125 Elsinore combined ultra-light weight and mega-inch (for the day) suspension to create a motocrosser that handled so well it took years for the other manufacturers to catch up.

The Elsinore Grand Prix near Lake Elsinore, California.

★ ★ ★ ★ ★

How many leather jackets can you get? It's not enough. And don't forget: this was back when you actually did wear leathers in a motocross race.

Engine: Air-cooled, two-stroke, single-cylinder
Horsepower: 19.7 at 8,000 rpm
Top Speed: n/a
Weight: 188 pounds
Value Now: $$

### Twenty-horsepower feather

There are those who say the first 125 Elsinore changed the face of modern motorcycle manufacturing. The suspension revolution was still a few years away, but this is the production bike that blew up the whole power-to-weight ratio thing. First came the CR250M. Everybody loved it— 214 pounds of the best-handling motocross bike Joe Public could buy. Then Honda introduced the baby Elsinore, and the world of motorcycling was never the same. At 19.7 horsepower, it was the class leader, but weighing in at only 188 pounds, it literally left all the other 125 motocross bikes in the dust. And more than a few 250s.

# Honda

## GL1000 Gold Wing

**The once and future king—of touring, that is**

To begin with, all Honda really wanted to do was build a bitchin' bike, a "king motorcycle" as they put it. Problem was, the engineers at Honda honestly did not know what such a glorious thing should be, or who its audience was. Seeing as how it was still a time when a motorcycle's worth was gauged by its peak horsepower and quarter-mile figures, the engineers at least had some guidance. Ultimately, they decided certain automobile-like features were warranted, such as liquid cooling and shaft drive. And, briefly, the GL1000 Gold Wing was the quickest and most sophisticated bike the world had seen. Still, it would be a few years before customers showed Honda the GL's true mission as maximum tourer nonpareil.

 Honda's now-closed plant in Marysville, Ohio, was originally built specifically with the notion of assembling Gold Wings there.

 Honda used more automotive technology on the GL1000 than on any other motorcycle before it and ended up creating a touring dynasty—although no one knew it at the time.

 Route 66 would probably do just fine.

 ★ ★ ★ ★
By using so much car "stuff"—liquid cooling, shaft drive, belt cam drive, and so on—the Gold Wing flew in the face of what was then contemporary motorcycle design.

Engine: Liquid-cooled, SOHC, eight-valve, horizontally opposed four
Horsepower: 82 at 7,500 rpm (claimed)
Top Speed: 125 miles per hour (estimated)
Weight: n/a
Value Now: $$$

In its last year in the United States, the 400's passenger pegs got their own subframe, rather than being mounted on the swingarm, as they were on earlier versions.

Honda's CB400F was in a class of its own when it debuted in 1975; nothing else looked like it, and only a few other Hondas had such an obvious link to the Golden Age of GP road racing in the 1960s.

Preferably, moderately long sweepers—nothing too fast or too slow, and certainly not too bumpy.

★ ★ ★ ★
The CB400F broke new ground for sportbike styling

| | |
|---|---|
| Engine: Air-cooled, SOHC, eight-valve, transverse inline-four | Top Speed: 95 miles per hour |
| Horsepower: 32.3 at 9,000 rpm | Weight: n/a |
| | Value Now: $$$ |

## Honda gets it right

Honda's CB400F marked the first time the Japanese manufacturers finally got the sportbike look *just right*. The little 400 had just the right amount of brightwork, along with tasteful monochrome paint on its perfectly shaped bread-loaf tank, with no unnecessary stripes, candy colors, or metalflake. Mechanically, though, the CB400F was little more than a bored-out CB350F with a sixth gear, along with a new fork and swingarm. Yet even with those changes it wasn't a match for RD Yamahas in performance. Still, the CB400F provided the closest street-legal link to Honda's fabled GP bikes of the 1960s, with its four-cylinder engine and 10,000-rpm redline, wrapped in the sexiest styling the Japanese had ever produced.

# Honda

## CB500T

**For Honda in the 1970s, refinement almost invariably meant reduced performance. Not all customers were thrilled.**

By the mid 1970s, Honda had created enough volume-selling motorcycles that several of them—especially in larger displacements—no longer needed to be updated or outright replaced as often. What that led to was refinement. That is, making the bikes quieter, more reliable, more urbane. Unfortunately, that also meant they were heavier and slower, and the CB500T makes for an illustrative example. Although the engine boasted a minor displacement increase over the CB450, the 500T lost out in virtually every measurable area of performance, while increased vibration took its toll on comfort, and a poorly placed centerstand badly inhibited cornering clearance. On top of that, the overtly baroque styling did little to increase the bike's appeal. The CB500T was in Honda's lineup for two short years. Few mourned its passing.

 To gain its 54cc-greater displacement over the CB450, the 500's stroke increased by 7mm, rather than achieving this increase via the more common avenue of a larger bore.

 Apart from the metallic-brown paint and brown quilt-pattern seat cover? Not much, except for being less capable than its CB450 predecessor in almost every way.

 To the mall, perhaps. Or the bingo parlor. Or the VFW lodge.

 More Brougham LTD than bad boy, the CB500T didn't have a rebellious bone in its metaphorical body.

Engine: Air-cooled, DOHC, four-valve, vertical twin
Horsepower: 34 at 8,500 rpm

Top Speed: 103 miles per hour (estimated)
Weight: 455 pounds
Value Now: $$

The Monkey has come in off-road/Baja, road-race-replica, and commuter-bike platforms. One intrepid owner even fabricated a 125cc inline four engine for a Monkey.

 The Monkey was and is famous for being a small, whimsical, fun bike anyone can master instantly. And—at first, at least—for being inexpensive.

 Anywhere you won't be tempted to take yourself seriously.

 ★ ★ ★ ★
Why four? Because Honda's Monkey, in all of its various forms over the years, really can be almost anything to any rider.

Engine: Air-cooled, pushrod-operated, two-valve, horizontal single
Horsepower: 3.4 at 8,500 rpm

Top Speed: 22 miles per hour (estimated)
Weight: 150 pounds
Value Now: $$$

### Do the Monkey-Doodle-Doo!

Few other motorcycles embody whimsy the way Honda's Z50, a.k.a. Monkey, has done ever since its introduction in 1961. Just look at it: a Monkey seems an improbable marsupial, and the bike's every appearance should be accompanied by the music "Entry of the Gladiators." The Z50 started out using the 50cc engine with three-speed gearbox and automatic clutch of Honda's well-known Cub, but it has since evolved to take on a manual clutch and four-speed transmission. For 2009, Honda built two versions for its domestic market: a standard model and a limited edition with special paint and chrome as well as a Tartan plaid saddle cover. Both Monkeys got Honda's PGM-FI fuel injection, which helped boost power to 3.4 and fuel economy to 250 mpg-plus. MSRP was . . . wait for it . . . almost $3,500.

## 750A Automatic

### No comparison

"Nothing but nothing can be compared with riding the new 750 Automatic," reads the first line of a two-page magazine ad introducing Honda's "revolutionary new" bike. Think about that claim for a second, though. It doesn't qualify, it just quantifies. With the benefit of hindsight, we can see how prescient that was, but this was written before the bike had tanked. Either the copywriter had ESP or he'd ridden the bike and was trying to preserve his job and his integrity at the same time. Sold as a tourer, the 750A's strength was really in the city—especially if your commute involved lots of traffic jams. It was a toaster you rode to work, and nothing but nothing should be compared with riding a toaster. On the plus side, a good portion of the Hondamatics that Honda did manage to sell were put to good use powering three-wheeled rigs for physically disabled riders.

 It isn't really an automatic, it's a two-speed; you just don't have to use the clutch when you shift. First gear is good for 60 miles per hour.

 Thinking it was a good thing, Honda made riding so easy that anyone could do it.

 In some nonriding marketing executive's mind.

 *
When Moto Guzzi did it a year earlier it was rebellious. This time around, it was just a bad idea.

Engine: Air-cooled, 736cc, SOHC, four-stroke, inline four
Horsepower: 67 at 8,500 rpm
Top Speed: 119 miles per hour
Weight: n/a
Value Now: $$

The CBX only saw four years of production, the final two as a sport-tourer.

Ridden by a young Ed Harris in George Romero's sublimely ridiculous *Knightriders*, a film about a troupe of motorcycle-riding Ren-Fest rejects.

California Coast Highway 1.

★ ★ ★

For Honda, huge. The CBX was Honda's statement, "We can build anything we can imagine."

| | |
|---|---|
| Engine: Air-cooled, DOHC, 24-valve, inline six-cylinder | Top Speed: 140 miles per hour |
| Horsepower: 85.6 at 9,000 rpm | Weight: n/a |
| | Value Now: $1,050 |

### Six appeal

In late 1978, Honda's six-cylinder CBX burst onto motorcycling's scene like a supernova, marking one of the first times Honda built a streetbike this exotic, this thoroughly outrageous, simply because it could. Shoichiro Irimajiri, architect of Honda's fabulous six-cylinder GP bikes of the sixties, also head-honchoed the CBX project, using what he'd learned in those heady times to speed the CBX into production. Still, even though the CBX was (briefly) the quickest production bike on earth, it's perhaps most important for being a stop-gap measure to boost Honda's image until the company introduced the VF750F Interceptor in 1983.

# Honda

## CM185T Twinstar

### Just say, "Charge it!"

"What possible significance," you might be asking, "could this little entry-level chopper-wannabe box-o'-poo have?" Curious you should ask. Honda's little (181cc) CM185T Twinstar might seem unprepossessing by sniffy superior sportbike snobs, and it is rather, well, slow. The real significance of the Twinstar was its sub-$1,000 MSRP. That meant, for a whole lot of Americans, the Twinstar represented the easiest, most expedient, and certainly least expensive route into motorcycling.

 Some couples (usually older ones, of course, with higher credit limits than most) bought pairs of Twinstars, a his and hers.

 Simple: it was one of the few brand-new motorcycles (not a scooter or a moped), with a warranty and all, that could be paid for with a credit card.

 *Anywhere*—as long as it was *away* from your bank's loan officer.

 ★ ★ ★
Yes, sadly, only two. What it did—to make it absurdly easy to purchase a new motorcycle—was uniquely subversive, but virtually nothing followed in its wake.

Engine: Air-cooled, SOHC, four-valve V-twin
Horsepower: 10 at 7,500 rpm
Top Speed: 58 miles per hour

Weight: 294 pounds (with half a tank of fuel)
Value Now: $

# Honda

## CMX250 Rebel

### A totem to mediocrity

It almost seems unfair to skewer the Rebel from the viewpoint of an experienced rider. The thing is, apart from a commendably low seat height and a certain agility, plus the reliability of its thoroughly phlegmatic and barely adequately powered engine, there's precious little left to recommend the Rebel. While it can be argued that the Rebel offers the beginning rider everything he or she needs, it's just as valid to say it offers little else at that crucial time of a rider's development.

 The Rebel has been in production for more than 20 years.

 The Rebel is as unthreatening—and subsequently as uninspiring—a ride for novices to the sport as Honda's vast technology could create.

 Actually, an MSF course, which is where you'll find most Rebels.

 ★
One jacket is generous; the Rebel doesn't even deserve a single leather jacket for its me-too cruiser styling and uninspiring performance.

Engine: Air-cooled, SOHC, four-valve, transverse twin
Horsepower: 17.5 at 8,250 rpm

Top Speed: 75 miles per hour
Weight: 311 pounds (claimed, dry)
Value Now: $

The NR was under near-constant development, with two major engine redesigns and at least three frames, from the original shrimp-shell, to a conventional steel-tube configuration, to an unlikely collection of carbon-fiber strips.

The NR500 was as innovative as they came, with oval pistons, 16-inch wheels, and a front fork with easily changed springs—but all of these innovations fell by the wayside as the bike was developed.

It would have been perfect to ride the NR500 to victory on GP circuits—but that was never to be the NR's fate.

★ ★ ★ ★ ★
Talk about rebellion: the NR500 fought against conventional wisdom like Brando's Johnny in *The Wild One*: "What are you rebelling against?" "Whaddaya got?"

| | |
|---|---|
| Engine: Liquid-cooled, DOHC, 32-valve, oval-piston, 100-degree V-4 | Top Speed: 180 miles per hour |
| | Weight: n/a |
| | Value Now: More than priceless |
| Horsepower: 130 at 19,500 rpm | |

### NR for New Racing? Or Never Ready?

Compared to the men who toiled to make Honda's NR500 a Grand Prix road racer worthy of the name, the man of La Mancha was nothing but a third-rate, low-rent pretender. Long after two-strokes had established their dominance in road racing, Honda selected a team of young, inexperienced engineers to build a world-beating four-stroke. Their genius was to create a 32-valve oval-piston V-4 with the valve area of a V-8. But in its first GP, one of the NRs wheeled off the line, oil puked out of the breather and onto the rear tire, and the bike crashed. Things could only improve, and they did—but not by much. Expected to win a world championship in its third year, the NR instead was ignominiously sent home.

# Honda

## CB750F Sport

### The best-handling motorcycle in 1980

Honda launched its second-generation 750 four in 1979, but it was the 1980 model that got everybody's attention. A reinforced swingarm supporting adjustable rear shock absorbers made the CB750F, in the words of *Cycle Guide* magazine's editors in their October 1979 issue, "the best-handling, most-nimble street superbike you can buy." They reached that decision after pitting the CB750F head to head against a Ducati Desmo 900 Super Sport at Willow Springs Raceway. When the smoke cleared, the CB750F was deemed the best-handling bike of the duo—and the world. The Honda was also quick through the standing quarter-mile, posting a time of 12.41 seconds at 106.8 miles per hour. Who said that every early Japanese bike with an inline, four-cylinder engine handled poorly?

 The CB750F was Honda's first official mount for AMA Superbike racing.

 The first Honda road bike to sport adjustable rear shock absorbers.

 Your favorite twisty canyon road.

 ★ ★ ★ ★
One good turn deserves another . . .

Engine: Air-cooled, 749cc, four-stroke, inline four
Horsepower: 75 at 9,500 rpm

Top Speed: 128 miles per hour
Weight: 524 pounds
Value Now: $$$

The Motocompo starred in the movie *You're Under Arrest.*

 It's more useful than a spare tire!

 Pack the Motocompo in your luggage for a trip to Bermuda, where scooters are common transportation.

 *
Fold your jacket neatly so there are no wrinkles.

| | |
|---|---|
| Engine: Air-cooled, 49cc, two-stroke single-cylinder | Top Speed: Faster than walking |
| | Weight: 93 pounds |
| Horsepower: 2.5 at 5,000 rpm | Value Now: $$ |

**Giving new meaning to the term *travel trunk***

Whoever said you can't take it with you must not have heard about Honda's Motocompo, a collapsible scooter that could fit in the trunk of a car. Fittingly, the Motocompo was also known as the "trunk bike" because, in 1981, Honda developed a car—the Honda City—specifically to accommodate a Motocompo in its trunk space. The scooter's rectangular body was designed to swallow the folding handlebars, seat, and footpegs, leaving only the smooth, plastic body and two exposed tires. The compact package was then easy to stash inside the car's trunk, allowing you to take your extra mode of transportation with you. The Motocompo wasn't exactly a smashing success, but it helped prove the versatility of a properly designed small scooter.

## Sabre V45

### Honda's V-4 dynasty begins

In 1982, Honda unleashed a salvo it doubtless expected to ride far into the future: the V-4 engine. In this case, it powered the Sabre V45. Honda planned to make the V-4 powerplant a common—and desirable—part of motorcycling's lexicon. And as a motive unit, the Sabre's V-4 was a corker. It displayed the breadth of powerband normally associated with V-twins, with the high-rev ability of inline fours. And with that came an almost ethereal smoothness, largely due to the perfect primary balance of the 90-degree configuration. The rest of the bike, though, wasn't quite up to the engine's performance, with slow steering and slightly harsh suspension response. Worst of all, the engines suffered a vast number of camshaft failures (more in Europe and the U.K.), which left Honda on the back foot for years and almost snuffed the Great V-4 Experiment before it had started.

 The *45* in V45 refers to the cubic-inch displacement.

 The V45 Sabre was the vanguard of Honda's V-4 brigade, the very first of its kind.

 Well, pavement, certainly, but it's best if it's neither too rough nor too challenging. The bike's 18-inch front wheel, conservative geometry, and weight made it reluctant to snap into corners.

 ★ ★ ★
Only three? Well, yes. Even if the Sabre did kick off Honda's love affair with the V-4 engine configuration, the rest of the bike wasn't really up to the sophistication of its powerplant.

Engine: Liquid-cooled, DOHC, 16-valve, 90-degree V-4
Horsepower: 82 at 9,500 rpm (claimed)
Top Speed: 125 miles per hour (claimed)
Weight: 542 pounds (claimed, wet)
Value Now: $$

At an F1 race in 1982, an FWS hurled an exhaust spring into a cylinder. Said spring was ejected through an exhaust pipe like a watermelon seed, with the engine none the worse for the experience.

Built to be all-conquering at Daytona, in the U.S. Formula 1 title competition, and at the Isle of Man, the FWS1000 so thoroughly outclassed its opponents that it was effectively Honda's Doomsday Weapon for 1982–1983.

Daytona, of course, or the Isle of Man Mountain Course. Almost anywhere else would be a waste.

★ ★ ★ ★ ★
Yes, a full five because the FWS exploded the inline four convention and, in so doing, paved the way for Honda's street-going V-4s.

Engine: Liquid-cooled, DOHC,
  16-valve V-4
Horsepower: 148 at 11,000 rpm
Top Speed: 180 miles per hour
  (estimated)

Weight: 364 pounds
Value Now: Priceless, and not
  for sale

**Yeah, just like an old tractor—a stinking fast old tractor**

True, the FWS only finished second at Daytona, but, partnered with Mike Baldwin, it swept the American F1 championship, and in the hands of the legendary Joey Dunlop, the FWS annihilated the opposition at the Isle of Man. The liter-size FWS was hugely powerful, had sweet handling, and included a level of fit and finish like that of a Honda street machine.

# Honda

## VF1000R

### Be careful what you wish for

Sadly, Honda's VF1000R never really had a chance in the United States. How can you say that about such Honda exotica, with its gear cam drive, its quick-release front-axle holders, and its distinct relationship to Honda's brutally fast Daytona weapon, the FWS1000? The problem was bad timing. The 92-brake-horsepower, 610-pound (wet) VF-R hit these shores in 1985—one year after Kawasaki's 115-brake-horsepower, 566-pound Ninja 900 and Yamaha's 125-brake-horsepower, 575-pound FJ1100. With competition like that, the VF1000R simply never stood a chance.

 For motorcyclists in the United States, the VF1000R was the "one that got away," the "forbidden fruit," and a host of other hoary clichés. When American Honda did import the bike in 1985, it was too little, too late, and too expensive.

 Some unhappy Honda dealers still had a VF1000R on their floors as late as 1990. And the earlier VF1000F that *was* available in the United States was a better bike.

 Fast, open, flowing, and well-paved roads of almost any sort. Even the autobahn works well for this low-flying missile. What certainly doesn't work are ultra-tight back roads, where the bike's weight bedevils it and the rider.

 ★ ★ ★
Three, simply because of the geared-cam drivetrain, the first such use on a modern production motorcycle.

Engine: Liquid-cooled, DOHC, 16-valve, V-4
Horsepower: 92 at 9,500 rpm

Top Speed: 150 miles per hour (estimated)
Weight: 610 pounds (wet)
Value Now: $$$

# Honda

Honda supplied a security lock and cable with each Magna.

A V-4 hot rod that kicked every V-twin cruiser's butt.

Woodward Boulevard, the hippest boulevard for hot rod cruising.

★ ★ ★
Prepare for an 11.4-second quarter-mile time.

Engine: Liquid-cooled, 1,098cc, four-stroke, 90-degree V-4
Horsepower: n/a

Top Speed: 142 miles per hour
Weight: 566 pounds
Value Now: $$

**A hot rod with cool styling**

Honda drew on two primary elements—horsepower and traditional American styling—for its V65 Magna, and the combination proved a winner in terms of sales. But the Magna was more than just a boorish, big-bore cruiser. It had the heart and soul of a hot rod, and it tapped into an artery that ran directly to the heart of American motor culture. In short, the Magna had the speed and power of a hot rod bike mixed with the cool styling of a roughneck boulevard cruiser. Moreover, it could wreak havoc in impromptu stoplight-to-stoplight drag races, yet it remained docile and friendly enough for milk runs to the corner grocery store.

# Honda

## NSR500

**Honda gambles big on an idea, and loses likewise**

Despite having a crack cadre of engineers, endless rows of dynos, and a stream of money pumped into R&D as if from a fire hose, Honda occasionally creates a dog, and the 1984 NSR500 GP bike was an epic barker. At the time, a low center of gravity was believed to be the key to good handling. So Honda created an upside-down bike, with the gas tank slung under the engine and exhausts running over the top of it. Unfortunately, the original hypothesis was badly flawed and created other problems: exhaust-pipe heat meant rider Freddie Spencer finished races with his forearms done to a turn, and mechanics despised working on a hot engine. At one point, Spencer practically begged Honda for his 1983 NS500 triple back.

 The NSR GP bike couldn't match the results of its predecessor, but Honda couldn't simply scrap the NSR and carry on with the NS500 in 1984. To all the Japanese manufacturers going backward instead of forward was an admission of failure, and a huge loss of face.

 The NSR500 was built to prove that a low center of gravity would imbue a two-wheel single-track vehicle with superior handling. Honda could hardly have been more wrong.

 Any of the high-speed European tracks with long straights, and what some referred to as "Honda Lanes" because they let the NSR stretch its legs and use its formidable peak power and top-end acceleration.

★ ★ ★ ★ ★
 The NSR500 easily deserves five jackets just for being a race bike built on such a narrow premise, one quickly found to fly in the face of reality.

| | |
|---|---|
| Engine: Two-stroke, 90-degree V-4 with reed-valve induction | Top Speed: 200-plus miles per hour (with fuel injection) |
| Horsepower: 140 at 11,000 rpm | Weight: n/a |
| | Value Now: Priceless |

*Cycle Guide* magazine named the Interceptor V45 "Bike of the Year" and, to commemorate it, had one chromed. That's right; except for rubber parts (tires and hoses) and the clear-plastic screen, *everything* got chromed.

At a single stroke, Honda's Interceptor made sportbikes that had been cutting edge suddenly seem terribly old hat.

The Interceptor raised the bar so much that the road is almost immaterial. If you must decide, however, consider California's Angeles Crest, as well as Highway 1 along the coast.

★ ★ ★ ★ ★

Yes, a full five because the Interceptor—with its smooth V-4, mile-wide powerband, near-no-fault handling, and overall rider-friendly nature—pointed the way to the future, not only for sportbikes, but for race bikes as well.

| | |
|---|---|
| Engine: Liquid-cooled, DOHC, 16-valve, 90-degree V-4 | Top Speed: 134 miles per hour |
| Horsepower: 86 at 10,000 rpm | Weight: 487 pounds (dry) |
| | Value Now: $$$ |

## Honda changes motorcycling forever—again

When it debuted in 1983, Honda's V45 Interceptor was nothing short of a revelation. Based—at least as a loose concept—on the previous year's Sabre V45, the Interceptor quickly went about establishing its bona fides: it made the highest peak power of any proddie 750, in part because it was the first well-tuned modern 750 and a V-4 at that, in a landscape awash with identikit inline fours. And yet that mighty motor still possessed monstrous midrange. The industry's first perimeter box-section frame wrapped around that prime mover and contributed heavily to the bike's stellar handling. Still, for all its techno touchstones, the Interceptor was hardly a high-strung bitch goddess of a sportbike, unlike some in the European mold. No, the Interceptor's broad powerband and confidence-inspiring road manners practically introduced the modern concept of rider-friendly machines, both for the street and for the racetrack.

# Honda

## VT750C Shadow

**Who knows what lurks in the heart of Honda? The Shadow does.**

Other motorcycle companies should beware when Honda gets its jaws into an idea and begins to ruminate on it, in both definitions of the word, as it did with cruisers in the early 1980s. After suitable reflection, Honda spit out the 1983 Shadow 750, a.k.a. VT750C. Where other Japanese cruisers tried—and failed—to imitate Milwaukee/Harley styling, the Shadow came much closer without appearing to be a caricature of itself. To the styling, Honda added a fair dollop of engineering: twin, offset crank pins for perfect primary balance; hydraulic valve adjusters and shaft drive for minimal maintenance; and a decent turn of speed from the 750cc, liquid-cooled, three-valves-per-cylinder, 45-degree V-twin. Never mind the 1970s-style wallow in cornering or the dreadfully compromised—but perfectly cool on the showroom floor—ergonomics. Customers loved the Shadow, and it went on to sire future versions. We've not seen their end yet.

 At the press intro, every single member of the press who climbed on the display bike went to put his or her feet on the footpegs . . . and missed. The pegs were mounted *that* far forward.

 The Shadow 750 was Honda's first proper V-twin–powered Harley fighter. It was also quick and as technically advanced as one would expect of a Honda.

 Oh, city boulevards mostly, especially if they have plenty of reflective mirrors for the rider to see him or herself in. And the occasional country lane, at a relaxed pace, of course.

 ★ ★ ★ ★ ★
Why so many? Because it was such a radical departure for Honda, the engineering company. Yes, Honda had built customs before, but nothing like *this*.

Engine: Liquid-cooled, SOHC, six-valve, 45-degree V-twin
Horsepower: 66 at 7,500 rpm (claimed)
Top Speed: 138 miles per hour (estimated)
Weight: 503 pounds (wet)
Value Now: $$

# Honda

Hank Scott was the first rider to win aboard an RS750. Ironically, he was a substitute for injured factory rider Mike Kidd during the 1983 season.

The bike that finally gave Honda its Number One Plate in AMA Grand National competition.

The Springfield Mile where Ricky Graham was oh-so-fast on his RS750.

★ ★ ★ ★ ★
Do a feet-up slide all the way around Springfield like Graham did in 1985, and you'll earn those jackets.

Engine: Air-cooled, 749.5cc, four-stroke, 52-degree V-twin
Horsepower: n/a
Top Speed: 130 miles per hour
Weight: n/a
Value Now: $$$$

**The bike that dethroned Harley-Davidson's XR750**

It was no coincidence that Honda's RS750 engine shared the same bore and stroke specs with Harley-Davidson's XR750. Harley had discovered the secret to telegraphing its 100-or-so horsepower to the hard-packed dirt of American oval tracks shortly after the XR750 bowed in 1972, so Honda took a shortcut to catch up in 1983. The gamble paid off, and for the next 20 or so years, riders on RS and XR flat trackers put on some dazzling shows for American race fans.

## VF500F Interceptor

### Perfection is attainable

Some motorcycles are just . . . perfect. A synergy exists between the engine and chassis that transforms a simple machine of steel, alloy, and plastic into something sublime. That describes Honda's VF500F Interceptor to the proverbial T. That broadband V-4 engine, bolted to a rigid, square-section, steel-tube frame is a perfect example of what Aristotle described as, "the whole is more than the sum of its parts." The little Interceptor had both midrange (something apparently lost on today's middleweights) and a soaring top end, allied to superb road manners. You didn't have to be the next Freddie Spencer to use everything it had to give. There have been faster motorcycles, but few have had the spherelike perfection of the VF500F.

The VF500F descended from Honda's domestic-model VF400F, which limited its displacement increase. It would have required wet liners, or a complete redesign, to get to the 550cc–600cc other manufacturers were fielding at the time.

One of the most complete, easy-to-ride-fast middleweights ever sold.

Anywhere that twists and turns—from California's Angeles Crest to Maine's Northern Route 201.

★ ★ ★
The VF500F Interceptor only really rebelled against other motorcycles—unlike them, the little VF made everything it had accessible to its rider, holding nothing back.

Engine: Liquid-cooled, DOHC, 16-valve, 90-degree V-4
Horsepower: 53 at 11,000 rpm

Top Speed: 129 miles per hour (estimated)
Weight: n/a
Value Now: $$

Tariffs on heavyweight motorcycles went from 4.4 percent to 49.4 percent in 1984.

This bike proved that shaft-driven motorcycles could actually handle well.

Around the Beltway, Washington, D.C.

★ ★ ★
Destroking a 750 is just a sneaky way to get around a rule.

| Engine: Air-cooled, 696cc, DOHC, four-stroke, inline four | Top Speed: 147 miles per hour |
| Horsepower: 80 at 9,500 rpm | Weight: n/a |
| | Value Now: $$ |

### The Honda that Harley built

There were almost 6 million motorcyclists on America's roads in 1981, and Harley-Davidson was still operating at a loss. What to do? Build a better bike? Or petition the U.S. International Trade Commission for relief? Harley chose the latter, and on April 1, 1983, President Ronald Reagan adopted a plan recommended by the ITC to save the American motorcycle manufacturing industry from extinction. Although enacted on April Fools' Day, it was no joke: tariffs on heavyweight bikes increased over tenfold. Thus did 750cc bikes become 700s overnight. While the rest of the world got Honda's CBX750, we got the CB700SC Nighthawk S, a version that was destroked 3.9mm. Not that U.S. riders suffered much from the slight neutering of the bike; the Nighthawk S was one of the fastest, best-handling middleweights on the market and would remain so until Suzuki redefined the term *sportbike* with its GSX-R series.

# Honda

## CX500T/CX650T Turbo

### Get your thrill on Boost Hill

Occasionally, Honda will build a motorcycle simply because it is the only company that *can*. Such an act not only showcases Honda's engineering expertise, it also precisely demonstrates to other manufacturers just who the Big Dog is. The CX650T Turbo is one such example. Small-displacement V-twins are notoriously difficult to turbocharge, which led Honda to introduce another first for the company: electronic fuel injection. Honda's first attempt, the 1982 CX500T, can only be described as a failure, an unsatisfying motorcycle in every respect, but when Honda took a boring bar to the engine and reprogrammed the fuel injection, the Turbo delivered its power as sensuously as a *Star Wars* jump to light speed. While the original 500cc version suffered terminal turbo lag, when the rider twisted the throttle of the 650cc version, the CX grabbed its skirt and launched itself toward the horizon. Now, *that's* entertainment.

 According legend, Honda sent 600 CX650Ts to Honda tech schools and junior college mechanics programs. The bikes were never intended to leave the schools, certainly not to be sold to civilians—but apparently many were.

 To create a turbobike, Honda picked the motorcycle least likely to succeed in such a makeover. Then did a bang-up job to come up with not only fierce midrange but one of the most sensuous power deliveries ever seen.

 Nothing too tight and twisty, please. Smooth, flowing, sweeping river roads like those in the U.S. Southeast.

 ★ ★ ★ ★
Yes, four, simply because of Honda's sheer obstinacy—and ultimate success—in making something work that should have been an unqualified disaster.

Engine: Liquid-cooled, turbocharged, transverse, 80-degree V-twin with eight pushrod-actuated valves

Horsepower: 100 at 8,000 rpm
Top Speed: 139 miles per hour
Weight: 571 pounds
Value Now: $$$$

In the hands of a talented pilot, and on a tight, twisty back road, a Helix can humiliate a lesser light on a big-bore sportbike.

 The C1 is famous simply for being one of the most versatile and easy-to-use scooters ever.

 Truly, almost anywhere with pavement.

 ★ ★ ★
Three? Surely. Not that there's much really rebellious about the Helix. No, the three is just for the way this scooter can consistently punch above its weight.

Engine: Liquid-cooled, SOHC, two-valve single
Horsepower: 19 at 7,500 rpm

Top Speed: 70 miles per hour
Weight: 349 pounds (claimed, dry)
Value Now: $

### Scooterus maximus

An intrepid reader might ask why Honda's Rebel received such harsh criticism here, whereas a scooter—Honda's Helix—gets described in far more glowing terms (as you shall see). It's pretty simple: the Helix surprises and delights because it exceeds expectations—comfortably so, in fact. Whereas the Rebel does neither. The Helix was one of the first Maxi-scooters, with a feet-forward riding position and a sizable trunk for weatherproof, lockable storage. Its drivetrain—a 250 single with CVT transmission—provided twist-and-go convenience, with just enough horsepower to enable freeway travel. The Helix possessed exemplary road manners as well, and not just "for a scooter." It was just as able, willing, and confidence-inspiring when commuting as it was for short-hop touring, and even the occasional back road sortie. In short, the Helix was one of those rare two-wheelers that was better than it had to be.

# Honda

## NS250R

### All that's missing is the checkered flag

You would be excused if you double-checked for number plates on Honda's NS250R. It looks every bit like a Grand Prix road racer. But make no mistake; this quarter-liter pocket rocket is a streetbike. You'll have to treat the engine as you would a race bike's; the tiny two-stroke's power doesn't kick in until about 8,000 rpm, peaking at its 10,500-rpm redline.

The NS250R was capable of a 13.1-second/101.6-mile-per-hour quarter-mile time.

A streetbike joined at the hip with Honda's dedicated road racer, the RS250.

A twisty road festooned with midgear corners and unsuspecting riders on larger bikes.

★ ★ ★ ★
An exceedingly narrow powerband will test your skills.

| | |
|---|---|
| Engine: Liquid-cooled, 249cc, two-stroke, 90-degree V-twin | Top Speed: 121 miles per hour |
| Horsepower: n/a | Weight: 339 pounds |
| | Value Now: $$$$ |

# Honda

## NS400R

### One of the finest-handling motorcycles of our time—that also just happens to have a firecracker of an engine

If you've never had the opportunity to ride a superlight middleweight streetbike, especially one powered by a potent, fast-winding two-stroke, then you really owe yourself the experience—especially if it's aboard a Honda NS400R. Honda even claimed the 400, with its V-3 engine configuration, was a road-going replica of the NS500 triple Freddie Spencer rode to his first world title in 1983. It wasn't, really, but Honda certainly provided the 400 with inspirational handling characteristics that would do justice to a race bike, with supple suspension and lightning-fast quick-flick steering that never deteriorated into nervousness. Allied to a 90-degree, two-stroke V-3 with a powerband broadened by reed valves in the intakes and Honda's version of exhaust power valves (named ATAC, for auto-controlled torque amplification chambers), the NS400R was a back road weapon that had precious few peers.

Owning a premium two-stroke streetbike like the NS isn't exactly cheap. They require more maintenance than an equivalently sized four-stroke, and high-quality (read: expensive) injector oil just makes good sense.

Handling—although the perky two-stroke mill is handy in its own right.

Everywhere from SoCal's Glendora Mountain Road to the switchbacks of the Dolomites—the twistier, the better.

★ ★ ★
Once such two-stroke race replicas were common, but restrictive legislation around the globe has made their numbers plummet. Apart from, perhaps, a stock Rothmans paint job, the NS400 was hardly a rebel.

| | |
|---|---|
| Engine: Liquid-cooled, reed-valve, two-stroke, transverse, 90-degree V-3 | Top Speed: 126 miles per hour |
| | Weight: 359 pounds (claimed) |
| | Value Now: $$$$ |
| Horsepower: 72 at 9,500 rpm (claimed) | |

The Gold Wing's predecessor, the M1, utilized a horizontally opposed six, and the engine was brought out of mothballs to test the six-cylinder Wing engine Honda was considering for the GL1500.

The first six-cylinder Gold Wing ushered in a new era of luxury touring and was so successful it reigned o'er the touring class for 13 years.

Smooth, paved roads that vanish over horizon after horizon. Why not Route 66? All of it.

★ ★ ★ ★ ★
Yes, five, because the 1500 exploded notions of how a big, luxurious touring bike should feel in engine performance and handling.

Engine: Liquid-cooled, SOHC, 12-valve, horizontally opposed six
Horsepower: 100 at 5,200 rpm (claimed)

Top Speed: 114 miles per hour (claimed)
Weight: 794 pounds (claimed, dry)
Value Now: $$$

**The next phase of Honda's touring dynasty**

So, just how good was Honda's first six-cylinder Gold Wing, the GL1500? Good enough to serve as the gold standard of touring for 13 years. First and foremost was that superb powerplant, like an electric motor in the way it dispensed mountain-flattening torque, with the additional refinement of a reverse gear. Add that to the bike's existing virtue of excellent road manners for such a Brobdingnagian device, plus its comfort, weather protection, and luggage capacity, and you have a dynasty virtually unequaled in the touring realm. Of course, what made the 1500 so good was the effort put into developing it. Five years in the making, the GL went through 15 iterations in 60 prototype stages for the most thorough development of any Honda motorcycle up to that time. Because the GL1500 could never be just good enough.

## GB500 Tourist Trophy

### Spooky

Designed to replicate an era rather than a specific machine, the GB500 captures "vintage" in every way but one: it's stone-cold reliable. Otherwise, it's just like the bikes it emulates, right down to achieving cult status. Go back in time and enter it in the Isle of Man TT. You'll fit right in. But what does it look like, exactly? A Velocette? A Vincent? An AJS? That tank looks so familiar. So does the seat. Spoked wheels, fork gators, clubman bars; it's a complete effort. Except you can rev the motor for days, and it still won't leave oil spots on the garage floor. And what is that on the front wheel, a disc brake? This thing must have wandered over from a parallel universe.

 *GB* stands for Great Britain.

 Confused the entire American market for two years.

 Fooling people at a vintage bike rally.

 ★ ★ ★ ★
It was a bold statement. Of some sort.

| | |
|---|---|
| Engine: Air-cooled, 499c, SOHC, four-stroke single | Top Speed: 103 miles per hour |
| | Weight: n/a |
| Horsepower: 38 at 7,500 rpm | Value Now: $$ |

The XRV750 actually had a most honorable *paterfamilias* in the NXR750, which won the Paris–Dakar Rally four times.

 Honda did its best to make the Africa Twin look as much as possible like the real-deal Paris–Dakar weapons.

 Stay on the pavement for the most part, but the odd dirt road shouldn't present much difficulty.

 ★ ★
Hardly a rebel in any sense, the Af-Twin was a jump-on-the-Dakar-bandwagon motorcycle from the start.

| | |
|---|---|
| Engine: Liquid-cooled, SOHC, six-valve, 52-degree V-twin | Top Speed: 110 miles per hour (claimed) |
| Horsepower: 61 at 7,500 rpm | Weight: 445 pounds (claimed) |
| | Value Now: $$ |

### Paris–Dakar for the masses

In the late 1980s, motorcyclists became enthralled with the exploits and bravery of men who competed in the now legendary Paris–Dakar Rally. Honda, like most manufacturers, came up with production bikes that resembled the P–D weapons, in this case the XRV750 Africa Twin. Despite its appearance, the Africa Twin was no more a serious off-road machine than its scrambler forebears. Yet because of its sheer size, plus a lightly tuned and torquey V-twin, the Af-Twin became a superior touring machine, much like many of its competitors. The bike had a remarkable production run, from 1989 to 2003, and earned an enviable reputation for comfort and reliability.

# Honda

## PC800 Pacific Coast

**The answer to . . . ah, what was the question again?**
To say that Honda's PC800 Pacific Coast was met with some bemusement is to understate to a near-fatal degree. Totally encased in Pearl Pacific White plastic—the color exaggerated the blobby PC's plumpness—it looked far too scooterlike for performance-obsessed world markets. But the PC handles just dandy. Given a sharp pilot, a well-ridden PC can keep a lesser rider on, say, an FZR1000 Yamaha at bay. And the trunk—another cleavage point—imbued the PC with remarkable practicality, but customers simply weren't ready for it. If there was one undeniable criticism to level at the PC, it was that its Shadow-sourced 800cc V-twin was just too anemic. If the Pacific Coast had been a stormer, chances are good it would be selling today.

 One U.S. magazine felt the white first-year Pacific Coast so resembled a porcelain convenience that they were compelled to attach as many stick-on toilet accessories (such as TP roll-holders and the like) as possible.

 Unfortunately, the Pacific Coast seemed to be the solution to a problem few riders realized they had. As practical as it could be, the blobby-looking bodywork that hid everything from sight alienated most longtime enthusiasts. It deserved better.

 Anywhere that's paved, really. Commute to work; shop for groceries afterward; join the monthly touring- or cruiser-bike ride out; or just go for a weekend ride, with or without the Missus. On the Coast, it really is all good.

 Truly, the PC's rebel factor can't be denied. Thing is, it seemed to be rebelling in the wrong direction.

Engine: Liquid-cooled, SOHC, six-valve, 45-degree V-twin
Horsepower: n/a
Top Speed: n/a
Weight: n/a
Value Now: $$

Fred Merkel won a World Superbike Championship on an RC30.

 Won two World Superbike titles before becoming available in America.

 Down a public street. Nobody ever does that on an RC30.

 ★ ★
The RC30 was built solely to satisfy World Superbike homologation rules. Rebels don't care about rules.

Engine: Liquid-cooled, 748cc, DOHC, four-stroke V-4
Horsepower: 118 at 11,000 rpm

Top Speed: 153 miles per hour
Weight: n/a
Value Now: $$$$

## Loss leader

Where the other manufacturers had 750cc sportbikes in their lineups, Honda appeared to have a hole. There were ZX-7s, GSX-R750s, and FZ750s, but no matching CBR750s. What Honda offered was the RC30. It weighed less than the other Japanese 750s and was faster and more nimble. It was also about twice as expensive, which explains why you've probably never seen one on the road. There were inherent flaws, such as overheating, seizing, warping, and stretching, and it took forever to get spare parts. But the bike was designed to win races, and win races it did. Honda lost money on every RC30 it sold, and showrooms around the world made up for it a thousand times over every time an RC30 won.

# Honda

## ST1100

**Virtually overnight, the ST1100 changed sport-touring forever**

For American motorcyclists, Honda's ST1100 was a happy accident. The ST originally was developed for the German/European market, where a big, fast, comfy-for-two, smooth, torquey sport-tourer would be perfectly suitable. But, in Peoria, for instance, not quite so much. Nonetheless, the ST is what the American market got—and it became a hit. Although ridiculously heavy for a clean-sheet-of-paper design (702 pounds wet versus 853 pounds for a Gold Wing), the ST became the sport-tourer of choice for many. Obviously, if your riding needs meshed neatly with the ST's capabilities, it was a match made in moto-heaven. But if needs and capabilities didn't match up as skillfully, the ST could seem to be a bit of an oddity: not quite comfy enough for Gold Wing devotees, yet a little too overstuffed and heavy for fully committed sport-touring riders.

 The ST utilized spring or rubber dampers in the clutch, mainshaft, and driveshaft to reduce noise, vibration, and driveline lash.

 At a single stroke, Honda altered the sport-touring landscape of the entire planet with its ST1100 in 1990.

 Any destination two to three states away.

 ** Apart from its V-4 powerplant, and the engine's longitudinal orientation, there's hardly a rebellious frame spar in the ST1100's makeup.

Engine: Liquid-cooled, longitudinally mounted, DOHC, 16-valve V-4
Horsepower: 100 at 7,500 rpm
Top Speed: 130 miles per hour
Weight: 658 pounds (dry)
Value Now: $$

The F2's cams were designed for midrange punch; superior head flow supplied the bike's impressive power at high revs.

 Won all nine AMA Supersport races in 1991. Miguel DuHamel took seven of them and the championship.

 Kicking a big, fat ZX-6's butt.

 ★ ★ ★ ★
Rebels dominate racetracks.

Engine: Liquid-cooled, 5,899cc, DOHC, four-stroke, inline four
Horsepower: 100 at 12,000 rpm

Top Speed: 154 miles per hour
Weight: n/a
Value Now: $$

## Delivery boy

If you want to know what makes a good bike, ask a motorcycle courier. He needs something that's efficient, durable, and easy to ride fast. Lots of couriers ride F2s. It might seem surprising, but 600cc sportbikes back in the early 1990s weren't the razor-sharp repli-racers they are today. The CBR600F2 was the fastest bike in its class, but it still got 42 miles per gallon. It was known for superb handling but was still comfortable after an hour of deliveries. The engine was a masterpiece of technology but couldn't be killed even when ridden with a dry cooling system at speed around a racetrack, as Doug Toland did during practice at an AMA Superbike round one year. An occasional courier probably did worse than that and lived to make another delivery.

# Honda

## NR750

### The most sublime motorcycle ever, or corporate willy waving?

When it comes to creating corporate jewelry—or willy waving, as some cynics refer to such exercises—it's tough indeed to top Honda's NR750 streetbike. Certainly the NR had the goods. It was a street-going version of Honda's NR500 road racer, which, although incredibly innovative, was hardly a success on the racetrack. And, like the NR500, the 750 boasted siamesed cylinders filled with oval pistons supported by two titanium rods each, beneath similarly oval combustion chambers with eight valves each, to make an ersatz V-8—with a 15,000-rpm redline. With breathtaking carbon-fiber bodywork and a single-side swingarm, topped off with Honda's legendary build quality, the NR750 became an *objet de lust* for motorcyclists the world over, and it remains so to this day. The fact that it never had world-beating performance is a testament to the power of corporate jewelry—or strenuous willy waving.

 The NR helped inspire the designer of Ducati's iconic and beautiful 916.

 It was a corporate icon, a halo bike, something with which Honda could show off lessons learned in its NR500 GP road-racing program.

 Medium-twisty, please, with good pavement and slow-in, fast-out corners to make the most of the V-4/8's supernaturally wide powerband.

 ★ ★ ★ ★
The NR deserves four because it embodied Honda's technological prowess.

| | |
|---|---|
| Engine: Liquid-cooled, DOHC, 32-valve, 90-degree V-4 | Top Speed: 160 miles per hour (claimed) |
| Horsepower: 125 at 14,000 rpm | Weight: 485 pounds (claimed, dry) |
| | Value Now: $$$$$ |

Baba-san does like a cigarette now and again. Not that there's really anything wrong with that. Much to his credit, he also prefers riding motorcycles to golf.

 By pursuing lightness, almost to the exclusion of anything else, Tadao Baba's first CBR900RR was a breakthrough machine.

 Almost any twisty road will do—fast or slow. As old as the 900 is, it can still give a good account of itself and dole out some surprises.

 ★ ★ ★ ★ ★
Baba's baby changed the trajectory of sportbike development—simple as that.

| | |
|---|---|
| Engine: Liquid-cooled, DOHC, 16-valve inline-four | Top Speed: n/a |
| | Weight: n/a |
| Horsepower: n/a | Value Now: $$ |

**The unbearable beating of lightness**

By the early 1990s, liter sportbikes had become porkers, swollen almost into caricatures of themselves. Honda's Tadao Baba changed that in a single stroke with his CBR900RR. This new motorcycle was as light as some 600s yet packed a big-bore punch, with an unrivaled power-to-weight ratio. It's not exaggeration to say Baba changed the course of motorcycling. The karaoke-loving, self-taught engineer became a celebrity, wholly identified with the 900 and its 918, 929, and 954 successors, something normally unheard of in Japan's consensus-building corporate culture. He let owners know just what he thought when he had the factory inscribe inside the 1998 and 1999 918 models: "For the people who want to know the meaning of light weight. Executive Project Leader Tadao Baba."

## RC45

### The Honda V-4 with more—and less

When Honda's RC45 was introduced in 1994, a sea change had already occurred in World Superbike competition. Thanks to rule changes (and Ducati ingenuity), V-twins had become the dominant force in WSB. And that's only one of the reasons the RC45 was up against it from the beginning. Combine that with the need to throw bales of cash at a bike to make it properly competitive, and the fact that the RC45 was developed as a road bike first—not a race bike—and it's easy to see why the RC45 only won a single World Superbike title. Apart from that white-hot cauldron of competition, the RC45 did manage to distinguish itself, with five Suzuka 8-Hour wins, two World Endurance titles, a pair of AMA Superbike Championships, and two Daytona 200 wins. Not too bad for something developed as a road bike, eh?

 After experiencing much difficulty converting the RC45 from a road bike to a race bike, race teams were involved in development of its V-twin–powered successor, the RC51, early on.

 The last—for a while, anyway—battle cry for Honda's V-4 powerplant, successor to the much-beloved RC30, was meant to be a step forward but ended up being more of a step sideways.

 Racetracks, please, such as Laguna, Assen, Phillip Island, Monza—you get the picture.

 ★ ★ ★
The RC45 was a rebel only because it was powered by Honda's favorite engine, the V-4, in an era when inline fours and V-twins were the norm.

Engine: Liquid-cooled, DOHC, 16-valve, 90-degree V-4
Horsepower: 97 at 10,000 rpm

Top Speed: 147 miles per hour
Weight: 448 pounds (dry)
Value Now: $$$$

Inside the Valkyrie's long mufflers were three separate pipes per side, essentially giving a six-into-six exhaust for a unique Porsche-like tone and added punch.

The Valkyrie was the first power cruiser—or just plain urban cruiser—with that magnificent flat six engine, sourced from Honda's GL1500 Gold Wing.

Boulevards, boulevards, boulevards, preferably stoplight to stoplight, for pinks if you so dare.

★ ★ ★

Only two because, while the use of a flat six broke new ground in the cruiser category, the rest of the bike was utterly conventional and, frankly, a bit too lardy for some tastes.

Engine: Liquid-cooled, SOHC, 12-valve, horizontally opposed six
Horsepower: 101 at 8,500 (claimed)
Top Speed: 130 miles per hour (estimated)
Weight: 739 pounds (wet)
Value Now: $$

### The power cruiser with the Wurlitzer motor

Imagine you're Honda. You've got this nifty, modern, six-cylinder engine that's already a knockout in its intended home, the Gold Wing GL1500. But what if you could put that engine to another use? What could you create, and how cool would it be? After the ritual wearing of thinking caps (and prodigious market research), Honda came up with this: the Valkyrie (standard) and Valkyrie Tourer. To say they went over a treat is to defame with underestimation. With the cruiser segment crowded with V-twins, and the power cruiser class populated largely by inline fours, the flat six Valkyrie—hot rodded from GL specs—cut a unique and impressive figure. And while Honda's Valkyrie didn't start the power cruiser class, it certainly defined it for a time.

# Honda

## CBR1100XX

### Speed—and life after speed

The CBR1100XX's mother ship's name was Honda *Motor* Company Ltd., and there's a reason for that. This was definitely a motorcycle wherein the motor was the message. In the mid-1990s, Honda decided it wanted to kick Kawasaki off its throne as maker of the quickest and fastest motorcycle in all of Christendom. It came up with the CBR1100XX and its ultra-potent 1,137cc inline four, which barked out a claimed 164 horsepower at 10,000 rpm, enough to do the trick. But, just as there's always a faster gunfighter, another bike took the Honda's place as reigning speed king. No matter, because the XX—with its still impressive speed and quality road manners—then found its natural market niche as one of the speediest sport-tourers around, a position it comfortably held for years. And it will still pin your ears back when you pull the wire.

 Honda has a private test facility in the Mojave Desert with a high-speed test track where the CBR1100XX underwent part of its development.

 For a brief moment, it was the quickest and fastest motorcycle on any showroom floor.

 Anything fast and flowing, or just fast—from California's 166 to France's Route Napoleon to Germany's autobahn.

 ★ ★ ★
Yes, the CBR1100XX displaced Kawasaki's ZX-11 as the quickest and fastest production bike, but its reign was brief.

Engine: Liquid-cooled, 1,137cc, DOHC, 16-valve, inline four
Horsepower: 164 at 10,000 rpm
Top Speed: 171 miles per hour
Weight: 550 pounds (wet)
Value Now: $$

# Honda

Until the introduction of the GL1800, all Gold Wing engines were built at Honda's Anna Engine Plant, on a separate, dedicated line. Although the location changed to Honda's Marysville main plant, the Gold Wing's engine remained essentially hand-built.

Not merely the most athletic Gold Wing ever but the most athletic touring bike ever. Quite an achievement for an 800-plus-pound blunderbuss of a motorcycle.

Anywhere paved, preferably at a great distance. And if the route takes in tortuous twisties, all the better.

★ ★ ★ ★

The GL1800's back road behavior broke down a lot of the barriers erected in the minds of people who'd never actually ridden a Wing before, which stemmed largely from the effects the new aluminum frame had on the GL's handling.

Engine: Liquid-cooled, SOHC, 12-valve, horizontally opposed six
Horsepower: 118 (claimed) at 7,500 rpm
Top Speed: 123 miles per hour
Weight: 898 pounds (wet)
Value Now: $$$$

**The Wing gets its sport groove on**

After 13 years at the top of the long-distance luxury touring class, Honda's six-cylinder GL1500 needed . . . something. But what? How about a little more power and character, courtesy of a displacement increase to 1,832cc, fuel injection, and tuning to make it more free-revving? Good, but not enough. Then how about a new, tauter chassis with revamped suspension and, crucially, a nice, stiff aluminum frame, 25 pounds lighter than the previous steel item? Yes, that was definitely the ticket. Plus new bodywork that brought the Wing decidedly into the new millennium. All fine and dandy. But how did it *work*? Glad you asked. The revitalized Wing owned a newfound athleticism that transformed its handling characteristics on twisty back roads. Just to give you an idea of the magnitude of the change, even soon-to-be AMA Superbike champ Nicky Hayden was impressed.

# Honda

## RC51

### Poor man's Ducati

If you can't beat 'em, join 'em. Ducati was winning World Superbike title after World Superbike title, thanks to the rule that let 999cc V-twins compete against 750cc multis, and Honda was sick of it. So Honda engineers built their own big V-twin and won another World Superbike Championship. Soon the rules would change yet again, giving everyone the same displacement limit no matter how many cylinders their engines had. Before that happened, though, RC51s took another world and one AMA championship, the latter propelling Nicky Hayden into MotoGP. Sadly, it wasn't enough to counter the lighter, flashier inline four repli-racers from the other Japanese manufacturers in the world's showrooms. Proving nobody really wants a poor man's Ducati.

 As of this writing, the RC51 was the last non-Suzuki to win an AMA Superbike Championship.

 Proved Honda could out-Ducati Ducati.

 Autodromo Enzo e Dino Ferrari, Imola, Italy.

 ★ ★ ★ ★
Showed Ducati where they could shove it.

Engine: Liquid-cooled, 996cc, DOHC V-twin
Horsepower: 139 at 9,750 rpm
Top Speed: 161 miles per hour
Weight: n/a
Value Now: $$$

The first prototype of the RC211V was so violent that test riders felt it was all but unrideable, but they were afraid to tell supervisors at Honda R&D.

 Being perhaps the easiest to ride, and therefore the most successful, of the new era of MotoGP four-strokes. The RC211V took 48 wins out of a possible 82 from 2002 to 2006, or 59 percent of the races held.

 Any racetrack with lots of frighteningly fast corners, such as Spa in Belgium or Australia's Philip Island.

 ★ ★ ★
Honda interpreted the rulebook to its best advantage and did all the preliminary testing and R&D work necessary to create one of the fastest, friendliest race bikes ever made.

| | |
|---|---|
| Engine: Liquid-cooled, DOHC, 20-valve V-5 | Top Speed: 205-plus miles per hour (claimed) |
| Horsepower: 220 at 15,500 rpm (claimed) | Weight: n/a |
| | Value Now: Pricey, if not priceless |

## Easy does it

When the four-stroke MotoGP era began in 2002, Honda had its rivals *covered*. Honda Racing Corporation (HRC) conjured the simply brilliant V-5 RC211V, which would be ridden by then-current world champion Valentino Rossi. After so many years of developing the churlish, semi-demonic NSR500 two-stroke, some bright sparks at Honda realized if they made the new four-stroke more user-friendly, it would be easier to ride—and win—on. The V-5 aided in that quest, tuned as it was not for maximum horsepower but for *manageable* horsepower the rider actually could use. Its firing intervals—not firing order—also aided rear tire traction, while Honda's increasing emphasis on mass centralization made the bike flickable. Allied with Rossi's monumental talent, the pairing could win almost at will.

# Honda

## Rune

### What sayeth the Rune?

Even though we might not all be in love with the custom-cruiser type of motorcycling perhaps best represented by Honda's Rune, we'd like to think we're at least adult enough to appreciate what went into getting it to dealers' showrooms. See, almost all manufacturers come up with show bikes, wild and extreme custom creations, often the result of a single person who hasn't the slightest concern with how it fits the production line. That was the case with Honda's Rune. Modeled after a Honda custom bike called the T2, which had been shown to test audiences effusive with praise, the Rune was to be produced with as little compromise as possible. Normally, all the best of intentions cannot forestall the near-total failure of such projects. But, with the Rune, Honda pulled off the trick quite nicely, as you can see.

The Rune is a near-as-dammit production version of the T2, a styling-exercise show bike never intended to see the merciless, near-ceaseless flow of a factory production line.

Simple: to recreate for public sale Honda's well-received T2 one-off custom show bike. It might have been easier to replicate cold fusion.

Any metropolitan city during rush hour so that you and the Rune can be admired by the greatest number of people.

★ ★ ★ ★
Yes, only four because, as outlandish as the Rune is, it's typically Honda mass-produced rebellion.

Engine: Liquid-cooled, SOHC, 12-valve, horizontally opposed sx
Horsepower: 91 at 5,250 rpm

Top Speed: 123 miles per hour
Weight: 794 pounds (claimed, dry)
Value Now: $$$

Honda was the last company to field a competitive two-stroke off-road racebike?

 Brought two-stroke emissions down to four-stroke levels by making the engine burn fuel more efficiently.

 From Grenada, Spain, to Dakar, Africa—the EXP-2 took first place in the two-stroke class in the 1995 Dakar Rally.

 ★ ★ ★ ★ ★
Introducing something as politically incorrect as a two-stroke motorcycle in the mid-1990s was most definitely a big eff you to the status quo.

| | |
|---|---|
| Engine: Liquid-cooled 400cc two-stroke single | Top Speed: NA |
| Horsepower: 54 at 10,000 rpm | Weight: NA |
| | Value Now: $$$$$ |

**Honda attempts to revive the "stink wheel"**

Much of the history of Honda motorcycles is a history of trying to put a stake in the heart of the two-stroke motorcycle, the direct result of the fact that Soichiro Honda, the company's founder, despised two-strokes, which he called "stink wheels." Honda tried to field a four-stroke racer at the highest levels of Grand Prix racing decades before regulations killed the two stroke, and they led the pack when it came to fielding competitive off-road four-stroke bikes, so imagine everyone's surprise when Honda introduced the EXP-2, a two-stroke with a special valve designed to reduce the unburned hydrocarbons inherent in the two-stroke design. The press hailed the EXP-2 as the rebirth of the two-stroke, but even though Honda took much of the stink out of the stink wheel, it wasn't enough to revitalize the design.

# Honda

## CBR600RR

**Real MotoGP influence, not mere marketspeak**

Honda's first MotoGP weapon, the RC211V, doubtless will be remembered as one of the finest race bikes ever made. The bike won 88 percent of the races in its and MotoGP's debut year, 2002. The development of both the RC211V and the CBR600RR paralleled each other, with great heaps of MotoGP technology—such as the unit pro-link rear suspension, programmed dual-stage fuel injection (PGM-DSFI), fuel tank placement, and especially mass centralization—transferring from the race bike to the road bike.

 Though Honda claimed that shock loads didn't get fed into the bike's frame simply because its unit pro-link rear end isolated the shock mounts to the swing arm, chassis and suspension guru Tony Foale has said that's complete bollocks. It has the whiff of being written by marketing, not engineering. And virtually every member of the press swallowed it whole.

 When it debuted as a 2003 model, the CBR600RR's significance stemmed from being Honda's first RR (race replica) middleweight motorcycle.

 As long as it's paved and twisty, the 600RR can hardly be equaled.

 ★ ★ ★
Although it's an extremely conventional motorcycle overall, the CBR600RR scores three jackets because of its many MotoGP influences.

Engine: Liquid-cooled, DOHC, 16-valve, inline four
Horsepower: 117 at 13,000 rpm (claimed)
Top Speed: 160 miles per hour (claimed)
Weight: 373 pounds (claimed, dry)
Value Now: $$$

# Honda

## CBR1000RR

**Vindication**

For years, motorcycle journalists around the globe labeled Honda's extremely capable CBR1000RR liter sportbike as being, well, dull. Most of the stick the bike got came from U.K. magazines, with writers slagging off the previous bike with epithets of "bland" and "lacks excitement/involvement." For 2008, Honda dug in to create the latest version of the CBR1000RR. And, finally, it was acclaimed as *good*: "The greatest sportbike in the world? It ain't far off."

 Thanks to a Honda-developed casting process called hollow fine die-casting, the RR's frame comprises only four sections.

 Famous for being the easiest-to-use big-bore sportbike the world has seen.

 Once again, it just doesn't make that much of a difference. As long as the road surface is concrete or tarmac, bike and rider will be as happy as 12 dogs.

 ★ ★
Yes, only two. This is a completely conventional sportbike; the number could have been lower.

Engine: Liquid-cooled, DOHC, 16-valve, inline four
Horsepower: 166 at 12,000 rpm
Top Speed: 179 miles per hour
Weight: 439 pounds (claimed, wet)
Value Now: $$$

In developing the VFR1200F, Honda specifically benchmarked BMW's K1300S, which should be further evidence that this latest VFR really isn't the sportbike many V-4 fans hoped it would be, or thought it had to be.

Nothing less than the return of the prodigal powerplant, the V-4, Honda's prime mover. That, and the VFR1200F offered Honda a huge canvas onto which it could paint a dizzying array of new-tech features.

Something on the order of Pashnit Tours' three-day Sierra Nevada Weekend Tour. When some of the routes in Central California are tied together properly, it's possible to explore a dizzying succession of near-perfect corners without using main highways for more than about a mile.

★ ★

The VFR1200F represents another mixed bag of accomplishments: while the bike can boast impressive technical credentials compared to other Hondas, that doesn't hold up when it gets compared to other motorcycles that can be counted as rivals on the showroom floor.

| | |
|---|---|
| Engine: Liquid-cooled, SOHC, 16-valve, 76-degree V-4 | Top Speed: 170 miles per hour (claimed) |
| Horsepower: 170 at 10,000 rpm (claimed) | Weight: n/a |
| | Value Now: $$$$ |

**The V-4 never really went away at Honda.**

Even before the all-new VFR1200F hit showroom floors, it looked to be in trouble due to a toxic sludge of hype, artificially swollen expectations, and a remarkable dollop of corporate confusion. Honda has portrayed the VFR1200F as "revolutionary," "game-changing," and an "evolutionary shift in the future of high-performance sport-touring motorcycles." Yet, except for the (optional) dual-clutch shift system (which many high-end cars have had for years), almost none of the latest VFR's features are truly new. What's more, Honda seems uncertain about the VFR's core mission, referring to the bike as a sport-tourer, then calling it the "world's best streetbike," and then grouping it with Honda's pure-sport CBR1000RR. Unquestionably, the VFR1200F is an impressive piece of engineering and an exceptional road tool. But for buyers who've long beseeched Honda to really pin everyone's ears back with an RC211V replica, the VFR is rather small beer indeed.

# Husaberg

## F450

### Rethinking the way off-road bikes are made

KTM's acquisition of Sweden-based Husaberg paved the way for the Austrian company to develop a new line of upscale motorcycles. The Husaberg F450 was the first of the new-generation off-road bikes to hit the market, and the bike showcased some interesting design features, chief among them a fuel-injected engine that centralized the bike's weight distribution. The engine itself took its cylinder and piston design from KTM's 450 XC-W, and by tilting the cylinder 70 degrees forward and moving the crankshaft up 100mm and back 160mm, the transmission could be positioned beneath the cylinder and crank assembly. The engine was nestled in a semi-parameter frame with a plastic subframe to help reduce weight. The rear shock absorber was mounted to a crossmember between the frame rails, helping soften the ride.

Husaberg was formed in 1988 after Cagiva bought Husqvarna.

This was the first model to result from KTM's acquisition of Husaberg.

The Novemberkåsan, Sweden's legendary enduro.

★ ★ ★ ★
If you enjoy off-road riding, you'll enjoy the F450.

Engine: Liquid-cooled, 449cc, four-stroke single-cylinder
Horsepower: 45 at 8,000 rpm
Top Speed: n/a
Weight: 261 pounds
Value Now: $$$

# Husqvarna

 To combat the Huskys, BSA built Jeff Smith a 255-pound motocrosser in 1963.

 Won the 1960 500cc European Grand Prix MX championship.

 Unadilla Valley Sports Center MX track, New Berlin, New York.

 ★ ★ ★ ★ ★
Made America safe for motocross.

Engine: Air-cooled, 500cc, two-stroke single
Horsepower: n/a
Top Speed: n/a
Weight: n/a
Value Now: $$$$

### Revolution

Sweden dominated the 1960 European Grand Prix season. At the end of the year, the top three places were held by Swedes, each on a Swedish bike. Sten Lundin took second overall on his Monark/Lito; on either side of him were Husqvarna-mounted riders Bill Nillson and Rolf Tibblin. In America, entrepreneur Edison Dye got expert rider Malcolm Smith to test a Husky. It was over 60 pounds lighter and light years ahead of the BSAs and Triumphs and Harleys available in the United States at the time. Smith raved, and a revolution began. The next 30 years saw motocross technology expand at an exponential rate. If not for an enterprising entrepreneur and an otherworldly rider he knew, Americans might never have known.

# Husqvarna

### With a capital T

When Husqvarna made its lead role in the motocross revolution the firm's sole focus, red tanks with shiny, silver sides started popping up everywhere, and Huskys dominated races on both sides of the Atlantic. In 1968, Husqvarna brought works performance to amateur motocrossers with the Viking 360 and, in keeping with the pillaging rapists it's named for, got a lot of riders in trouble on tracks around the world.

 In the ultimate tribute, Steve McQueen traded his beloved Triumph dirtbike for the Husqvarna 400 he rode in *On Any Sunday*.

 This bike scared the crap out of riders not named Torsten Hallman.

 An AHRMA Classic 500 race.

 ★ ★ ★ ★
Rebels are scary. This bike is scary. Therefore, this bike is a rebel.

Engine: Air-cooled, 351cc, two-stroke single
Horsepower: 33 at 5,500 rpm
Top Speed: n/a
Weight: n/a
Value Now: $$

# Husqvarna

## 250 CR MAG

### Long-legged Swede

Long-travel rear (LTR) suspensions for motocross bikes came into vogue in the early 1970s, but it took the manufacturers a few years to catch up and incorporate them into production bikes. It was a race in itself, then, to see who could do so first. Husqvarna won, with its 1974 250 CR MAG, its rear shocks moved a cautious distance forward. But LTR only counted a fraction toward what made the 250 CR so desirable then, as it is now for AHRMA competitors. Husqvarna also equipped the bike with a new reed-valve induction almost big enough to stick a fist through, magnesium engine cases (hence MAG), a new frame, and increased fork travel. Back in the day, the 250 CR MAG was about as close to a production works bike as a customer could buy.

 If anything, the 250 CR MAG is just as popular and desirable—if not more so—a race bike now as it was when it was introduced.

 The first mass-production motocrosser with long-travel rear suspension.

 Certainly not a supercross track. No, look for something more like Unadilla, from back in the day, when suspension travel was about 3–4 inches.

 ★ ★ ★ ★ ★
Although the Japanese manufacturers certainly caught up in double time, the fact remains that a rather small Swedish motorcycle company got the drop on them in rushing LTR to the production line.

Engine: Air-cooled, two-stroke, reed-valve single-cylinder
Horsepower: n/a
Top Speed: n/a
Weight: 214 pounds (claimed)
Value Now: $$$

Two-strokes lack engine braking, automatic transmissions compound that trait, and brakes weren't all that great back then, especially if they got wet.

 Could get through bogs like no other bike—just point it and twist the throttle.

 Through the woods while talking on a mobile phone.

 ★ ★ ★ ★ ★
This bike flew in the face of convention.

Engine: Air-cooled, 384cc, reed-valve, two-stroke single
Horsepower: 35 at 6,000 rpm

Top Speed: 80 miles per hour
Weight: n/a
Value Now: $$$

### Shiftless

Fleet operations have spawned a few memorable motorcycle designs. The Ducati Apollo was conceived for use by American law enforcement agencies, and Moto Guzzi developed its automatic transmission for the Italian military. The 390 Auto traces its roots to a Swedish army edict that recruits become proficient on a motorcycle within a week of joining up. Not in a way that allowed them to cruise around delivering letters and picking up girls, but in a way that enabled them to go cross-country—on snow if needed. Husqvarna built them some bikes with automatic transmissions, and away they went. Off-road riding enthusiasts have different demands than people who have to ride off roads, though, and the offshoot 390 Auto was never accepted by the civilian world.

# Indian

## Scout

**A landmark design that led to an even more significant model, the Scout 101**

Talk to anybody who has ridden an early Indian Scout, and you'll probably hear nothing but words of praise. For good reason too, because, for its time, the Scout mixed a quality ride and predictable handling with a smooth, powerful, 37-cubic-inch engine. The Scout served well throughout the 1920s until it was replaced in 1928 by a version with a slightly larger engine (45 cubic inches), which ultimately led to the Scout 101, considered by many enthusiasts to be one of the all-time great motorcycles.

 Indian dropped the popular V-twin–powered Scout from its model lineup after 1948, the same year that Floyd Emde won the Daytona 200 on a Daytona Sports Scout.

 The 1920 Scout offered such a balanced package that many consider it the first truly modern motorcycle.

 Eastern Iowa, where you can enjoy the bridges of Madison County.

 ★ ★ ★
The first Scout links early motorcycle design with the modern era.

| | |
|---|---|
| Engine: Air-cooled, 596cc, four-stroke, 42-degree V-twin | Top Speed: 55 miles per hour |
| Horsepower: 11 at 2,500 rpm | Weight: 315 pounds |
| ¼ Mile: n/a | Price New: n/a |
| | Value Now: $$$ |

# Indian

## Scout

**More displacement for more performance**

Because it represented the technological state of the art in its heyday, there really wasn't much to improve upon with Indian's Scout. Consequently, only minor improvements followed it through the 1920s. The biggest change occurred in 1928 when engine displacement was bumped to 45 cubic inches. Overnight, something good got even better. But the best was yet to come, and by lengthening and lowering the frame, Indian produced the Scout 101, a bike considered to be one of the best road bikes of the era.

 A popular limerick among Indian owners stated, "You can't wear out an Indian Scout or its brother, the Indian Chief. They are built like rocks to take hard knocks; it's the Harleys that cause grief."

 The Scout led to the Scout 101, considered to be among the great motorcycle designs of all time.

 Joshua Tree National Monument to make use of the Scout's power and predictable handling through the park's many sweeping curves.

 ★ ★ ★ ★
Once you master the left-hand throttle, left-foot clutch, and right-hand tank shifter, you'll love this bike.

| | |
|---|---|
| Engine: Air-cooled, 45-cubic-inch, four-stroke, 42-degree V-twin | Top Speed: 75 miles per hour |
| Horsepower: 18 at 3,000 rpm | Weight: 370 pounds |
| | Value Now: $$$$ |

## Boardtrack Racer

 Indian held the American land speed record of 132 miles per hour until Joe Petrali and Harley-Davidson broke it in 1937.

 For maximum power, the engines had four valves per cylinder head.

 There are no boardtracks anymore, but a lap around the Indianapolis Mile will suffice.

 ★ ★ ★ ★ ★
Remember, this racer was capable of 120 miles per hour, and it had direct drive, skinny tires, and no brakes.

Engine: Air-cooled, 994cc, four-stroke V-twin
Horsepower: 7 (early model); 20 (late model) at 4,500 rpm
Top Speed: 60 miles per hour (early model); 130 miles per hour (late model)
Weight: 240 pounds (early model); 260 pounds (late model)
Value Now: $$$$$

### Chairman of the board for many years

Among the most popular forms of motorcycle racing during the 1910s and '20s, boardtrack racing took place on circular, steeply banked courses consisting of wood planks laid side by side. The same race bikes that competed on the dirt ovals, such as the Dodge Mile, also raced in those wood motordromes. As you might guess, it took a rider with nerves of steel to race those 120-mile-per-hour boardtrackers; the bikes had engines with direct drive to the rear wheel, spindly tires that were two inches across at the tread, and no brakes. Indian produced many racers during that era, powered by both single- and twin-cylinder engines.

## Big Chief

**The Big Chief was just that, a model with a bigger engine than the original Chief's**

The original Indian Chief debuted in 1922 with a 61-cubic-inch engine. That classic liter motor offered plenty of power, but customer demand—heavily swayed by Harley's JD model that had a 74-cubic-inch engine—led to a bigger Indian engine for 1924. The result was the Big Chief, powered by a 74-cubic-inch engine that became the standard to which Indian and Harley-Davidson, and customers, adhered for performance and excellence for years to come. Indian offered the Chief and Big Chief for 1924, but eventually the smaller engine was dropped, as was the Big name.

 The American Motorcyclist Association was formed in 1924.

 The first Indian to use a 74-cubic-inch engine.

 A cruise to Pickerington, Ohio, to the AMA Motorcycle Hall of Fame.

 ★ ★ ★ ★
Bigger is always better.

Engine: Air-cooled, 74-cubic-inch, four-stroke, 42-degree V-twin
Horsepower: 34 at 3,000 rpm
Top Speed: 75 miles per hour
Weight: 440 pounds
Value Now: $$$$

## The *Munro Special*

Some speculate that Burt fabricated his engine cylinders from underground gas pipe, and he fashioned the bike's cooling fins from aluminum slices that he shrank over the pipe.

The bike made doubly famous in 2005 by the movie *The World's Fastest Indian*.

Following the black line over the Bonneville Salt Flats—in Burt's honor, of course.

★ ★ ★ ★ ★
Would you really slip inside that streamlined body to attempt a 200-mile-per-hour pass?

Engine: Air-cooled, 58-cubic-inch, four-stroke, 42-degree V-twin
Horsepower: n/a
Top Speed: 190.07 miles per hour (qualifying speed for record)
Weight: n/a
Value Now: $$$$$

### Proof that age has no limits

Without doubt, the *Munro Special* is the most famous Indian motorcycle of all time. It's also the fastest, as commemorated in the film *The World's Fastest Indian*. Indeed, the *Special* pays tribute to one man's passion: going as fast as he could with a motorcycle that he built, tuned, and rode himself. Burt Munro toiled with the bike for 57 years, the final dozen or so years spent racing it at Bonneville on a quest for a class record, which he achieved in 1967 with a speed of 183.586 miles per hour.

# Indian

## Indian Scout

**An all-new design that, sadly, became old all too quickly**

Shortly after World War II ended, Ralph Rogers led a small group of investors who bought Indian Motorcycle Company. The first order of business was to introduce new models, among them the Arrow (with a single-cylinder, 220cc engine) and the Scout (440cc twin). The bikes boasted innovative features (by American motorcycle design standards), such as foot shifters, hand-operated clutch levers, and lightweight chassis. The Scout was offered in three models: the standard Scout, the Sports Scout with a few accessories tacked on, and the Super Scout, which offered a windshield and saddlebags. For various reasons, the new models couldn't compete against the British imports, and by 1953, Indian was shutting down its operations in Springfield, Massachusetts.

 The new postwar Indian engines were designed by the company's former chief of engineering, G. Briggs Weaver.

 The Scout was one of three engine designs based on the "modular" concept that was conceived by Ralph Rogers.

 Springfield, Massachusetts, with your sights on Hendee Street, named in honor of the company's co-founder. Stop to visit the Indian Motorcycle Museum.

 ★ ★
This bike will offer you a taste of what the American motorcycle market could have been, had Indian survived.

Engine: Air-cooled, 440cc, four-stroke, vertical parallel twin
Horsepower: 20 at 4,000 rpm
¼ Mile: n/a

Top Speed: 85 miles per hour
Weight: 280 pounds
Value Now: $$

# Indian

 This was Indian's first model to have a right-hand throttle and left-side shifter as standard equipment.

 The model that Indian customers preferred at the time.

 Sturgis, South Dakota, where we'll visit the Chief Crazy Horse Monument.

 ✱ ✱ ✱
You'll be rewarded with a rather smooth ride backed by plenty of Indian heritage.

Engine: Air-cooled, 80-cubic-inch, four-stroke, 42-degree V-twin
Horsepower: 50 at 4,800 rpm
Top Speed: 92 miles per hour
Weight: 570 pounds
Value Now: $$$$

**Packing an 80-cubic-inch engine, this was the biggest Chief of them all**

While the bulk of Indian's resources were focused on developing the parallel twin-cylinder engine during the late 1940s, the remainder of the tribe busied themselves refining the company's leading seller, the Chief. The revised model sported a telescopic fork, revised shifter and clutch operation, and an 80-cubic-inch engine courtesy of stroker flywheels. The Chief's reliability remained intact too, but none of this was enough to save the company from financial ruin. By the dawn of the 1950s, the side-valve (flathead) engine represented antiquated technology, and the last remaining Chiefs found few buyers. This, combined with the poor reception and dismal reliability of the company's vertical twins, doomed the fabled marque; in 1953, Indian went out of business.

# Indian

## Gilroy Chief

**An Indian with a (gasp!) Harley-clone engine**

After its original demise in the 1950s, the Indian name was dragged though the mud by a long series of charlatans and ne'er-do-wells, more than one of whom ended up in prison for his efforts. With the rare exception that usually came in the form of some low-rent minibike built in a third-world sweatshop, few actual motorcycles bore the proud *Indian* name on their fuel tanks. Perhaps the closest thing to a real new Indian in the pipeline was an innovative clean-sheet design created by James Parker in the 1990s, but before that machine ever became a reality, a company called *California Motorcycle Company* (CMC) snatched up the Indian trademark by convincing a gullible judge that it had an Indian motorcycle that was ready for production. Which it did, but only because CMC already produced Harley clones using aftermarket engines; the new Indian was simply a Harley clone with goofy skirted fenders, and a not-particularly good one at that. Alas, the motorcycling public didn't want Harley-Indians; the rechristened Indian Motorcycle Company of America declared bankruptcy in 2003.

 In an attempt to change the public's perception that the new Indians were just Harley clones, Indian reshaped the cylinders on later versions to disguise the engines' Harley origins.

 The Indian Motorcycle Company of America was born as the result of an extremely ill-conceived court decision.

 To a Harley dealership to trade it in on the real deal.

 Real rebels don't need to resort to bullshit lawsuits to start businesses.

Engine: Air-cooled, 80-cubic-inch, four-stroke, 45-degree V-twin
Horsepower: 60 at 4,800 rpm
Top Speed: 102 miles per hour
Weight: 670 pounds
Value Now: $

The A1 had oil injection, so you didn't need to premix fuel.

 This was the first of Kawasaki's power bikes.

 Sneaking up behind Bonnevilles and then blowing past them.

★ ★ ★
It was the King's grandpa.

Engine: Air-cooled, 247cc, rotary-valve, two-stroke twin
Horsepower: 31 at 8,000 rpm

Top Speed: 103 miles per hour
Weight: n/a
Value Now: $$

### Chameleon

Able to stick with four-stroke 650 twins of the day, the Samurai started Kawasaki down the primrose path of power. Its two-stroke strength paved the way for the Mach III and Mach IV's straight-line supremacy, and the two steering dampers foreshadowed the Kawi two-strokes' inferiority when those lines started to curve. Kawasaki sold standard A1s and scrambler A1s, and in 1967 the company came out with a 350cc version, the A7. But the A1R was the coolest version. Made for road racing, it had 43 horsepower, thanks to bigger carbs and higher compression, and was good for speeds of over 125 miles per hour. At Daytona in 1969, Cal Rayborn raced the little two-stroke and then jumped onto his Harley and won the 200. Talk about changing colors.

# Kawasaki

## H1 Mach III 500

### Evil, wicked, mean, and nasty

Kawasaki started working on a new four-stroke, four-cylinder engine design in the late 1960s. It was going to be blisteringly fast. Then engineers caught wind of Honda's prototype 750 and changed course. Out went the four-cylinder four-stroke, in came a three-cylinder two-stroke intended to provide maximum power and minimum weight, and a cult of speed was born by accident.

You could easily graft more cylinders onto Kawasaki triples. People did it all the time, ending up with as many as 48 of them Frankensteined together.

Fastest bike available at the time. Wheelied whether you wanted it to or not.

Lion's Associated Drag Strip, Long Beach, California.

★ ★ ★ ★ ★
Chewed unassuming riders up and spit them out.

Engine: Air-cooled, 498cc, two-stroke, inline triple
Horsepower: 60 at 7,500 rpm
Top Speed: 114 miles per hour
Weight: n/a
Value Now: $$

# Kawasaki

## H2 Mach IV 750

### Flexible flyer

The year 1972 was very good for 750s—Ducati 750SS, Suzuki GT750 Water Buffalo, MV Agusta 750S, Moto Guzzi V7 Sport, Norton Commando Combat—but none could match the power of Kawasaki's H2 Mach IV. But the bike was a powerful engine wrapped in an inadequate chassis. The swingarm flexed, the forks flexed—you could even watch as the frame flexed at the steering head—and the bike wheelied, weaved, and tank-slapped its way into a very bad reputation.

A new H2 was $300 cheaper than a new Norton Commando.

For many years, the H2 held the quarter-mile records for nitrous-injected and normally aspirated 750cc motorcycles (7.776 seconds at 170 miles per hour and 8.240 seconds at 153 miles per hour, respectively).

U.S. Highway 129, Deal's Gap, North Carolina. Just kidding.

★ ★ ★ ★ ★
Unleashing 74 horsepower in a 2,800-rpm powerband is rebellious.

Engine: Air-cooled, 748cc, piston-port, two-stroke, inline triple
Horsepower: 74 at 6,800 rpm
Top Speed: 120 miles per hour
Weight: n/a
Value Now: $$

Yvonne DuHamel lapped the Daytona oval on a Z1 at 160.199 miles per hour in 1973, a new record.

From its inline four to its swoopy styling, the Z1 was really the first of what we now call superbikes.

Daytona International Speedway, Daytona Beach, Florida.

★ ★ ★ ★
All the cool bikes wanted to be the King.

| | |
|---|---|
| Engine: Air-cooled, 903cc, DOHC, four-stroke, inline four | Top Speed: 133 miles per hour |
| Horsepower: 82 at 8,500 rpm | Weight: n/a |
| | Value Now: $$$ |

## "New York Steak"

Kawasaki was developing a 750cc, four-stroke, inline four in the late 1960s but caught wind of Honda's 750 and launched a line of two-stroke triples instead. It turned out to be the right move, and *Kawasaki* became synonymous with *acceleration*. But *two-strokes* and *emissions* were becoming equally synonymous. Re-enter the four-stroke project. This time, there would be no upstaging. Given the code name "New York Steak," the new/old mission was kept top secret—Z1s in America during preproduction testing even wore Honda tanks and badges. Though bolted into an H2 Mach IV frame, the Z1's engine was much more civil. The nicknames each bike earned tell the tale: The H2's moniker was "Widowmaker"; the Z1 was called "the King." Got twice the gas mileage too.

# Kawasaki

## KZ1300/6

**Butt kicker**

When the KZ1300 came out, *Cycle* magazine asked if it made sense to add 100 pounds of engine just to move an extra 100 pounds of engine. You ended up with a big, long, heavy bike, but given Kawasaki's history, yes, it made perfect sense. Honda has a new 750cc inline four? Build a 500cc two-stroke triple that'll kick its butt. Suzuki has a new 1,340cc, 170-horsepower bike named for a bird that can hit 300 kilometers per hour in a dive? Build a 1,354cc, 180-horsepower bike that'll kick its butt. Honda has a new 1,046cc, inline six? Build a 1,286cc, inline six that'll kick its butt. See the pattern? That's how manly men do it, and Kawasaki is a manly man's company.

 At 286 pounds, the KZ1300 engine weighed more than some imported bikes. And, at 130 horsepower, it was more powerful than lots of imported cars.

 Biggest, most powerful—and most complicated—Japanese motorcycle engine at the time.

 Bonneville Speedway, Wendover, Utah.

 ★ ★ ★ ★ ★
It was built to kick butt.

Engine: Liquid-cooled, 1,286cc, DOHC, four-stroke, inline six
Horsepower: 130 at 8,000 rpm
Top Speed: 135 miles per hour
Weight: n/a
Value Now: $$

There was no suggested retail price for an Eddie Lawson Replica. You paid what the dealer wanted for it.

 This was the first replica to generate a replica.

 Down memory lane.

 *
Marketing ploys aren't rebellious.

Engine: Air-cooled, 1,015cc, DOHC, four-stroke, inline four
Horsepower: 89 at 8,500 rpm

Top Speed: 131 miles per hour
Weight: n/a
Value Now: $$$$

### Mockup

Eddie Lawson won the 1981 AMA Superbike title on a KZ1000. Kawasaki commemorated the feat by tarting up a KZ1000J with some cosmetic parts and selling it as the KZ1000R Eddie Lawson Replica. The real replica, of course, was the KZ1000S (pictured below). Right down to the twin-plug head and magnesium wheels, it was the bike Lawson and Wayne Rainey raced in 1982. Only 30 were made, and they sold for $10,999, a privateer's dream. The ELR itself would be channeled a couple of decades later through the ZRX1100, a bike on which you could have beaten Eddie if you'd had it in 1982 and he'd had his namesake replica. Despite their mechanical normalcy, ELRs are valuable these days, which speaks to their association with a legend more than their capabilities.

# Kawasaki

## GPz750 Turbo

### Best of the turbobikes

During the Great Turbo Experiment of the mid-1980s, only one manufacturer really understood how a turbobike should act; it had to have a real, unmistakable boost in power, and it had to be a sportbike. That was the initial promise of turbocharging, after all. Well, Kawasaki's GPz750 Turbo fulfilled that promise. It was just as quick as the maker's own GPz1100. What's more, the 750 T-bike slaughtered the opposition, all of which made too little power and were plagued with excessive turbo lag. Although turbocharging ended up being a dead-end for motorcycling, at least briefly, Kawasaki's GPz750 Turbo showed everyone just how it should be done.

 Kawasaki initially produced a handout/ad quoting about a half-dozen of the company's engineers who had developed the 750 Turbo, but the quotes were in badly translated English. One engineer was allegedly quoted as saying, "Please come to try to ride our son."

 More than any other turbocharged motorcycle, Kawasaki's GPz750 Turbo came the closest to fulfilling the original promise of turbo technology.

 Preferably billiard-smooth tarmac, with gentle, broad-radius corners so that you can keep the turbo on the boil—ecstasy.

 ★ ★ ★ ★
Honda, Yamaha, and Suzuki's turbobikes preceded Kawasaki's. Given that these bikes constituted the conventional wisdom, Kawasaki's 750 Turbo flaunted it and showed them how turbocharging should be done.

Engine: Liquid-cooled, DOHC, eight-valve, turbocharged inline-four
Horsepower: n/a
Top Speed: n/a
Weight: n/a
Value Now: $$$

## GPz900R Ninja 900

 The Ninja name was added for the North American market.

 Ten years after the Z1, the Ninja 900 was clocked at 151 miles per hour, reclaiming the "world's fastest production motorcycle" mantle for Kawasaki.

 University Avenue, Anytown, USA.

 ★ ★ ★ ★
A guy nicknamed Maverick rode one.

Engine: Liquid-cooled, 908cc, DOHC, four-stroke, inline four
Horsepower: 115 at 9,500 rpm

Top Speed: 154 miles per hour
Weight: n/a
Value Now: $$

### The first squid bike

Tom Cruise rode a Ninja sans helmet in *Top Gun*, and a generation of squids was born. At least Maverick wore his bomber jacket. While Cruise changed attitudes toward riding gear, the original Ninja—the GPz900R—changed bikes. Kawasaki engineers had discovered that frame downtubes could be eliminated if the engine became a stressed member. Thousands of road-test miles later, the diamond frame was born. Horsepower is heat, and air-cooled engines don't like heat, so the GPz900R made liquid cooling standard sportbike fare. Then there was the fairing. Aerodynamic research pointed to a more radically dolphin-like design, but market research pointed away from it, so a compromise was reached. And frat boys in flip-flops would forever be drawn to the power.

# Kawasaki

## ZL900 Eliminator

### That's *amore*

First there was the motorcycle. Soon after came the racing motorcycle. Next was the economical motorcycle. Then the powerful motorcycle. By the 1980s, niches were being carved out of niches. There were sportbikes and sport-tourers, standards and cruisers, enduros and dual-sports—in 1985, Kawasaki sold more than 30 different models in the United States, and each needed its own engine. Two-stroke, four-stroke, single, twin, four; the trick was designing an engine flexible enough to fit multiple applications. Like Kawi's big Z-series multi. With 36mm carbs, it's a Ninja; but stick on some 32s, and it's an Eliminator. Depending on tune or bore, that same engine powered Concours, Ninjas, and Eliminators. That's more than *amore*. That's amortization.

 At 2.9 gallons, the tank was good for about 100 miles at most. Half that if you twisted your wrist with any sort of vigor.

 The Eliminator was a drag race bike with lights.

 To the gas station.

 ★ ★
It's just a Concours without the bags.

Engine: Liquid-cooled, 908cc, DOHC, four-stroke, inline four
Horsepower: 105 at 9,500 rpm

Top Speed: 134 miles per hour
Weight: n/a
Value Now: $$

The Concours won *Cycle Guide* magazine's Bike of the Year Award when it was introduced in 1986.

 Speed and distance with style and grace.

 Lake Superior Circle Tour.

 ★ ★
Nothing terribly rebellious here.

| | |
|---|---|
| Engine: Liquid-cooled, 997cc, DOHC, four-stroke, inline four | Top Speed: 125 miles per hour |
| Horsepower: 100 at 9,000 rpm | Weight: n/a |
| | Value Now: $$ |

### Endurance runner

Kawasaki introduced the Concours for the 1986 model. You could still buy the same basic machine virtually unchanged for the next 21 years, and you can still buy the redesigned version introduced in 2007 today. With the exception of Royal Enfield's Bullet, which is still being built in India in more or less the same configuration that it has been in since early man first started pounding on metal with stone hammers, and Honda's Rebel 250, which has remained in production since 1985 simply because it's so nondescript that Honda's product planners forgot it was there, few bikes have enjoyed that kind of longevity. For the original Concours to have sustained a production run of over 20 years is remarkable. It's a testament not only to the bike but to the marketing prowess that discovered the bike's niche. "Kawasaki has entered touring at full throttle," screamed the giant, block letters on the saddlebag-wearing, shaft-drive Ninja's first sales brochure. And so began the Connie's marathon.

# Kawasaki

## GPz600R Ninja

### Sportbike prototype

It's doubtful Kawasaki had in mind what it eventually accomplished with its 1985 GPz600R Ninja: permanently shifting motorcycling's middleweight class from 500–550cc to 600cc and basically set the template for sportbike development to follow, even to the present and beyond. That's some serious history, and an equally serious legacy. On top of which, the middleweight Ninja was a proper cracking motorcycle as well. At the time, it was a near-revelation of what buyers could come to expect from a middleweight.

 During the road test of the GPz600R's U.S. introduction, one magazine editor (who just happens to be writing this) realized he was on his own, was lost (despite the map Kawasaki provided), was low on fuel, and had left his wallet at the hotel.

 It was certainly not claimed at the time of its introduction, but the GPz600R Ninja was a breakthrough motorcycle, one that would influence future sportbike design for a very long time.

 How about something like Stunt Road in the Malibu mountains? Suffice it to say, the road lives up to its name and would indeed be perfect for the 600R's potent motor and quick-flick handling.

 ★ ★ ★ ★ ★
The middleweight Ninja simply changed too much of the existing sportbike scenery to deserve any less.

| | |
|---|---|
| Engine: Liquid-cooled, DOHC, 16-valve, inline four | Top Speed: 128 miles per hour |
| | Weight: 430 pounds |
| Horsepower: 75 at 10,500 rpm | Value Now: $$$ |

# Kawasaki

## ZX-6R Ninja B1/B2

### Kawasaki's middleweight Ninja goes big

The 2003–2004 ZX-6R B1/B2 represented Kawasaki's renewed dedication to performance." The B1 and B2 models featured an extra 37cc of displacement for added midrange, as well as several firsts, both for Kawasaki and for the middleweight class: inverted front fork, radial-mount front four-pad brake calipers, and fuel injection, all in a lighter, more compact package. At a stroke, Kawasaki leapfrogged the competition to create the sharpest, most tightly focused, and most rawboned middleweight the class had yet seen.

 Kawasaki was the first—and only—Japanese manufacturer to offer a middleweight displacing more than 600cc.

 By ignoring the displacement limit artificially created for middleweight racing classes, Kawasaki was able to create a superlative road bike.

 The Texas Hill Country would do nicely: fast and pretty darn smooth. Or a racetrack, such as Laguna Seca.

 ★ ★ ★ ★
Surely four, because virtually overnight Kawasaki reconfigured its ZX-6R with racing-quality equipment that vaulted the bike to the top of the middleweight class.

| | |
|---|---|
| Engine: Liquid-cooled, DOHC, 16-valve, inline four | Top Speed: 165 miles per hour (estimated) |
| Horsepower: 125 at 13,000 rpm (claimed) | Weight: 355 pounds |
| | Value Now: $$ |

With the right tires, the KLR is a great urban bike.

Tamed the world for motorcyclists.

Around the world. Literally.

* *
Not terribly rebellious. Just stone-cold reliable.

Engine: Liquid-cooled, 651cc, DOHC, four-stroke single
Horsepower: 48 at 6,500 rpm

Top Speed: 95 miles per hour
Weight: n/a
Value Now: $$

**Funnest distance between two points**

If you could go anywhere, why wouldn't you? KLRs have been to the Arctic, crossed the Sahara, and circumnavigated the world. That's quite a testament, both to the bike's capability and to its reliability, as is the fact that the KLR went through two decades of production before getting a major makeover. A "400-pound dirt bike" might seem like an oxymoron, but that misinterprets the objective. No, it's not something you can fling sideways onto a berm. But it *is* something you can rely on to get you from Point A to Point B, no matter where either point might be. Thus did a whole cottage industry spring up to supply KLR owners with hard bags.

# Kawasaki

## ZX-11 C1 Ninja

**Fast enough to yank your arms off yet leave you happy about it**

*Cycle* magazine's road test pegged the essence of Kawasaki's 1991 ZX-11: "This machine is the speed freak's midnight fantasy, a ride on the blast wave of an endless explosion. . . . This is a bike for kicking ass." This is truly a motorcycle you must ride to get the proper sense of its mind-warping acceleration and phenomenal, 175-mile-per-hour top speed.

 Kawasaki held a world intro for the updated D model in 1993 that featured a ride to the Grand Canyon. On the very first day, Arizona state police were eavesdropping on Kawasaki's communications net, and several less-prudent members of the foreign bike press went to the slammer for speeding.

 Oh, nothing much—just being the quickest, fastest, and hardest-accelerating production road machine money could buy.

 Actually, almost anywhere; the ZX-11 is no one-trick pony, thanks to excellent handling and well-spec'd suspension rates. Still, it would be hard to beat a fast road with big sweepers that allow the big Ninja to really stretch its legs and run.

 ★ ★ ★ ★
The ZX deserves all four, not because of outrageous styling or futuristic, ground-breaking mechanicals, but instead for pure, wig-spinning, hoo-hah speed and acceleration.

Engine: Liquid-cooled, DOHC, 16-valve, inline four
Horsepower: 127 at 10,000 rpm
Top Speed: 175 miles per hour
Weight: 503 pounds
Value Now: $$$

---

# Kawasaki

## ZZR1400 ZX-14

**Metamorphosis**

Since its two-stroke triple days, Kawasaki's thing has been raw, unadulterated power. The ZX-12, successor to the fabled ZX-11, was right in character. If not for Suzuki, there'd have been no question about the big Kawi's place in history. But the always-pesky rival put the Hayabusa square in the middle of Kawasaki's road to world domination. So the ZX-12 changed into a ZX-14 and beat the 'Busa.

 The ZX-14 is actually quite docile around town.

 This was the world's fastest and most powerful production motorcycle in history at the time.

 Las Vegas Motor Speedway, Las Vegas, Nevada.

 ★ ★ ★
Fast and friendly isn't a particularly rebellious combination.

Engine: Liquid-cooled, 1,352cc, DOHC, four-stroke, inline four
Horsepower: 187 at 9,2500 rpm
Top Speed: 186 miles per hour (electronically limited)
Weight: n/a
Value Now: $$$

Back when Eddie Lawson was finishing his career with Kawasaki, Rob Muzzy was just starting his.

Everybody loves it.

Nowhere special. It's just fun to ride.

★ ★

It's a replica of a replica.

Engine: Liquid-cooled, 1,052cc, DOHC, four-stroke, inline four
Horsepower: 106 at 8,700 rpm
Top Speed: 143 miles per hour
Weight: n/a
Value Now: $$$

### Split personality

Twin shocks? Carburetors? What's all this about? Is the ZRX1100 a sportbike or an homage? Both, it turns out. Modern suspension and brakes carried on an old-school, double-cradle, tubular-steel frame typify the ZRX dichotomy. The engine is state of the art, but its roots are solidly in 1972's Z1. It looks like the 1982 Eddie Lawson Replica, yet it makes no attempt to be a racer. The ZRX is one of those bikes that works way better than it looks on paper. It's heavy but surprisingly nimble. The engine is a detuned performance mill, but the added torque keeps it exciting. The tubular-steel frame flexes a bit, but the bike still handles relatively well. The ZRX is a paradox wrapped in a riddle and clothed in wicked-cool Eddie Lawson racing livery.

# KTM

## LC4

### Easy start, thanks to the "electric leg"

KTM's first proprietary engines were single-cylinder thumpers, and weren't easy to kick-start, so the company attached an electric starter to the engine. That happened in 1996 with the LC4 (liquid-cooled, four valves), and KTM's popularity (read: growing sales) has been on the rise ever since.

 KTM's 620 engine actually displaces 609cc, and the 640's displacement is 625cc.

 KTM's first electric-start engine.

 No matter where you ride the LC4, the adventure begins with your right thumb.

 ★★
Electric starting takes a lot of the work out of the ride.

Engine: Liquid-cooled, 609cc, four-stroke single-cylinder
Horsepower: n/a
Top Speed: n/a
Weight: n/a
Value Now: $

---

# KTM

## 990 Adventure R

### More power for more adventure

The lads at KTM made one of the best adventure-touring bikes better by giving it slightly more height and more power. The end result was the 990 Adventure R. Power was increased by about eight horsepower, and the R's rider could sit higher in the saddle thanks to slightly longer suspension travel. The sum total is one of the best big-bore adventure-tour bikes you'll find.

 The Paris–Dakar Rally spawned the adventure-tour market.

 The first bike to challenge BMW's R1200GS for supremacy in the class.

 Into California's Sierra Nevada Mountains, following J41 from Highway 395 to Kennedy Meadows. Take a side trip on Jackass Trail for a real adventure.

 ★★
One jacket for the road, the other for the off-road.

Engine: Liquid-cooled, 999cc, four-stroke, 75-degree V-twin
Horsepower: 113 at 8,750 rpm
Top Speed: 130 miles per hour
Weight: 456 pounds
Value Now: $$$

## 690 Duke R

KTM originated in 1937 at a metal shop in Austria run by Hans Trunkenpolz. The company's official name was Kraftfahrzeuge Trunkenpolz Mattighofen. Yes, we prefer to say KTM too.

The fastest Duke to date.

What better place than a quick pass across the Dragon's Tail, Highway 129 near Deal's Gap, Tennessee?

★ ★ ★
To earn more jackets, you'll need to slide both tires through the turns. It can be done.

Engine: Liquid-cooled, 690cc, four-stroke single-cylinder
Horsepower: 70 at 7,000 rpm
Top Speed: n/a
Weight: 326 pounds
Value Now: $$$

### Making a great supermotard model even greater

The editors from *Cycle World* once stated that KTM "is always honing and improving its line [of motorcycles]." The 690 Duke R is proof of that, checking in with more power and better handling than ever before. Chalk one up for refusing to settle.

## Super Duke 990R

For many years, KTM manufactured scooters.

A bike with a big engine that has a big appetite for the racetrack.

A technical racetrack, such as the Streets of Willow, where handling and low- and midrange power prevail.

★ ★ ★ ★
A 130-horsepower bike built for the express purpose of popping wheelies—four leather jackets is conservative.

Engine: Liquid cooled, 999cc, four-stroke V-twin
Horsepower: 130 at 10,000 rpm
Top Speed: 140 miles per hour
Weight: 410 pounds
Value Now: $$$

### "Built for the love of it." —KTM

KTM claims the Super Duke 990R is "ready to race." That might explain why the Super Duke delivers such precision steering into corners, or why the suspension delivers a rock-steady ride, or why the V-twin engine's powerband is so broad, or, well, you get the picture.

# KTM

## 1190 RC8

**A superbike for the super-serious rider**

KTM's first superbike offers all that you'd expect in terms of on-track performance. The engine, especially, is quick to oblige as power builds to a crescendo throughout the rev range. KTM made its name by building off-road motorcycles that were capable of winning races right out of the box. When the company got into the business of building road bikes, it came as no surprise that KTM built machines that would be just as competitive in Superbike racing. For any customers planning to use KTM's road machines as intended, the company offers various speed components for the 1190 RC8 too, among them a Club Race Kit that includes altered valve timing, different cylinder head sealing, and free-flow Akrapovic exhaust pipes.

*Cycle World* ran the RC8 through the quarter-mile in 10.07 seconds at 137.97 miles per hour.

KTM's first-ever superbike.

Track day at Mazda Laguna Seca Raceway, where the 1190 RC8 first bowed to the American press.

★ ★ ★ ★
You'll need all that leather for protection.

Engine: Liquid-cooled, 1,148cc, four-stroke, 75-degree V-twin
Horsepower: 155 at 10,000 rpm
Top Speed: 166 miles per hour
Weight: 401 pounds
Value Now: $$$$

SFC stands for *super freni competizione*. Something about holding back the competition in a superior way.

 According to a Laverda brochure, the SFC is a "production racer for those who ride very hard."

 The Iron Butt Rally.

 ★ ★ ★ ★
Only neglect can destroy it.

| | |
|---|---|
| Engine: Air-cooled, 744cc, chain-driven SOHC, four-stroke, parallel twin Horsepower: 70 at 7,400 rpm | Top Speed: 130 miles per hour Weight: n/a Value Now: $$$$$ |

## Bulletproof

Rebuilding engines on kitchen tables is common among racers. Francesco Laverda took the practice a bit further, actually casting new parts in his kitchen at night. Why the fascination with racing? Simple: racing improves the breed. Riders looking for reliable streetbikes are best served by looking at those based on successful racing motorcycles. Like the Laverda 750 SFC.

 After purchasing the company in 2000, Aprilia erased all evidence of Laverda's Breganze, Italy, operations, destroying everything down to the last mold.

 This bike hit 175.46 miles per hour on the Mistral Straight at the Paul Ricard Circuit while practicing for the 1977 Bol d'Or 24-hour endurance race.

 There are only two, and one doesn't run. The other is insured for half a million bucks, and only people whose last names end in "Laverda" get to ride it.

 ★ ★
If they'd kept going with it despite the rule change, it would have been rebellious.

| | |
|---|---|
| Engine: Liquid-cooled, 995cc, chain-driven DOHC, four-stroke V-6 Horsepower: 140 at 11,800 rpm | Top Speed: 177 miles per hour Weight: n/a Value Now: $$$$$ |

## Lambo, first blood

Often called the Lamborghini of Italian motorcycles, Laverda took that nickname literally and hired an actual Lamborghini technical director, Giulio Alfieri, to help design its new V-6 engine. Francesco Laverda had learned that bigger is better in the American market, and he figured we'd eat up a bike with a V-6 in it. In time-honored Laverda fashion, the plan was to conquer endurance racing, learn how to build a stronger bike, then release a production model. "You can learn in a day what would take four months of normal road testing," said Piero Laverda of endurance racing. Sadly, F.I.M. endurance racing rules were changed to disallow engines of more than four cylinders in 1979, and the world's fastest laboratory was abandoned.

# Laverda

## Jota

### Magnum opus

If you want durability, borrow from agriculture. Moto Guzzi took that advice literally and built a motorcycle around the company's tractor engine. Laverda was more figurative. Also a manufacturer of agricultural machinery, Laverda employed the basic principles of longevity—light weight, strength, ease of maintenance—rather than the actual parts. This allowed engineers to design heavy-duty bikes that were still, in riding terms, flickable. The Jota was intended to be lighter, narrower, and faster than the Honda CB750, and just as bulletproof. It ended up being technically superior and sounded way better. For many, it was and will forever be Laverda's masterpiece.

 In 1982, Jotas changed to crankshafts with a 120-degree firing interval to combat excessive vibration. They still sounded cool but weren't the same as the old 180-degree Jotas.

 Jotas won four of the next five Avon Tyre Production Race championships—the U.K.'s precursor to Superbike—after the bike was introduced in 1976.

 Through the foothills north of Breganze, Italy.

 ★ ★ ★ ★
But only for the Jotas with 180-degree cranks.

Engine: Air-cooled, 981cc, gear-driven DOHC, four-stroke, inline triple
Horsepower: 90 at 7,500 rpm
Top Speed: 140 miles per hour
Weight: n/a
Value Now: $$$$

Laverda also manufactures fairly high-quality agricultural equipment, such as combine harvesters.

Gives its rider triple-digit, continent-crushing speeds while cocooning him in comfortably stable composure.

Preferably, the nearest autobahn.

★ ★ ★ ★
The RGS gets four simply because of its single-minded purpose, and its execution of that purpose: speed with exceptional stability.

| | |
|---|---|
| Engine: Six-valve, DOHC, transverse inline-triple | Top Speed: 142 miles per hour (estimated) |
| Horsepower: 73.5 at 8,000 rpm | Weight: n/a |
| | Value Now: $$$ |

**An Italian stallion that ensures all your tours will be grand**

Seeing as how the term *gran turismo* originated in Italy, it's no surprise to find an Italian motorcycle that can give the term its fullest two-wheeled expression. That motorcycle is Laverda's 1983 RGS 1000. One of the primary virtues of a GT machine is its ability to cover distances at high rates of speed with ridiculous ease, a trait that's been bred deeply into this bike's DNA. Powered by a brawny triple housed in a chassis calibrated for stability, the RGS is at its most endearing when piloted at the ton, in utter and complete composure. It was the Laverda's very poise at speed that earned one magazine tester a 115-mile-per-hour speeding ticket. But that's another story.

# Maico

## K501

### Rooster tales

Manly men ride open-class motocrossers, and rich, manly men ride Maico open-class motocrossers. The biggest single-cylinder, two-stroke motocross bike available in 1971, the Maico K501 could kick up dirt like no other. That's what "sometimes uncontrollable power" can do for you, and irrepressible muscle is exactly what you get from this bike. The only way you can restrain a 501 is by twisting back the throttle. Otherwise it doesn't matter where you are—sand, loose dirt, a grass-covered field—ask it to accelerate, and accelerate it will. K501 riders have lots of tales to tell, usually involving giant plumes of dirt rising behind them, but at 15 miles per gallon plus the cost of admission, only the rich get to tell them.

 "Riding the 501 requires enormous strength, riding ability, and a great deal of prudence with the throttle." Thus did one magazine win a Yewey, the Understatement of the Year Award.

 The biggest single-cylinder, two-stroke motocross bike available at the time.

 Take this bike to the Baja 1000.

 ★ ★ ★ ★ ★
*You* break the news that it gets fewer.

Engine: Air-cooled, 501cc, piston-port, two-stroke single
Horsepower: 54 at 7,000 rpm
Top Speed: n/a
Weight: n/a
Value Now: $$$

# Maico

## GS125

### Blaues blut

Radial cylinder-head fins, a Maico trademark. Another Maico trait is that the smaller they get, the better they handle, and this is as small as they get. No surprise that everyone called it the best-handling motocross bike available. Of course, they all added "for the money" to the end of their appraisals, but Maico's GS125 was every serious motocrosser's dream. So what if it had flimsy foot controls and weak muffler and head stays, or that you had to tear apart the right side of the engine and take out the shifting mechanism—and then put it back in the same position—if you wanted to change the countershaft sprocket. Yeah, lots of problems; maybe you shouldn't ride one. Probably best not to know what you're missing.

 Until 1975, the European Motocross Championship didn't have a 125cc class.

 The best-handling 125cc production motocrosser available at the time.

 Red Bud MX track, Buchanan, Michigan.

 ★
Rebels aren't born with silver spoons in their mouths.

Engine: Air-cooled, 124cc, rotary-valve, two-stroke single
Horsepower: 21.2 at 8,800 rpm
Top Speed: 71.5 miles per hour
Weight: n/a
Value Now: $$

Like many French motorcycles of the period, Majestic used engines from a number of other manufacturers rather than building their own.

 Innovative full-coverage bodywork cloaked even more innovative technology.

 In big, loopy circles on the Place du Carrousel roundabout in front of the Louvre.

 ★ ★ ★ ★
While usually not profitable, being ahead of your time certainly is rebellious.

Engine: 350cc overhead-valve single
Horsepower: 11 at 4,000 rpm

Top Speed: 56 miles per hour
Weight: NA
Value Now: $$$$$

### Beating the Tesi by 60 years

When Bimota introduced its Tesi with center-hub steering replacing the traditional twin-tube fork arrangement, the bike was hailed as a technological breakthrough. But there really is nothing new under the sun; the Majestic 350 beat Bimota to the punch by six decades. In another move that foreshadowed developments that would take place over half a century after its introduction, the Majestic featured full-coverage bodywork. While other manufacturers tried to get the public to accept center-hub steering both before the Majestic's time and after the Tesi's (the most recent example is the Yamaha GTS1000), the design has never caught on, in part because it has never worked better than the traditional fork. Full-coverage bodywork did catch on, however, and today there are more motorcycles with bodywork than without.

# Matchless

## Silver Arrow

**High on cutting-edge design, low on performance and sales**

Designed by Charlie Collier, the Silver Arrow was an attempt to pack as much power into a compact engine as possible. The Silver Arrow engine was a monoblock design with cast-iron cylinder heads. Unfortunately, the 400cc, narrow-angle V-twin didn't perform to expectations, so it was back to the drawing board for the Collier clan to find more power. It also hurt that the stock market crash of 1929 occurred shortly before the bike was introduced to the motorcycle market. By 1933, Matchless threw in the towel on the Silver Arrow.

 During World War II, the Matchless factory shifted production from motorcycles to rifles and bayonets for His Majesty's army.

 Lackluster performance taught the Collier brothers a valuable lesson—there's no replacement for displacement, so the model to replace the Silver Arrow had a larger-displacement engine.

 Let's see, where can we find an English country road that has little traffic and no steep hills?

 *
A Rebel caught out of his or her own way.

| Engine: Air-cooled, 397cc, four-stroke, 26-degree V-twin | Top Speed: 63 miles per hour |
| Horsepower: 16 at 5,000 rpm | Weight: n/a |
| | Value Now: $$ |

# Matchless

## Silver Hawk

**A V-4 to square off against Ariel's Square Four**

The lackluster performance of the Silver Arrow prompted the people at Matchless to reach into the corporate quiver for something else. This time, it was younger brother Bert Collier's design that made it into production, the bike being the Silver Hawk. Powered by a 600cc V-4 engine, the Hawk soared, but it didn't fly fast, so to speak—the new Matchless still couldn't match the iconic Ariel Square Four's performance. Eventually, it would be a single-cylinder engine that would power Matchless to the forefront of Great Britain's great motorcycle industry in years to come.

 About the time that the Silver Hawk took flight, Matchless acquired AJS.

 Considered to be one of the smoothest-running motorcycles of its time. The engine also featured overhead cams, and the frame offered rear suspension—both novelties for the era.

 California Highway 154, heading north out of Santa Barbara. Destination: the Solvang Vintage Motorcycle Museum where we'll view a pristine Silver Hawk.

 **
The Silver Hawk's bland performance is overshadowed by its unique engine design.

| Engine: Air-cooled, 592cc, four-stroke, 26-degree V-4 | Top Speed: 80 miles per hour |
| Horsepower: n/a | Weight: 380 pounds |
| | Value Now: n/a |

Matchless was founded by the Collier family in 1899. Charlie Collier won the first-ever Isle of Man TT on a Matchless in 1907.

 A 1958 engine design that remained competitive on the racetrack through the mid-1960s.

 Southwest Wisconsin's scenic route through Wildcat Canyon Road to Bear Creek Road.

 ★ ★ ★
A streetbike designed to win races—that's at least somewhat rebellious.

| | |
|---|---|
| Engine: Air-cooled, 496cc, four-stroke single-cylinder | Top Speed: 135 miles per hour |
| Horsepower: 51 at 7,000 rpm | Weight: 290 pounds |
| | Value Now: $$$$ |

**Lightweight, rock-steady handling, agile steering, and adequate horsepower. What more could a bloke ask for?**

The venerable Matchless G50, introduced in 1958, was based on the AJS 7R, a 350cc single known as the "Boy Racer." The G50's main competitor at the time was Norton's Manx, but soon enough it was competing against the Japanese multi-cylinder race bikes too. The Matchless offered good power, but its forte was its weight, or actually, lack of it; a race-ready G50 checked in at only about 300 pounds. The G50 proved competitive well into the 1960s—just ask Dick Mann who used his small squadron of Matchless racers to help him win his first of two AMA Grand National Championships (1963 and 1971).

# Matchless

## G85 CS Scrambler

**As some motorcycle enthusiasts from the 1960s used to say, "Do it in the dirt."**

Four-stroke engines still dominated off-road racing during the late 1950s and early 1960s, and one of the more competitive bikes was the Matchless G85 CS. The bike was based on the successful G50 clubman road racer, and like its stablemate, the G85 was lightweight and offered good handling. The engine's long stroke produced plenty of torque, and when coupled with a 12:1 compression ratio, the G85 only contributed to the thumper legend that survives today.

 Matchless introduced the telescopic front fork to motorcycling when it equipped a 1941 model with the unique front end.

 One of the final designs from Matchless before it was absorbed by Norton-Villiers in 1966.

 A long, steep, natural-terrain hill where that long-legged engine can show off its torque.

 ★ ★ ★
If you can get this high-compression engine kick-started on the first try, you won't need any more jackets.

| | |
|---|---|
| Engine: Air-cooled, 496cc, four-stroke single-cylinder | Top Speed: 73 miles per hour |
| | Weight: 318 pounds |
| Horsepower: 41 at 6,500 rpm | Value Now: $$$$ |

Germany's hyperinflation put Megola under in 1926. By 1923, 100 trillion marks equaled about 25 U.S. dollars.

Perhaps the first—and only—motorcycle to have its engine mounted on the front wheel.

Visit the German National Bank Building on Vine Street in Cincinnati, Ohio.

\*
Once you've taken in the Megola's star-shaped engine, the bike's star quality fizzles.

Engine: Air-cooled, 640cc, four-stroke, radial five-cylinder
Horsepower: 14 at 3,000 rpm

Top Speed: 60 miles per hour
Weight: n/a
Value Now: $$$

## Totally radial, dude

Step aside Erik Buell, Fritz Egli, and other contemporary motorcycle designers with eccentric ideas. German-born Fritz Cockerell has you beat with the Megola, a bike that used a radial five-cylinder engine planted on its front wheel for power. Heir Fritz elected to *not* use a clutch or gearbox, either. Power was transferred as the engine and wheel rotated forward, and the crankshaft, which operated via the gear train, functioned six times as quickly in the opposite direction. This layout meant that the driving forces were equally distributed for a rather smooth ride. The design worked, with top speeds in excess of 60 miles per hour. Approximately 2,000 Megolas were built.

# Mission Motors

## Mission One Superbike

### Mission accomplished?

The Mission One looks like it was designed by the chairman of the industrial design department at the California College of the Arts. Which it was. Yves Behar's mission for the Mission was to "create a design that would be accepted by motorcycle enthusiasts while also being immediately recognizable as a vehicle fueled by alternative energy." Okay, it was. Mission number one accomplished. The new bike went to Bonneville and averaged 150.059 miles per hour, a world record. Then Thomas Montano rode it to a fourth-place finish in the inaugural TTXGP at the Isle of Man, a zero-emissions race during TT week meant to show the "high-speed, high-performance fun" you can get from electric bikes. Okay, it's entertaining. Mission number two accomplished. Mission number three? Mainstream acceptance. That's up to you.

 The Mission One has top-shelf Öhlins suspension components front and rear, as well as a fully integrated, wireless data acquisition system.

 The first electric motorcycle capable of power wheelies at 70 miles per hour, Mission Motors claims it costs about two bucks to fully charge the batteries, enough juice for 150 miles.

 Pennsylvania Highway 441 south along the Susquehanna River from Royalton, Pennsylvania, past the Three Mile Island nuclear power plant.

 ★ ★ ★ ★ ★
Adrenaline-pumping eco-rebels rejoice.

Engine: Liquid-cooled, three-phase, AC-induction electric
Horsepower: 123 at 6,500 rpm

Top Speed: 150 miles per hour
Weight: n/a
Value Now: $$$$$

## DOHC 125cc Road Racer

 A similar Mondial racer with a 175cc engine (used for national competition) is on display at the Solvang Vintage Motorcycle Museum (California).

 Among the first four-stroke bikes to beat the two-strokes in the Grand Prix World Championship.

 Bologna, Italy, to enter the Mondial 125 in the Motogiro d'Italia. Who cares about winning? We want to hear that engine fire up.

 ★ ★ ★
How fast can you ride a 12-horsepower motorcycle?

| Engine: Air-cooled, 123.5cc, four-stroke single-cylinder | Top Speed: 80-plus miles per hour |
| Horsepower: 12 at 9,000 rpm | Weight: n/a |
| | Value Now: $$$$ |

**A single-cylinder engine with two camshafts won three world championships**

When road racing resumed after World War II, two-stroke engines dominated the small-bore classes. Mondial, owned by the Bosselli brothers in Italy, changed that with their 125cc four-stroke engine that had double overhead camshafts. The bike proved so fast that it won three Grand Prix World Championships, 1949–1951, and in the process established the four-stroke engine as the one to beat in all classes. It wasn't until MZ brought out its two-strokers about 10 years later that the smokers returned to their winning ways.

# Montesa

## Impala 175

### Tough enough

Imagine a major motorcycle manufacturer deciding to prove just how tough its latest, cutting-edge sportbike design is by—wait for it—riding three of them from Cape Town, South Africa, to Cairo, Egypt. Well, that's precisely what young-at-the-time motorcycle manufacturer Montesa did with its then-new Impala 175 two-stroke streetbike in 1962. As a result, the Impala's durability became legendary.

 *Operacion Impala* was covered by almost every European news agency and newspaper of the day. Several books have even been written about the remarkable undertaking. Only in the United States was it ignored.

 Being one of the stoutest two-stroke streetbikes ever conceived—possibly even more indestructible than Honda's legendary Super Cub.

 Inner-city roads for commuting, super-tight back roads for scratching, and . . . apparently South Africa, believe it or not.

 ★ ★ ★
Mid-displacement Spanish two-strokes were virtually dime-a-dozen when the Impala 175 debuted. Its one standout feature—admittedly a huge one—was the bike's performance on *Operacion Impala*.

Engine: Two-stroke, air-cooled, piston-port single-cylinder
Horsepower: n/a
Top Speed: n/a
Weight: n/a
Value Now: $$$

# Montesa

## Cota

### Last bike standing

In 1945, three friends began manufacturing motorcycles in Barcelona. In 1968, Pedro Pi won the company's first Spanish trials championship on the company's first trials bike, built a year earlier. Under Pi's direction as a rider and engineer, they became the bikes to beat. This winning tradition is carried on by the Cota, the only Montesa still built today.

 One of the original Montesa partners, Francisco Bulto, jilted the company in 1958 to start his own company, Bultaco.

 Won Montesa's third World Trials Championship in 1969.

 Across, well, anything.

 ★ ★ ★ ★ ★
It can climb walls. Just like Spiderman.

Engine: Air-cooled, 249cc, two-stroke single
Horsepower: 17.5 at 5,000 rpm
Top Speed: n/a
Weight: n/a
Value Now: $$

# Morbidelli

 Dutchman Jorg Muller, who helped Kriedler be competitive in the 50cc class, was primarily responsible for developing the Morbidelli 125 twin.

 Winner of the 125 Grand Prix World Championship in 1975, 1976, and 1977.

 The Isle of Man TT, sadly the place where Morbidelli's legendary factory rider Gilberto Parlotti lost his life in 1972 while leading the 125cc race.

 ★ ★ ★ ★
Remember, there are no on-board diagnostics to assist the rider in his quest for speed with this bike.

| | |
|---|---|
| Engine: Liquid-cooled, 124cc, two-stroke, parallel twin | Top Speed: 150 miles per hour |
| Horsepower: 42 at 14,000 rpm | Weight: n/a |
| | Value Now: $$$$ |

## Built for the love of racing

Who would have thought that a company specializing in woodworking machinery would win three Grand Prix road race world championships? That's exactly what happened between 1975 and 1977 when Morbidelli beat the road-racing world with its 125cc twin. Given the phenomenal success of its road-racing motorcycles, one can't help but think that the company must have screwed together one hell of a spice rack.

---

# Morbidelli

 The V-8 was one of the featured bikes in Guggenheim Museum's Art of the Motorcycle exhibit.

 The Guinness Book of World Records lists the Morbidelli V-8 as the world's most expensive motorcycle.

 The Barber Museum near Birmingham, Alabama, is said to possess a Morbidelli V-8, so we'll sneak it out the back door and roam the nearby roads that offer rewarding curves.

 ★ ★ ★ ★
The bike's price tag in 1994 was $60,000. Talk about big round ones.

| | |
|---|---|
| Engine: Liquid-cooled, 847cc, four-stroke, 990-degree V-8 | Top Speed: n/a |
| Horsepower: 120 at 11,000 rpm | Weight: 442 pounds |
| | Value Now: $$$$$ |

## The world's most expensive motorcycle

In 1994 Morbidelli had a better idea—it would build a motorcycle with a V-8 engine for sport touring. It was a good idea until the bean counters tallied up manufacturing costs, which they ultimately deemed prohibitive, so the bike never saw production; even with a retail price of $60,000, the company couldn't break even.

# Moto Guzzi

## Motoleggera 65

### Mobility for the masses

Italy was starving for small, efficient transportation after World War II. Until Fiat introduced the Cinquecento in 1957, the market was dominated by small, lightweight motorcycles like the Motoleggera, which was basically a bicycle with a tiny motor and no pedals. The Motoleggera was nicknamed "Guzzina" (Little Guzzi), and a 1951 review of the mechanical creature touted "a speed of 25 mph from rest could be reached with a slickness comparable with average four-wheel vehicles, so that in built-up areas one could remain comfortably with the rest of the traffic." Of course, the review went on to say "considerably higher speeds" were "practicable in only slightly favourable conditions." They were talking about going downhill with a tailwind. In unfavourable conditions, "one had the option of making good use of the gearbox."

 When Moto-Hispania licensed the Guzzina, it was produced in two countries at the same time.

 The Guzzina was the smallest-capacity full-fledged motorcycle being built at the time.

 Around the plaza at dusk.

 ★ ★ ★
This bike kept a generation of Italians independently mobile.

Engine: Air-cooled, 64cc, two-stroke single
Horsepower: 2 at 5,500 rpm
Top Speed: 37 miles per hour (downhill with a tailwind)
Weight: n/a
Value Now: $$$

# Moto Guzzi

## Falcone

### Dirty, dirty bike

OMG, its flywheel is showing! While modern naked bikes show off their radiators and plumbing and bra straps and such, the Falcone's actual flywheel is right there, hanging off the left side for all the world to see. (Don't wear a scarf if you ride one. Or loose pants.) This Moto Guzzi has no shame.

 Most Falcones were produced around 1957, the year legendary Italian femme fatale Luisa Casati died.

 The Falcone is a direct descendent of the first bike Carlo Guzzi and Giorgio Parodi built in 1919.

 Chasing robbers who held up the Banco d'Italia.

 ★ ★ ★
Conflicted. It's a cop bike, but it's flashing its flywheel at us.

Engine: Air-cooled, 499cc, OHV, four-stroke single
Horsepower: 23 at 4,500 rpm
Top Speed: 85 miles per hour
Weight: n/a
Value Now: $$$

# Moto Guzzi

Moto Guzzi pioneered the swingarm rear suspension.

Won the Freccia Azzurra, awarded to bikes that held total-distance-traveled and top-speed records simultaneously.

SS36 north along the coast of Lake Como from Mandello del Lario, Italy.

★ ★ ★ ★
A supercharged 250 single? It should probably get five.

| | |
|---|---|
| Engine: Air-cooled, 250cc, supercharged, F-head, four-stroke single | Top Speed: n/a |
| | Weight: n/a |
| | Value Now: $$$$$ |
| Horsepower: n/a | |

## An important story

Once upon a time, a wealthy ship owner and a motorcycle enthusiast who couldn't find a bike he liked teamed up to build a magical prototype. It was powered by a 500cc, four-valves-per-cylinder, OHC single, and it could fly. More bikes were made, a company came to be, and racing history was written. One day, a little 250—the Aerone Sport—was born. Its parents were racers, and its parent's parents were racers. So Aerone, too, became a racer. It tried, and it tried, but not until it got a supercharger and became a 250 Compressore did anyone ever notice the little bike. Then, they all lived happily ever after. Until the Japanese came along and wrecked everything.

# Moto Guzzi

If the tires back then could have coped, and the brakes hadn't sucked, and the suspension had been better, there might be a lot more V-8s in motorcycle racing today.

Ken Kavanagh refused to ride it again after the 1956 Grand Prix at Spa-Francorchamps.

Lion's Associated Drag Strip, Los Angeles, California.

★ ★ ★ ★ ★ ★
And put on the rest of your protective gear too.

| | |
|---|---|
| Engine: Liquid-cooled, 499cc, DOHC, four-stroke V-8 | Top Speed: 187 miles per hour |
| | Weight: n/a |
| Horsepower: 78 at 12,000 rpm | Value Now: $$$$$ |

## Otto's crazy

Moto Guzzi built a 500cc V-8 engine for their 1955 Grand Prix contender. It took 20 years for another GP bike to best the Otto's top speed; its sound is still unmatched, and nobody has ever flattered it with imitation. It was insane. Fergus Anderson got bucked off in its first race at Modena. It broke its crankshafts, seized its tiny pistons, and boiled its coolant. By 1957, nobody would ride it.

# Moto Guzzi

## V7 Sport

### World's most fun exercise machine

It's kind of funny when you think about it: a sportbike powered by a tractor engine. And that's exactly what the V7 Sport is. Its transverse-mounted V-twin was originally designed for use in an Italian Ministry of Defense utility vehicle called the *Mullo Mechanico*. Still, for lots of us, our first ride was on a mini-bike powered by a lawnmower engine, so why not a motorcycle with a tractor engine? Tractor engine or not, the V7 Sport is a hoot to ride. And, at 500 pounds, it's also quite invigorating. It's a big, stable bike that likes long, fast sweepers, but if you want to work out some muscles you didn't know you had, go get sweaty on some tight, twisty corners. Way more fun than a stair climber.

 Only 104 V7 Sports were produced in 1971.

 This was the first production bike to top 124 miles per hour.

 SP62 north from Lecco, Italy.

 ★ ★ ★
Sportbike, tractor engine. Sportbike, tractor engine. Still hard to reconcile.

Engine: Air-cooled, 748cc, OHV, four-stroke V-twin
Horsepower: 70 at 7,000 rpm

Top Speed: 125 miles per hour
Weight: n/a
Value Now: $$$$

First gear was good for 85 miles per hour.

The Convert beat Honda's automatic to market by a year.

To the Moto Guzzi shop to trade it in for a different model.

★ ★ ★ ★
C'mon, think about it for a second. Yep, that's why.

| | |
|---|---|
| Engine: Air-cooled, 949cc, OHV, four-stroke V-twin | Top Speed: 110 miles per hour |
| Horsepower: 71 at 6,500 rpm | Weight: n/a |
| | Value Now: $$ |

## La-Z-Boy

"That transmission can be very handy in city traffic or when you get caught behind a bus or truck on a mountain grade." You're in trouble if that's the best thing a motojournalist can say about your bike, and with the V1000 Convert, Moto Guzzi was in trouble. With its automatic transmission that was really a two-speed, the V1000 Convert was a joy to ride in traffic. Or behind big things plugging up cool roads. At least in theory. In reality, the transmission took so long to spool up that you had time to finish your cigarette before the bike started to generate any serious forward momentum. The fact that people like cars with automatic transmissions isn't a very good foundation for motorcycle design, and motorcycles with automatic transmissions have never caught on; still, companies continue to try to foist automatic transmissions onto the motorcycle-buying public to this day. Fortunately, most work better than Moto Guzzi's Convert. But the Convert wasn't completely awful. According to *Cycle*, "Its seat is as good as, if not better than, a BMW's."

# Moto Guzzi

## California II

### Italia Glide

Now we're talkin'. There's a reason they're called Italian Harley-Davidsons. Make no mistake about Moto Guzzi's racing heritage—their singles were legendary, and their V-8 was . . . unique—but their giant V-twin is far better suited to relaxed jaunts than angry attacks. A 5-ton tractor motor is scary in a sportbike costume. Luckily, Americans are said to love riding with their feet out front and their hands held high. According to the California II brochure/Declaration of Independence, we demand "the basic American features of high and wide handlebars" because they lead to "an upright riding position." Later, we claim an inalienable right to floorboards and a wide saddle. There's nothing in there about horsepower, though. Just torque. Good ol', V-twin, tractor-pullin' torque. We're doin' it Harley style.

 Moto Guzzi built the first wind tunnel designed specifically for motorcycles. Came in handy for the California models.

 Yet another Italian motorcycle manufacturer saved by a bike designed for the ultimate cliché of the U.S. market. Spooky.

 SS1 down the west coast of Italy.

 ★ ★
Let freedom ring. Another tired cliché.

| Engine: Air-cooled, 948cc, OHV, four-stroke V-twin | Top Speed: 119 miles per hour |
| Horsepower: 59 at 6,750 rpm | Weight: n/a |
| | Value Now: $$ |

Way back in 1935, Moto Guzzi was the first Italian marque to win an Isle of Man Senior TT.

 Nothing, really. Just a cool, old bike.

 SR1 down the west coast of California.

 ★ ★ ★ ★ ★
It takes major cojones to offer this up as an answer to the GSX-R750.

| | |
|---|---|
| Engine: Air-cooled, 992cc, belt-driven SOHC, four-stroke V-twin | Top Speed: 143 miles per hour |
| Horsepower: 95 at 8,000 rpm | Weight: n/a |
| | Value Now: $$$$ |

**If you can't say something nice . . .**

"Sure-footed, if rather ponderous."

"It still feels quaintly old-fashioned, an endearing mixture of old and new."

"Riding the Daytona is a curious experience."

"It handles surprisingly well for a Moto Guzzi."

"A relatively flickable, yet very stable nature despite its 502-pound weight."

"The Guzzi is an altogether different animal."

"A polished and thoroughly updated version of a machine many had left for dead."

"There is no more charismatic motorcycle on the market today."

"Easy to fall in love with."

## V10 Centauro

### The Fountainhead

Luciano Marabese designed the Centauro to be an uncompromising motorcycle, one that doesn't bow to traditions of motorcycle design. Intended to commemorate Moto Guzzi's 75th anniversary, the Centauro defines the term *bold statement* but ends up more cartoon than classic.

 Moto Guzzi was never really the same after Carlo Guzzi died in 1964.

 Moto Guzzi had survived 75 years when the Centauro came out.

 Main Street, Toontown.

 ★
Howard Roark was a real rebel. The Centauro is a cartoon rebel.

Engine: Air-cooled, 992cc, belt-driven SOHC, four-stroke V-twin
Horsepower: 97 at 7,400 rpm
Top Speed: 135 miles per hour
Weight: n/a
Value Now: $$$

# Moto Guzzi

## MGS-01 Corsa

### Beautiful dreamer

Racing is in Moto Guzzi's DNA, so it shouldn't come as much of a shock that Gianfranco Guareschi rode an MGS-01 Corsa to a win in its first race, a Battle of the Twins event at Daytona in 2006. Finally, Moto Guzzi had a bike that was fast enough to win races that weren't held in a previous century. Or our wildest dreams.

 At last count, Moto Guzzi had recorded 3,329 victories in international competition.

 Won the 2006 AHRMA Battle of the Twins championship.

 Blowing by a Buell at Barber Motorsports Park, Birmingham, Alabama.

 ★ ★ ★ ★
Brings exhilaration to each and every sense.

Engine: Air-cooled, 1,225cc, belt-driven SOHC, four-stroke V-twin
Horsepower: 122 at 8,000 rpm
Top Speed: n/a
Weight: n/a
Value Now: $$$$

## Rebello 175

A military target, the Moto Morini factory was bombed by the Allies in 1943.

Nobody really knows how many races 175 Rebellos won.

Through the streets of Bologna at midnight. During the work week. At 10,000 rpm. Next to a 1964 Ducati 250 Mark 3 Diana.

★ ★ ★ ★ ★
Look at the name.

Engine: Air-cooled, 175cc, DOHC, four-stroke single
Horsepower: 25 at 10,000 rpm
Top Speed: 125 miles per hour
Weight: n/a
Value Now: $$$$

### M-M-M-Milestone

Home to the oldest university in the Western world, Bologna has always teemed with students. Students are everywhere, drinking coffee and "studying," walking, riding bicycles. Around the turn of the nineteenth century, when Alfonso Morini was a wide-eyed, impressionable child, students were zipping around the streets on motorized bicycles. He grew to love their sound. In 1925, he built a 125cc race bike with Mario Mazzetti, and over the next 12 years, a legend started taking shape. Mussolini made him manufacture airplane parts for a while, but Morini got back to racing when the war ended, this time without Mazzetti. About 10 years later, the 175 Rebello hit the track. It took second in its first event, the Milano–Taranto endurance race; a Gilera 500cc four took first. Just another Moto Morini milestone.

## Corsaro

Moto Morini patriarch Alfonso Morini's second bike, the MM175, set a world motorcycle speed record in 1933.

Flagship for the relaunch of a legendary marque.

Into the corner 'til you see God, brake hard, flick it over, then open the throttle as wide as you dare on the way out. With all that torque, there's probably no need to downshift.

★ ★ ★
Great engine. Adequate looks.

Engine: Liquid-cooled, 1,187cc, chain-driven DOHC, four-stroke V-twin
Horsepower: 140 at 8,500 rpm
Top Speed: 148 miles per hour
Weight: n/a
Value Now: $$$

### Second Coming

Having apparently learned his lesson with the Moto Guzzi Centauro, motorcycle stylist Luciano Marabese took no chances with the Corsaro. Well, the overall design involved risks, but Miguel Galuzzi's Ducati Monster had taken all of those risks 15 years earlier. Now it was just flattery via imitation. The engine, on the other hand, is a masterpiece. Moto Morini scion Maurizzio Morini lured legendary Moto Morini engineer Franco Lambertini back into the fold to design it. Called the Bialbero CorsaCorta, it's especially impressive when you consider how tiny Moto Morini's operations are these days, having been relegated to born-again status. It's even legal for World Superbike. Perhaps signaling the start of a rapturous new era?

# Munch

## Mammoth

### Mammuthus primigenius

There's no replacement for displacement; that was obviously the theory behind Friedl Munch's primeval Mammoth. Inspiring comments like "a nice looking bike in a brutish sort of way" because of its voluminous car engine, you'd think supercharging would have been overkill. Which it was, but you could still get a blown Mammoth if you wanted one. Munch started with an NSU Prinz engine and went from there. At around 630 pounds, handling wasn't the Mammoth's strong suit. No real surprise there; just look at the thing. While today there are clubs around the world dedicated to preserving the fossils, the company was extinct by the mid-1970s. Munch would be back a few years later, but nobody really cared anymore.

 Friedl Munch and American motorsports publisher Floyd Clymer teamed up to try to relaunch the Indian brand in 1967.

 The Mammoth was the fastest production motorcycle at the time.

 To a bike show, where you can park it and let people gawk.

 ★ ★
Sometimes ideas like this are rebellious. Sometimes they're just dumb.

Engine: Air-cooled, 1,289cc, DOHC, four-stroke, inline four
Horsepower: 88 at 6,000 rpm
Top Speed: 169 miles per hour
Weight: 630 pounds
Value Now: $$$$

MV launched a 600 four in 1966, but its styling didn't resemble that of the team racers. As you might guess, it was a sales flop.

MV Agusta's first bike that paid homage to the company's Grand Prix racers.

Utah's Highway 12, where steep canyon walls will echo the melodic tones from the MV's exhausts.

★ ★ ★ ★
Just to hear the howl from those four shiny exhaust pipes is worth the ride.

| | |
|---|---|
| Engine: Air-cooled, 743cc, four-stroke, inline four | Top Speed: 120 miles per hour |
| Horsepower: 69 at 7,900 rpm | Weight: 506 pounds |
| | Value Now: $$$$ |

### A tribute to the factory team racers

A year after Honda's CB750 rocked the world, MV Agusta upped the ante with its four-cylinder 750S (or Sport). The 750S shared many of the features found on the company's factory racers that dominated the 500cc Grand Prix class from 1958 through 1974, including clip-on handlebars, alloy wheels, and a race-style seat.

MV Agusta went out of business in 1980. Cagiva assumed control a few years later.

As the name suggests, the MV Agusta America was developed specifically for the U.S. market.

Even though it's called the America, it's more at home on the Italian Autostrada.

★ ★ ★
Its angular lines aren't nearly as sexy as those on the original 750S.

| | |
|---|---|
| Engine: Air-cooled, 789cc, four-stroke, inline four-cylinder | Top Speed: 130 miles per hour |
| Horsepower: 75 at 7,900 rpm | Weight: n/a |
| | Value Now: $$ |

### As American as meatballs and spaghetti

When MV launched the 750S America in 1975, the company aimed it at the right country but at the wrong time. Simply put, America's motorcycle market was not yet ripe for such a bike. It would be another 10 years before the sportbike concept was accepted on these shores, so the America turned out to be a foreign idea that was ahead of its time.

# MV Agusta

## F4 750 Serie Oro

### MV once again strikes gold

MV Agusta marked its return to the sportbike market in 1999 with the F4 750 Gold Series. The first 300 bikes that were built utilized many magnesium parts (swingarm, frame side plates, and wheels, to name a few) that were anodized gold, accounting for the bike's name. The exotica didn't end there. All painted parts, such as fairing, seat tail, front fender, fuel tank, and airbox, were made of carbon fiber.

 *Serie Oro* means "Gold Series" in Italian.

 The bike that brought MV Agusta back to the forefront of the exotic bike market.

 Nevada's Highway 318 from Lund to Hiko, site of the Silver State Classic. It's a good place to exercise the F4's horsepower.

 ★ ★ ★
It's like riding a two-wheeled Ferrari.

| | |
|---|---|
| Engine: Liquid-cooled, 749.5cc, four-stroke, inline four | Top Speed: 180 mile per hour |
| Horsepower: 129 at 12,500 rpm | Weight: 397 pounds |
| | Value Now: $$$$ |

---

# MV Agusta

## F4 750 Serie Oro

### Built with the spirit of Ayrton Senna, a true champion

One of the greatest race car drivers ever was Brazil's Ayrton Senna, who lost his life in a racing accident in 1994. Cagiva's figurehead, Claudio Castiglioni, was a friend of the Formula 1 star, and in 2002 he instructed the MV Agusta arm of his company to build a tribute bike in Senna's honor.

 Formula 1 racer Ayrton Senna died racing in Italy in 1994. Count Domenico Agusta died of a heart attack in 1971.

 Despite the Senna's near $30,000 price, the most expensive MV Agusta was the F4 CC, tagged at $120,000!

 Track day at the Autodromo Enzo e Dino Ferrari racing circuit near the Italian town of Imola, Italy, site of Senna's fatal accident.

 ★ ★ ★ ★
There's real excitement riding a $30,000 motorcycle as fast as you can on a racetrack.

| | |
|---|---|
| Engine: Liquid-cooled, 998cc, four-stroke, inline four | Top Speed: 180 miles per hour |
| Horsepower: 174 at 11,900 rpm | Weight: 418 pounds |
| | Value Now: $$$$ |

MV was founded in the village of Verghera, Italy, and *MV* stood for *Meccanica Verghera* (Verghera mechanics).

At $18,000 MSRP, this bike is affordable—by MV Agusta standards.

Take a breather on the Midland Trail/Highway 60 that parallels the Great Kanawha River in West Virginia, enjoying the Brutale's wide powerband in the process.

★ ★ ★ ★
Ride it hard enough, and you can slide both tires.

| | |
|---|---|
| Engine: Liquid-cooled, 1,078cc, four-stroke, inline four | Top Speed: 165 miles per hour |
| Horsepower: 144 at 10,600 rpm | Weight: 419 pounds |
| | Value Now: $$$ |

### An MV for the masses

The naked truth about naked bikes is that they are typically fun to ride. MV Agusta's Brutale 1090RR is no exception, and its engine delivers power through a wide rpm range, making it easy to ride fast on the road. Need power? Just twist the throttle, and you'll be rewarded quickly—no waiting for the engine to spool up to maximum rpm. The Brutale doesn't necessarily share the same sexy styling as MV's F4 line of sportbikes, but that's okay. This bike still delivers an exciting ride, no matter what the road conditions.

# MZ

## 250cc Works Racer

**Once upon a time there was an East Germany, and this is the bike that represented that repressed communist country at the Grand Prix**

When Grand Prix world championship racing resumed after World War II, the formula for winning usually involved a four-stroke engine. But in 1958, the East German company of MZ brought a pair of two-stroke models—a 125cc and 250cc—to the track, and the face of motorcycle Grand Prix was about to change. The MZ racers were fast, and in the capable hands of such riders as Horst Fügner and Gary Hocking, they were winners. But the communist-bloc company was always plagued by bad luck—enough that they never won a world championship. Even so, MZ's pioneering spirit led Suzuki and Yamaha to produce some of the fastest two-stroke racers of the 1960s and 1970s.

The *M* stood for *Motoraderwerke*, and the *Z* was for *Zschopau*, the East German city where the factory was situated.

MZ's 125cc and 250cc engine designs prompted the return of the two-stroke engine to Grand Prix road racing.

To truly appreciate the MZ 250, you'll need to ride this bike on public roads. Best bet: the Ulster Grand Prix in Ireland, where they still host *real* road races.

★ ★ ★ ★
Hold your breath while those treaded tires try to grip on the cast-iron manhole cover up ahead!

Engine: Air-cooled, 249cc, two-stroke two-cylinder
Horsepower: 45 at 10,500 rpm

Top Speed: 140 miles per hour
Weight: n/a
Value Now: $$$$

# MZ

## 1000S

**A sporting alternative to cookie-cutter sport-touring bikes**

MZ is quick to point out that the company's 1000S is a sport-tourer, with emphasis on sport. And at that kind of riding the 1000S excels, offering crisp handling and precise steering over a windy road. Mount the soft luggage of your choice to hold all your personal items, fill the 5.3-gallon gas tank with regular (yes!) blend, and you're good to go for miles and miles. Keep your eyes on the road ahead to enjoy the view; those mirrors buzz enough to distort the view behind you.

The bodywork for the 1000S was designed by the same engineer who laid out the lines for the F-117 Stealth Fighter.

MZ's first large-bore motorcycle, and it offers snappy handling.

Venture into the Forest Heritage National Scenic Byway near Greenville, South Carolina, stopping at Looking Glass Falls for a quick swim in the pool at the base of the falls.

★ ★
There's nothing daunting about this bike—just a solid ride for a fun time.

Engine: Liquid-cooled, 998cc, four-stroke, parallel twin
Horsepower: 117 at 9,000 rpm

Top Speed: n/a
Weight: 510 pounds
Value Now: $$

Two Belfast brothers, Rex and Cromie McCandless, developed the Featherbed frame. After an initial test on the Isle of Man, Norton team leader Harold Daniels said it had a "featherbed ride," and the name stuck.

 Took first, second, and third places in the Junior and Senior TTs at the Isle of Man in 1950.

 Mountain Course, Isle of Man.

 ★ ★ ★ ★
Standing up to the AMA is rebellious, especially if you lose.

Engine: Air-cooled, 499cc, DOHC, four-stroke single
Horsepower: 50 at 7,200 rpm

Top Speed: 150 miles per hour
Weight: n/a
Value Now: $$$$$

## AMA versus Norton

In December 1957, the AMA Competition Committee came together for its annual meeting. According to the minutes, there was general discussion about developing a Southern California road-racing program; the rule restricting "girl riders from speed competition" was retained; and a 1955 ruling that the Norton Manx Model 30 was ineligible for Class C racing was upheld. The original Manx 500 had been approved in 1946, but the Model 30's engine had two overhead cams and an oversquare bore. Not to mention the new Featherbed frame. It was allowed to race at Daytona in 1950, but in 1957 there still weren't any road-going Model 30s being produced. So, by a vote of a 19 to 8, the application for approval was rejected. AMA: 1. Norton: 0.

# Norton

## Dominator Model 7

### Underwhelming

Norton was founded in 1898 to be a manufacturer of "fittings and parts for the two-wheel trade." By 1947, it had hired Bert Hopwood away from Triumph. Hopwood was on Triumph's Speed Twin design team. When he went to Norton, he used the knowledge gained at Triumph to help him develop the Dominator engine, Norton's first twin. He and Norton parted ways in 1948, but the Dominator went into production anyway. It was underpowered and didn't handle particularly well. In fact, until Don Hele built the *Domiracer* in 1960, the Dominator was anything but dominant, regularly getting schooled on the track even by Norton's single-cylinder Manx. After the Dominator Model 88 was introduced, Model 7s were most often used as places to hang sidecars.

 Hopwood returned to Norton in 1955 but left again as the Associated Motorcycles fiasco began to unfold. He then began a second stint at Triumph, during which he designed the Trident/Rocket 3 engine.

 The Dominator Model 7 was Norton's first twin. They got better.

 Following a 500cc single around a racetrack.

 *
Just not that rebellious.

| | |
|---|---|
| Engine: Air-cooled, 497cc, OHV, four-stroke twin | Top Speed: 95 miles per hour |
| Horsepower: 30 at 7,000 rpm | Weight: n/a |
| | Value Now: $$$$ |

# Norton

## Mark 1 Atlas

### Getting there

Bert Hopwood's original 500cc twin was first stroked into a 600 and then bored into a 650. Finally, it was stroked again, and Norton's first 750 was born. The Atlas might have been just a 500 with bigger jugs and carbs, but it had the Featherbed frame. According to *Cycle* magazine, "Riding the Atlas is an experience that cannot be understood short of the deed itself." The bike was only available in the United States for its first two years. It came with high-rise bars—and lots of vibration when it hit the upper rpm ranges. Originally called the 750SS, it was Norton's transition between the Dominator and the Commando. Like any good steppingstone, it was better than the first but not as good as the last.

 An "off-road" version of the Atlas, the P-11, used the 750cc motor in a Matchless Scrambler frame. It worked better as a streetbike and could hit 113 miles per hour.

 Norton's first 750.

 Take this bike down U.S. Route 66.

 * *
Not there yet.

| | |
|---|---|
| Engine: Air-cooled, 745cc, DOHC, four-stroke twin | Top Speed: 119 miles per hour |
| Horsepower: 58 at 6,800 rpm | Weight: n/a |
| | Value Now: $$$$ |

## Commando 750 Hi.rider

Some lucky motorcycle cops in the 1970s got to ride Commando 750 Interpols.

It looked like a chopper.

Anyplace where the sun is shining and you don't have to turn much.

★ ★
Choppers were rebellious back then. But the Hi.rider was just made to look like a chopper.

Engine: Air-cooled, 745cc, OHV, four-stroke twin
Horsepower: 58 at 6,800 rpm
Top Speed: 125 miles per hour
Weight: n/a
Value Now: $$$

### Atlas shrugged

In the early 1960s, Joe Berliner of Berliner Motor Corporation told the Norton brass they should build a 750cc bike for the U.S. market. They did. It was called the Atlas, perhaps because it had the weight of the world's biggest motorcycle bazaar on its shoulders. Next came the Commando, a vast improvement on the Atlas, if only because of the Isolastic engine mounts. Anticipating the worldwide web phenomenon that would take us all by storm two or so decades later, Norton introduced a new Commando in 1971, the strangely spelled Hi.rider. By that time, the whole world wanted high-rise handlebars and upswept seats with tiny sissy bars on bikes with big engines. Because everyone knew that's how we did it in the States.

## Commando Fastback

Dr. Bauer was a Rolls Royce engineer before he started working for Norton.

This bike was named *Motor Cycle News* Machine of the Year for five straight years after it was introduced.

Donington Park, Leicestershire, England.

★ ★ ★ ★
Now we're getting somewhere.

Engine: Air-cooled, 745cc, DOHC, four-stroke twin
Horsepower: 60 at 6,800 rpm
Top Speed: 125 miles per hour
Weight: n/a
Value Now: $$$$

### Supercalifragilisticexpialidocious

From Edward Turner's 1938 Speed Twin on, British parallel twins vibrated a lot. Dr. Stephen Bauer decided that the Featherbed frame countered all known engineering principles and designed a new frame for the Commando that used special rubber fittings to isolate the engine, gearbox, and swingarm. It was dubbed the "Isolastic Anti-Vibration Super-Ride" system. It worked well—as long as it was adjusted properly.

# Norton

## Commando Rotary

### Geography lesson

Clever people are always trying to find a better way. Thus the Wankel craze of the mid-1970s. Primarily an answer to the piston engine for cars, rotary engines spilled over into bikes every now and then. We all remember Suzuki's RE-5; less known are Norton's attempts at reinventing the wheel. The first was the Interpol II police bike. Next up was the Classic, which was moderately successful, and then came the Commander, basically the second generation of the rotary police bike but without the lights and siren. The Commander had three flaws: The brakes and suspension weren't up to par; the first production models had non-removable saddlebags; and Norton was known for fire-breathing race bikes. Touring bikes were supposed to come from Germany.

 At about 500 machines, the Interpol II was the most-produced Norton rotary.

 This bike looked like a BMW RT. The way a Ford Grenada looked like a Mercedes.

 Trans-Canada Highway.

 ★ ★ ★ ★ ★
Going touring when everyone expects you to go racing is rebellious, if only in an ass-backwards sort of way.

Engine: Liquid-cooled, 588cc, twin-chamber rotary
Horsepower: 85 at 9,000 rpm
Top Speed: 145 miles per hour
Weight: n/a
Value Now: $$$$

# Norton

 The model name is in reference to the John Player Tobacco Company, sponsors of Norton's factory road racers in 1974.

 The JPS looked just like the bikes Peter Williams and Phil Read raced in Formula 750.

 Track Day at Brands Hatch, keeping in mind that you're riding a rather stock-performing Norton.

 ★ ★ ★
If you really want to play the part on the Norton JPS, wear a Phil Read replica helmet.

Engine: Air-cooled, 828cc, four-stroke, parallel twin
Horsepower: 48 at 5,500 rpm
Top Speed: 115 miles per hour
Weight: 476 pounds
Value Now: $$$$

## A standard Commando dressed up like a factory racer

In its 1974 road test of the Norton JPS, *Cycle* magazine's editors noted, "Hooking down a winding road is probably the most pleasant thing you can do with the JPS." Hmm, not a bad summation of a bike that was modeled after Norton's factory-team road racers of 1974. The key phrase, however, is "modeled after" because beneath that flashy bodywork sits a rather stock Commando chassis. Not a bad thing, though. As the *Cycle* staff pointed out, the JPS welcomed a twisty road and put a smile on its rider's face.

# NSU

## Max

### Knit one, race two

The *S* in *NSU* stands for *Strickmaschinen*. It's the German word for "knitting machines," the first products NSU manufactured. NSU built its first motorcycle in 1901, its first water-cooled bike in 1905, and, in 1920, a 1,000cc V-twin that put out 15 horsepower. It hired Walter William Moore away from Norton in 1929 and then produced a 500cc, bevel-gear-driven, SOHC single. Some say it's basically a Norton Manx. After World War II, NSU built a 500cc, DOHC, inline four. Rather than race the 500cc four, NSU engineers split the engine design into 125cc singles and 250cc twins (supermax shown). Werner Haas won the Isle of Man 250 TT on one, plus two world championships, but you might not have heard of Germany's first world champion motorcycle racer. He died at the age of 29.

 Mike Hailwood, Sammy Miller, and John Surtees all raced NSU Max motorcycles.

 Took first, second, and third at the Isle of Man Lightweight TT for 250s in 1954.

 Beating a Norton Manx at Silverstone.

 ★ ★ ★ ★ ★
Mike the Bike rode one.

Engine: Air-cooled, 247cc, SOHC, four-stroke single
Horsepower: 28 at 9,000 rpm
Top Speed: 118 miles per hour
Weight: n/a
Value Now: $$$$

## Six Days Replica

Ossa started in 1924 by manufacturing movie projectors.

This bike showed that even low-volume manufacturers could make special-edition replicas.

Forest Road 247, Chequamegon National Forest, Wisconsin.

★★
Replicas can be cool, but they aren't rebellious.

| | |
|---|---|
| Engine: Air-cooled, 244cc, piston-port, two-stroke single | Top Speed: n/a |
| | Weight: n/a |
| Horsepower: 24 at 8,000 rpm | Value Now: $$$ |

### Be careful what you wish for

In 1949, Ossa introduced its first motorcycle. With Ossa being a Spanish company, and observed trials being basically the Spanish national sport, it was only natural that Ossa and trials should become inextricably linked. Ossa won its first European Trials Championship in 1971, followed by another the next year. Ossa also successfully competed in motocross: Buzz McMillian rode an Ossa Stiletto in the first Supercross event. Given their reliability, Ossas made great enduro bikes too. The Six Days Replica is basically a Pioneer with a fancy seat/fender treatment, but it looks just like the factory Ossas used in the 1972 International Six Days Enduro. Ten years later, the entire Ossa workforce walked off the factory floor, citing "inhospitable working conditions." Thus ended Ossa.

# Ossa

## 250 GP Bike

**It could have been more than just a contender**

When you first clap eyes on Ossa's 250 Grand Prix bike, all the visual clues seem wonky—badly so, in fact. It has a true monocoque frame carrying an air-cooled engine that has a *huge* head and cylinder, way out of scale for a 250 single, as is the preternaturally corpulent expansion chamber that looks like something off a motocrosser rather than a road racer. The bike just looks wrong, and it especially did in 1969. It came from a tiny Spanish company that started out selling movie projectors, but that odd Ossa went like stink, and bloodied the nose of the Japanese manufacturers, until the pilot, Santi Herrero, died at the Isle of Man in 1970. And with his passing went Ossa's road-race program, forever.

 The 250 GP bike—and other Ossas—was designed by Eduardo Giro, son of founder Manuel Giro.

 It was the first truly successful monocoque race bike, and the single two-stroke engine's 45 horsepower was sufficient to beat Japanese and European 250s of twin- and four-cylinder configurations, even at the frighteningly fast Spa circuit.

 Any European racetrack—except the Isle of Man Snaefell Mountain Course.

 ★ ★ ★ ★ ★
Five, because the experimentation Ossa did with its monocoque frame was off the charts compared to the efforts of its contemporaries and compared to modern motorcycles.

Engine: Two-stroke,
   disc-valve single
Horsepower: 45 (claimed) at
   9,500 rpm

Top Speed: n/a
Weight: n/a
Value Now: Priceless

# Penton

 In 1977, Penton made the K-R, a short-tracker designed with—you guessed it—King Kenny Roberts himself.

 Showed that Triumph rep a thing or two.

 Over the hills and through the woods to Grandmother's house.

 ★ ★ ★ ★ ★
Building your own bike because the Triumph rep made you mad is rebellious.

Engine: Air-cooled, 122cc,    Top Speed: n/a
   piston-port, two-stroke single   Weight: n/a
Horsepower: n/a    Value Now: $$$$

## DIY

John Penton was a man, a big man. He had to be. He rode off-road races on Harleys, BSAs, NSUs, and BMWs. One day he berated a Triumph sales rep, telling him everything that was wrong with racing big, heavy streetbikes on dirt. The sales rep told Penton to build his own bike if he knew so much. So he did. Well, he had KTM put the bikes together out of parts he chose after he put up $6,000 of his own money. The first bike, the 125 Six Day, went on sale in 1968. It was eventually joined by sister bikes as big as 400cc and as small as 100cc. By 1978, KTM had absorbed Penton, but by then the big man had made his point.

# Piaggio

## Vespa

**Cheap transportation for Italy and, later, the world**

When citizens of war-torn Italy needed affordable transportation in 1946, the Piaggio family answered the call with the Vespa scooter, a simple vehicle with a painted, pressed-steel frame that formed a protective cowling around the 98cc, two-stroke engine and integrated three-speed transmission unit. This simple machine came to define the concept of the motor scooter around the world.

 General Corradino D'Ascanio, who had been responsible for helicopter production for Count Agusta (MV Agusta) prior to World War II, designed the original Vespa.

 Vespa is to scooters what Honda is to motorcycles.

 Ride through Rome with a pretty Italian belle sidesaddle behind you, à la Audrey Hepburn behind Gregory Peck in the movie *Roman Holiday*.

 *
The original Vespa was as mischievous as a golden retriever puppy but hardly rebellious.

Engine: Air-cooled, 98cc, two-stroke single-cylinder
Horsepower: 4.5 at 6,500 rpm

Top Speed: 39 miles per hour (2008 LX 50)
Weight: 225 pounds (2008 LX 50)
Value Now: $$

# Piaggio

## Vespa GS 150

**Talkin' 'bout my ge-ge-ge-generation**

Mods and rockers, move aside; the star of this show is the Vespa GS 150, the scooter that made worldwide fame with The Who's 1979 rock-opera movie *Quadrophenia*. The scooter's faired handlebar/headlamp unit has become a styling icon among younger scooter riders today.

 The word *vespa* is Italian for *wasp*. More than 138 versions of the scooter have been produced worldwide since 1946.

 A popular model ridden by the mods during the 1960s.

 London, with a stop at the Ace Café, where you and other members of the mod squad can antagonize the rockers.

 **
Mods don't back down . . .

Engine: Air-cooled, 150cc, two-stroke single-cylinder
Horsepower: 8 at 7,000 rpm

Top Speed: n/a
Weight: n/a
Value Now: $$

Piaggio also offers the MP3 with 250cc and 400cc engines.

 An MP3 player that *really* rocks!

 South Dakota's Needles Highway (SR87), where you can enjoy the hairpins leading to Mt. Rushmore.

 *
Cool though it may be, it's still a tricycle.

Engine: Liquid-cooled, 492cc, four-stroke single-cylinder
Horsepower: 40 at 7,500 rpm

Top Speed: 90 miles per hour
Weight: 538 pounds
Value Now: $$

### Lean to the left, lean to the right!

One motorcycle website said about Piaggio's MP3, "We were skeptical, but the suspension engineering really works well—and the scooter's a blast to ride." In truth, the MP3 offers rather brisk handling, with a lean angle of 40 degrees to either side. The continuously variable transmission means that you won't have to worry about shifting gears, either. Simply twist the throttle, aim for the turn's apex, and then lean into it as you would a motorcycle. An electro-hydraulic locking mechanism assists in keeping the bike upright without a kickstand while parked. All in all, a pretty cool little tricycle.

# Royal Enfield

## Bullet 350

### Change is a four-letter word

The first Royal Enfield Bullet was sold in 1931. Yeah, they're not really the same bikes anymore; for a while, they even had—*gasp*—electronic ignitions. Still, you try "updating" a bike first built when the British monarchy split into realms of commonwealth. In 1949, the engine's cylinder was made upright and given an alloy head, the frame got a swinging arm in the rear (with shock absorbers!) and telescopic forks up front, and, well, that was pretty much it for improvements until the mid-1990s, when Royal Enfield introduced an all-alloy engine. Of course, that kind of radical change can cause chest pains, so Bullets today come with nice, familiar cast-iron blocks. And a set of contact breaker points with their trusty sidekick, the condenser.

 Siddhartha runs Royal Enfield. No, not that Siddhartha. Siddhartha Lal became CEO of Royal Enfield in 2001. Now he's the CEO of the parent company, Eicher Motors.

 Royal Enfield's Bullet has been in production longer than any other motorcycle in history.

 To Shady Acres, where you and your bike can enjoy your twilight years.

 ★ ★ ★ ★ ★
It has probably outlived more real bikers than you have.

Engine: Air-cooled, 346cc, OHV, four-stroke single
Horsepower: 18 at 5,000rpm
Top Speed: n/a
Weight: n/a
Value Now: $$

# Royal Enfield

## Super Meteor

### Who needs apehangers?

To build Royal Enfield's Super Meteor motor, engineers essentially fused two cylinders from 350cc singles to the bottom end of a 500cc Meteor Minor to create a 700cc vertical twin. The frame, also from a Meteor Minor, had to be strengthened, but the bike was said to cruise nicely at 80 miles per hour.

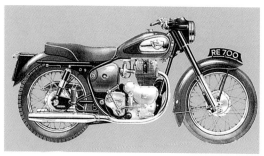

 The 500cc Minor version of the Meteor tested over 10 miles per hour faster than the Triumph Tiger at the MIRA proving grounds. For some reason, the Tiger still had more sex appeal.

 In 1958, Royal Enfield Super Meteors were used by Britain's Transport Research Laboratory to test the Dunlop Maxaret anti-lock braking system.

 East Coast Road from Cuddalore to Chennai, Tamil Nadu, India.

 ★ ★
Not even as sexy as a Triumph Tiger.

Engine: Air-cooled, 692cc, OHV, four-stroke twin
Horsepower: 40 at 4,500 rpm
Top Speed: 100 miles per hour
Weight: n/a
Value Now: $$$$

Rudge produced knockoff wheels for sports cars well into the 1960s.

 Took first, second, and third places in the 1934 Isle of Man Lightweight TT.

 Old Clady Circuit, County Antrim, Northern Ireland.

 ★ ★ ★
Rudges were badass, but the company's sales motto was lame.

Engine: n/a
Horsepower: n/a
Top Speed: n/a

Weight: n/a
Value Now: $$$$

**"The Broom"**

"Rudge it, don't trudge it" was the sales motto. Like so many motorcycle manufacturers, Rudge-Whitworth began by making bicycles. It made its first motorcycle in 1911. Rudges went on to win lots of races, from the Ulster Grand Prix to the Isle of Man TT; in fact, a whole model line was named for the Ulster Grand Prix after Graham Walker won the 1928 event with an average speed of over 80 miles per hour. In 1934, Rudge introduced the Ulster Sport 250, a single with a four-valve, radial head. It swept the first three places at the Isle of Man. But the Depression compounded some bad business decisions, and then World War II broke out. Rudge retooled to produce radar equipment and never really made motorcycles again.

# Scott

## Flying Squirrel TT Replica

### Unfair advantage

"What better advert is there than something so good it has to be banned?" read Scott's ad copy. Scott two-strokes were so much more advanced than their rival machines that if you raced a Scott, your bike's displacement was multiplied by 1.32 to determine its competition class. They were liquid cooled, had telescopic forks and three-speed transmissions, and won lots of races back in the day. Alfred Scott, the man behind the machines, didn't just think outside the box; he lived there. He left the company he founded to make three-wheelers in 1919. That didn't work out so well, but Scott Motors continued without him. In 1929, a Flying Squirrel took third place in the Isle of Man TT, leading to the TT Replica.

 Engines with red paint were road models; engines with green paint were for racing.

 The first, and perhaps only, race replica bike to commemorate a third-place finish.

 Take this to the 18th fairway, Pebble Beach Golf Links, Pebble Beach, California.

 ★ ★ ★ ★ ★
Steve McQueen used to own one. He rode it down to Salinas to pick up broads.

Engine: Liquid-cooled, 596cc, two-stroke twin
Horsepower: n/a

Top Speed: 70 miles per hour
Weight: n/a
Value Now: $$$$$

Sunbeam's S7 is actually considered the more desirable/collectible of the lineup, but the S8 is easier to restore.

The Sunbeam was originally intended to be a gentleman's motorcycle—high-quality, refined, and something that would instill pride of ownership. And it was—mostly, anyway.

A country lane, in late spring or early summer.

★ ★

Only two because, although it was completely different from anything else BSA (or other English motorcycle manufacturers) produced at the time, it was still essentially a prewar R75 with a quirky, low-output, tandem twin.

| | |
|---|---|
| Engine: Air-cooled, OHC, four-valve, tandem twin | Top Speed: 85 miles per hour |
| | Weight: 430 pounds |
| Horsepower: 24 at 6,000 rpm | Value Now: $$$$ |

**A prewar R75 built by BSA? With a tandem twin? That's Sunbeam.**

At heart, Sunbeam's S-series bikes were based on BMW's R75 (plans of which were turned over to England, and eventually BSA, as war reparations following World War II) but with a unique all-alloy, 487cc, tandem twin to retain use of shaft drive. But these bikes were slightly more too: BSA meant for the Sunbeams to have higher aspirations than the parent company's bikes in terms of quality and convenience. The best model in terms of practicality (for a vintage bike) is the S8 Sport model, produced from 1946 to 1956. It lacked some of the sophistication of the S7, but it lacked the handling-impairing balloon tires as well. The S8 was also lighter, had higher-compression pistons, and benefited from some standard BSA parts, such as front suspension, brakes, and wheels.

# Suzuki

## Stinger 125

**A street scrambler that was actually a street screamer**

Back in 1969, small-bore motorcycles like Suzuki's Stinger 125 were popular in America. Hot on the success of its high-performing 250cc X-6 Hustler and 200cc X-5 Invader, Suzuki produced the Stinger, an affordable street bike that rewarded its rider with stellar performance—for its displacement class. As time went by, American motorcycle enthusiasts' tastes leaned more toward bikes with larger engines, eventually relegating 125cc bikes to beginner status.

 Suzuki's first 250cc X-6 Hustler was among the quickest street bikes from 0 to 60 miles per hour.

 One of the last popular 125cc street bikes in America.

 Take a couple of minutes (or more) to enjoy Willow Springs Raceway's nine turns. That's the same track where club racers on Stingers dominated the 125cc Modified Production class in 1969 and 1970.

 ★ ★ ★
Spend too much time in the saddle, and you could suffer from Stinger envy.

Engine: Air-cooled, 124cc, two-stroke, parallel twin-cylinder
Horsepower: 15 at 8,500 rpm

Top Speed: 75 miles per hour
Weight: 211 pounds
Value Now: $$

# Suzuki

## X6 Hustler

**The Little Engine that Could**

The X-6 Hustler's (in America: T20 in the rest of the world) engine was designed by Suzuki's first racing director, Masano Shimizu. Suzuki won a world title in its first year, so Shimizu was obviously no slouch. His goal for the new engine was to develop 100 horsepower per liter of displacement. He exceeded his goal: the little 250 could generate 29 horsepower.

 This was the first mass-produced bike with a six-speed transmission. Thus the X-6 and Super Six monikers.

 Over 30,000 X6/T20s were sold around the world. Many are still ridden—even raced—today.

 Manx Grand Prix on the Mountain Circuit, Isle of Man.

 First mass-produced motorcycle engine to generate 1 horsepower per 10cc of displacement.

Engine: Air-cooled, 247cc, two-stroke twin
Horsepower: 29 at 7,500 rpm

Top Speed: 100 miles per hour
Weight: n/a
Value Now: $$

## T500II Titan

According to one sales brochure, the Posi-Force oil-injection system spewed raw oil over the big end.

The Titan was a multi-level oxymoron: a reliable two-stroke road bike from the early 1970s that handled as if it didn't want to kill you.

This bike is best for losing a Kawasaki Mach III on a winding country road.

★ ★ ★
Two-stroke power and decent handling to boot.

Engine: Air-cooled, 492cc, two-stroke twin
Horsepower: 47 at 7,000 rpm

Top Speed: 119 miles per hour
Weight: n/a
Value Now: $$$

### Powerful warrior, losing battle

"Built to take on the country," read the Titan ad. What they probably meant was Britain and the British 650cc four-strokes. First came the T500I Cobra, a 500cc two-stroke with a 57.3-inch wheelbase. While Kawasaki two-strokes were notoriously poor handlers, the long Suzuki was surefooted and stable. But the Cobra looked like something from the 1960s, so Suzuki built the T500II Titan. Not terribly different mechanically, its styling brought Suzuki into the 1970s. The Titan continued to evolve over the next eight years, getting electronic ignition, a front disc brake, and, strangely, less power as the years rolled by. It still kicked Triumph butt, but in the end it was American politics the Titan had to take on. It (and all other two-stroke road bikes) lost.

# Suzuki

## GT750

**My bike's better than yours is**

When Suzuki entered the 750cc class, there was lots of competition. There were four-strokes and two-strokes, inline fours, inline triples, V-twins, and parallel twins. What there wasn't was a liquid-cooled engine. Enter the GT750. Suzuki claimed it ran 30 percent cooler than any other two-stroke 750. "Costly crankshaft failures, not unheard of with competitive air-cooled machines, are virtually eliminated," read the ad copy. Take that, Kawasaki. Suzuki also claimed that a motorcycle is supposed to be "a sleek, beautiful machine that runs blazingly fast, under control, over any road." Okay, over any road might be stretching it, but *under control*? There you go, Kawasaki. The GT750 runs cooler, lasts longer, and handles better than your precious H2.

In 1973, the GT750 became the first mainstream production bike to offer dual disc brakes up front.

Although the GT750 was marketed as a touring bike, its engine was used in Suzuki's racing TR750. It pushed Yamaha's race-only TZ750 to the limit, and if not for some unimaginably consistent bad luck, it might have taken away a few of the Yammie's AMA championships.

You'll enjoy leading some guy who's scared out of his wits because he's on an H2 Mach IV around Daytona International Speedway.

★ ★ ★ ★ ★
Italian GT750 ads showed the bike with naked women.

Engine: Liquid-cooled, 738cc, piston-valve, two-stroke, inline triple
Horsepower: 67 at 6,500 rpm

Top Speed: 120 miles per hour
Weight: n/a
Value Now: $$$

### Motorcycle complex

Prototype rotary-engine bikes were built by all four Japanese motorcycle companies, but only one model made it into production. The RE-5 represented a typically Japanese approach to problem solving: each solution created another layer of technology. This meant the RE-5 was a complex machine, with systems and subsystems all trying to work together. For example, the twist-grip throttle controlled five cables that operated carburetor primary butterflies, secondary valves, even an oil pump to lubricate the engine's tip seals. But despite its mechanical intricacy, the RE-5 was fun to ride. *Cycle World* called it "the absolute king of the heavyweight Japanese handlers." Notice how the writer avoided comparing it to any Italian bikes. Still, the RE-5's frame would eventually be used in the GS750, which set a new standard for sportbike roadworthiness.

 The motor was produced by NSU, Felix Wankel's employer.

 Ed Mitchell, the sixth man to walk on the moon, introduced the RE-5 at its launch.

 The road less traveled.

 ★ ★ ★ ★ ★
Although the word sounds like "wanker," Wankel engines can be scary fast.

Engine: Liquid-cooled, 497cc, single-chamber rotary
Horsepower: 62 at 6,500 rpm
Top Speed: 105 miles per hour
Weight: n/a
Value Now: $$$

# Suzuki

## GS1000S

### Jingoism 101

The GS1000S came with air forks. Each fork leg had to be within 1.4 psi of the other. The maximum pressure you could run in them was 17.1. Recommended pressure for British riders was 14.2. Recommended pressure for American riders was 11.4, which was also the minimum pressure you could run. What*ever*. While the GS1000E came with air shocks in back, the S did not, seceding another chance to bash bikers in the United States. The S came with a bikini fairing, which meant flat bars to clear it. Flat bars work better with higher and more rearward pegs. Flat bars, rear-sets, fancy suspension—hey, what is this, an Italian bike? No, it couldn't be. The engine's too reliable, and all the switches work.

Wes Cooley followed Pops Yoshimura from Kawasaki to Suzuki in 1978. Cooley started winning regularly after the switch. Take that, Kawasaki.

Looked like those Yosh Suzukis Wes Cooley rode when he was winning AMA Superbike titles in 1979 and 1980.

Mazda Laguna Seca Raceway, Monterey, California.

★ ★ ★ ★
And 16 psi in the forks too.

Engine: Air-cooled, 987cc, DOHC, four-stroke, inline four
Horsepower: 90 at 9,000 rpm

Top Speed: 135 miles per hour
Weight: n/a
Value Now: $$$

The first American to ride a GS1100 was one of this book's authors, Dain Gingerelli, at Suzuki's test track in Japan.

 Suzuki's first road bike with a four-valve engine.

 Ryuyo, Suzuki's test course in Hamamatsu, Japan.

 ★ ★ ★
Ridden fast or slow, you'll enjoy the ride.

Engine: Air-cooled, 1,075cc, four-stroke, inline four
Horsepower: 105 at 8,000 rpm

Top Speed: 140 miles per hour
Weight: 544 pounds
Value Now: $$$

### The bike that ushered in a whole new era

Motorcycle historians can identify 1980 as the landmark year in which handling began to catch up with horsepower. Honda's 1980 CB750F laid the groundwork for balancing the handling/horsepower equation, but it was Suzuki's GS1100—introduced later that year—that properly addressed the problem, for this was the first *really* fast motorcycle capable of harnessing the *h* word through corners. The GS1100's solid frame, suspended by an air-adjustable fork and fully adjustable rear shocks, meant that the rider could put as much of the 105 crankshaft horsepower to the rear tire as possible. Today's sportbikes can leave the GS1100 in the dust, but truth be told, Suzuki's 1980 model was the bike that paved the way for today's hyper-handlers.

# Suzuki

## Katana GS1000SV

### Silver dream machine

To say Suzuki's GS1000SV Katana divided opinions over its looks is an understatement of global proportions. Styled by Hans Muth and named after a particularly vicious samurai sword, the Katana took two-wheel aesthetics to a place not everyone was sure they were meant to go. As a halo bike, then, something to draw traffic to Suzuki showrooms, the Katana was a smash hit. Ergonomically, though—with its clip-ons and high-for-the-day footpegs—not so much. And while the styling was *outré*, the basic bike underneath was essentially a GS1100, albeit with 2.0mm-narrower bore and 1.2mm-shorter stroke, supposedly to qualify for AMA Superbike racing with its 1,000cc displacement limit. Those changes weakened the normally Godzilla-like torque of the GS1100 and chased horsepower up the rpm band. For 1983, displacement returned to 1,100cc. None of that really mattered, though. For its short time on sale (1982–1983), the Katana made the engineers at Suzuki look like visionaries.

 Although hardly a sales success in the United States, the Katana has long had a rather rabid following in its homeland. That's why Suzuki kept pumping out big-bore Katanas up until the Final Edition model in 2000.

 What else but its Hans Muth rocket-ship styling.

 Anywhere with fast, gentle sweepers—preferably with billiard-table-smooth pavement.

 ★ ★ ★ ★ ★
There's never been anything styled like the Katana before, or since. There's not likely to be either.

Engine: Air-cooled, DOHC, 16-valve, inline four
Horsepower: 108 at 8,500 rpm (claimed)
1/4 Mile: n/a

Top Speed: 141 miles per hour (estimated)
Weight: 557 pounds (claimed, wet)
Price New: n/a
Value Now: $$$$

*Motorcyclist* magazine raved about the XN85's handling prowess, declaring: "Nothing works better in the corners."

Really just a placeholder, an entrant in the turbo bike market to say that Suzuki had an entrant in the turbo bike market.

To any one of a number of gatherings of early-1980s turbocharged motorcycles.

*

A parts-bin engineered bike thrown together as a last-minute entrant in the turbo wars of the early 1980s is not very rebellious.

Engine: Air-cooled, 673cc, DOHC, four-stroke, inline four
Horsepower: 85 at 10,500 rpm

Top Speed: 124 miles per hour
Weight: 543 pounds
Value Now: $$

### Placeholder

In 1983, turbocharging seemed the path that future motorcycles would take to getting more horsepower. Everyone else built a turbo, so Suzuki figured they'd better build one themselves. Suzuki combined the sci-fi bodywork from the Hans Muth–designed Katana, and the firm's reliable, if decidedly low-tech middleweight engine, then mounted a turbocharger pumping out 9.6 psi. To add to the XN85's tech cred, Suzuki used fuel injection. The result was a decent enough motorcycle, but an expensive one, and Suzuki sold very few examples.

# Suzuki

## RG500 Gamma

**Jailbait**

*Cycle* magazine said the RG500 Gamma's power had "the quality of an arrow shot from God's own crossbow." Then the writer rambled on about the difference between here and there blurring as it all became here, or some such nonsense. Apparently, that writer was smitten. Based on the RG500 Grand Prix racer, the Gamma might have been street legal, but most were probably ridden illegally when they did see a street. In fact, they may well have gotten a few folks thrown in jail. The Gamma had a typically peaky two-stroke powerband, but it also had a side-loading cassette gearbox, so you could find just the right gearing for whatever road you planned on riding to set your next new unofficial world record.

 Power output went from about 37 horsepower at 6,500 rpm to almost 90 horsepower at 9,000 rpm.

 From the aluminum frame to the square-four engine to the changeable gearbox, the Gamma was a direct relative of Suzuki's RG500 Grand Prix race bike.

 Suzuka International Racing Course, Ino, Japan.

 ★ ★ ★ ★ ★
The Gamma is criminal activity waiting to happen.

Engine: Liquid-cooled, 498cc, disc-valve, two-stroke, square four
Horsepower: 93 at 9,500 rpm

Top Speed: 142 miles per hour
Weight: n/a
Value Now: $$$$

*Motorcyclist* magazine chose the Tempter for its Bike of the Year Award.

A near-3-pound variable flywheel weight attached to the crankshaft engaged below 3,000 rpm for easier pulling away from a stop and disengaged above 3,000 rpm for better acceleration. That was the theory, at least.

To the crappy motorcycle burial grounds.

\*
A Japanese 650 vertical-twin with near-zero personality or character, save for that of a whiney four-year-old.

Engine: Air-cooled, DOHC,
    four-valve vertical-twin
Horsepower: 39 at 7,000 rpm

Top Speed: Yeah, right
Weight: n/a
Value Now: $

### The not-so-good die young too

The majority of the bikes in this book were selected to induce unbridled moto-lust. Some, though, such as Suzuki's Tempter, were chosen just to show motorcycling's darker side. Under the heading, "It Must Have Seemed Like a Good Idea at the Time," Suzuki created a modern interpretation of the classic 650 vertical-twin but jetted it so lean it almost squeaked. It also came with mismatched suspension rates, a mediocre single front-disc brake, and a pointless variable flywheel weight. The result? An unhappy motorcycle that appeared to do everything under duress. After two years, the Tempter died quietly, mourned by few.

# Suzuki

## GS1100ES

### Pleasantly competent has-been

Buyers of heavyweight bikes had choices in 1983. There was the sit-back, feet-forward, hands-in-the-air V65 Magna, Honda's powerful but wheelie-prone cruiser. At the other end of the Honda spectrum was the fine-handling but overweight CB1100F. Suzuki had the Katana, with its contortionist-inspired clip-ons and rear-sets. And there was Kawasaki's GPz1100, but who really cared? There were more powerful bikes than the GS1100ES; there were faster and lighter bikes too. But none were as quick or as comfortable. The big GS's frame and motor were on the road to obsolescence, but they were still perfect for whatever road you happened to be on, especially if you were going to be there for a while. Like a gracefully aging movie star, it could still hit its lines.

 The GS1100ES was 0.06 seconds faster than the Katana in the quarter-mile, but the Katana posted a 2.84-mile-per-hour faster trap speed. Same engine, different fairing and seating position.

 This was the first production bike tested by *Cycle World* to post a 10-second quarter-mile time.

 Leaving a V65 at the line while its front wheel reaches for the sky.

 ★ ★ ★
Surprisingly good, considering its technology was obsolete the day it hit the showroom floor.

Engine: Air-cooled, 1,075cc, DOHC, four-stroke, inline four
Horsepower: 111 at 8,500 rpm
Top Speed: 140 miles per hour
Weight: n/a
Value Now: $$$

# Suzuki

## RM250

As an homage to candied popcorn snacks, Suzuki called its RMs Screaming Yellow Zonkers in a 1977 magazine ad.

This bike began a long line of RM250s that would eventually become the liquid-cooled, monoshock, track-eating freaks of science you can buy today.

Trying to keep up with Joel Robert on a grass track.

★ ★
Nice racing heritage, but late to the party.

Engine: Air-cooled, 246cc,
    reed-valve, two-stroke single
Horsepower: 37 at 7,500 rpm

Top Speed: n/a
Weight: 217 pounds
Value Now: $$

### Keeping up with the Joneses

The world of motocross was changing fast, as YZs and Elsinores shifted everyone's notion of satisfactory power, weight, and suspension. It took 22 months before Suzuki designers, engineers, and test riders deemed the RM250 ready to market. The only parts it shared with its predecessor, the TM250, were the brakes. The shocks were mounted at a 42-degree angle, giving 8 inches of rear suspension travel. The engine put out 33 percent more horsepower and 20 percent more torque. Ready to race, the RM250 weighed only 217 pounds. And race it could. Suzuki had been a dominant force since taking its first world motocross title in 1970, and the RM was a direct descendent of those factory works bikes. It didn't set any new standards, but it kept pace.

# Suzuki

## GV1400GD Cavalcade

**A worthy touring bike—much like the baggers that were already on the market**

By the time Suzuki decided to join the turnkey touring party, Honda (Gold Wing), Yamaha (Venture), and Kawasaki (Voyager) already had established models. Harley-Davidson (FLTC) and BMW (various models) also were key players, so when the Cavalcade reported for duty (late), it pretty much confirmed the notion that baby boomers were seeking more efficient ways to address the matter of long-distance riding. In terms of performance, comfort, and design, the Cavalcade was equal to its contemporaries. It was nothing more and nothing less than a touring bike.

 The Cavalcade's V-4 engine was based on the Madura's high-revving powerplant. The touring edition was vastly detuned for tractability.

 Suzuki's first turnkey touring model.

 Extend your arm so that your thumb intersects the horizon. Now point the Cavalcade in that direction, and ride.

 ★ ★ Want to sample motorcycle touring from the 1980s? Here's one fine example.

Engine: Liquid-cooled, 1,360cc, four-stroke, 82-degree V-4
Horsepower: n/a
Top Speed: 115 miles per hour
Weight: 806 pounds
Value Now: $$

## GSX-R750

The GSX-R750 was designed by the same engineers who built the GS1000R factory endurance race bike.

First no-holds-barred superbike for the street. The brochure even made a point of mentioning that the engine had been detuned from 130 horsepower to 100.

Rush hour in Sao Paulo, Brazil. Just kidding.

★ ★ ★ ★
Brought badassedness to the street.

Engine: Air-cooled, 749cc, DOHC, four-stroke, inline four
Horsepower: 106 at 10,500 rpm
Top Speed: 130 miles per hour
Weight: n/a
Value Now: $$$

### Racer with lights and mirrors

The GSX-R750 was the first motorcycle that really could go straight from a crate to the track and win races without much fiddling beyond getting rid of its lights and mirrors. That and putting on a set of decent tires was all you really had to do. Anyone who wanted more just had to talk to Pops. Yoshimura, that is.

## GSX-R1000

The original GSX-R1100 debuted in 1985 at Laguna Seca Raceway.

The dominant brand in AMA Superbike racing since 2000.

Your favorite American road-race course.

★ ★ ★ ★ ★
Mat Mladin and Ben Spies won seven consecutive AMA Superbike Championships on GSX-R1000s.

Engine: Liquid-cooled, 998cc, four-stroke, inline four
Horsepower: 160 at 9,500 rpm
Top Speed: 179 miles per hour
Weight: 370 pounds
Value Now: $$$$

### As close to a race bike as you will get for the street

Suzuki redefined the liter-bike class in 2001 when it replaced the long-standing GSX-R1100 with the GSX-R1000. The new model's frame took many proven features from the frame of the GSX-R750 but used slightly thicker metal for less flex and a more stable ride. And with 160 horsepower kicking through the Suzuki's big rear tire, there was plenty of power to challenge the chassis. The combination was so good that between the AMA rule change that made the GSX-R1000 eligible for the U.S. Superbike Championship and U.S. Superbike racing disintegrating at the end of the 2009 season, the GSX-R1000 not only won every championship, but it also filled almost every podium spot. Few bikes in the history of motorcycle racing have been as dominant.

# Suzuki

## TL1000S

### Too terribly clever

England's *Motor Cycle News* likened the TL1000S to Freddie Kreuger. The motor lives on in today's SV1000, but, thankfully, the frame and its bizarre rear suspension were put down in 2001. Oddly, it took four years and who knows how many crashes for that to happen. Although 90-degree V-twins had already been burning up roads and tracks for decades, Suzuki felt some inexplicable need to reinvent the shock absorber in order to accommodate the engine design's inherent length. So they applied Formula 1 car technology to bikes. But bikes and cars have different suspension requirements. Bikes need more travel, making the damping components work harder, creating heat. The microscopic amount of fluid in the TL's damper couldn't cope, causing more than a few clenched buttocks.

 Like Freddie Kreuger, the TL has achieved cult status today.

 Scared the bejesus out of people and still attracted a loyal following.

 A very smooth, twisty road.

 ★ ★ ★ ★
Try not doing a wheelie on one of these outlaw machines.

Engine: Liquid-cooled, 996cc, DOHC, four-stroke single
Horsepower: 125 at 8,500 rpm

Top Speed: 161 miles per hour
Weight: n/a
Value Now: $$

# Suzuki

## SV650

A race-kitted SV650 will run circles around a 1000cc streetbike on a tight, twisty racetrack.

Dominated lightweight classes in club racing for a decade.

Any racetrack anywhere in the world where amateur road racers gather.

★★★★
Anything capable of this kind of speed on a racetrack is rebellious.

Engine: Liquid-cooled 645cc eight-valve V-twin
Horsepower: 70 at 9,000 rpm

Top Speed: NA
Weight: 364 pounfd
Value Now: $$

### A club racer for the ages
When Suzuki introduced its overachieving SV650, no one knew quite how to categorize the new lightweight Suzukis. The folks who really understood the little Suzuki's potential were members of road-racing clubs around the world, and the SV650 soon became the most popular platform for amateur road racing. If you really want to go fast, get yourself a track-ready SV650 and go racing.

# Suzuki

## DL1000 V-Strom

The reason the DL1000 V-Strom hasn't been more successful is because its little brother, the DL650 V-Strom, is even better.

Provided the virtues of BMW's R1200GS dual sport at a much more civilized price.

From Seattle to Anchorage, or pretty much anywhere else.

★ ★ ★
There's something at least a little rebellious about a 528-pound dirtbike.

Engine: Liquid-cooled 996cc eight-valve V-twin
Horsepower: 91 at 8,000 rpm

Top Speed: NA
Weight: 528 pounds
Value Now: $$$

### Suzuki finally gets it right
In the mid-1990s Suzuki designed a killer 996cc V-twin engine but never quite found a good home for it. The original TL1000S was an entertaining sportbike, but it was let down by a goofy rear suspension and a weak frame. The TL1000R fixed the frame but gained a ridiculous amount of weight. The SV1000 had a normal rear suspension but had tortuous sportbike ergonomics. Finally Suzuki got it right with the DL1000 V-Strom.

# Suzuki

## GSX-1300 Hayabusa

### Predator

Hayabusa is what the Japanese call the peregrine falcon. These hayabusas are said to reach 300 kilometers (186.4 miles) per hour when they fly in a dive, making them the fastest animals on earth; Suzuki Hayabusas were designed to go 300 kilometers per hour when they fly on a track, making them the fastest motorcycles on earth. Real hayabusas prey on blackbirds; Suzuki Hayabusas were designed to prey on Honda CB1100XX Blackbirds. You get the picture. Eventually there would be Kawasaki ZX-14s, however, and what the ZX-14 lacked in poetry, it made up for with velocity, leading the world's motorcycle manufacturers to voluntarily limit speeds to 300 kilometers per hour, lest the world's governments step in and do it themselves. Of course, just disconnect a couple of wires and the hunt is back on.

 As long as you don't accidentally whack open the throttle, the Hayabusa is quite docile around town.

 Thanks to the self-imposed speed limit, the 1999 Hayabusa remains the only production motorcycle to have surpassed the 300-kilometer-per-hour mark.

 Inching away from a ZX-14 while you both leave a CB1100XX in the dust.

 ★ ★ ★ ★ ★
The Hayabusa will probably forever remain the world's fastest production motorcycle.

Engine: Liquid-cooled, 1,298cc, DOHC, four-stroke, inline four
Horsepower: 175 at 9,800 rpm
Top Speed: 191 miles per hour
Weight: n/a
Value Now: $$$

Suzuki's first V-twin–powered cruiser was the 1985 Intruder 700.

A cruiser with cutting-edge styling.

Hollywood's Sunset Strip, and you won't have to worry about Dead Man's Curve.

★ ★ ★

Handling, horsepower, and hyper-brakes equate to a rewarding ride.

Engine: Liquid-cooled, 1,783cc, four-stroke, 54-degree V-twin
Horsepower: 127 at 6,200 rpm

Top Speed: n/a
Weight: 764 pounds
Value Now: $$

### Redefining the power-cruiser class

The Suzuki M109R is easy to spot by its streamlined, trapezoid-shaped headlight cover and bodywork, inverted front fork, and 240mm rear tire. It's a cruiser model loaded with top-shelf technology, such as Suzuki's dual throttle valve (SDTV) injection system and race-proven composite electrochemical material (SCEM) that lines the cylinders for better heat transfer and tighter piston-to-cylinder tolerances. Moreover, the M109R's two-into-one-into-two stainless-steel exhaust system features Suzuki's digitally controlled exhaust tuning (SET) that enhances the engine's exceptionally wide powerband. But beyond the engine's stunning performance, the M109R warrants a ride because it handles so well. In the words of one website ride review: "This is a motorcycle for guys who want hyper-bike performance in a cruiser riding style."

## Triton

### Chinese menu special

Norton's Featherbed frame was thought by many riders to offer the best handling of any production bike at the time. But Norton's 650cc and 750cc engines had an inherent mechanical limitation—when revved past 7,000 rpm, the length of the stroke made the pistons move too fast, and stuff broke. Triumph engines used more-square cylinders and had strong bottom ends. So pick a frame from column A and an engine from column B. Eventually, dropping Triumph twins into Featherbed frames became so popular you could buy kits to make the job easier. Or you could bring a frame and motor to a shop and they'd build a Triton for you. Some would even sell you a complete, already-built Triton. But where's the fun in that?

The trick was getting the Triumph engine positioned low enough in the frame. A low center of gravity was how the Featherbed worked its magic.

An incredibly cheap (at least in the 1970s) alternative to a high-priced Italian bike of comparable performance.

North Circular Road past the Ace Café, London, United Kingdom.

✴ or ✴✴✴✴✴
Depends on the bike. Some are wonderfully built; others are horribly wrong.

Engine: Various Triumph twins
Horsepower: Depends on engine and tuning
Top Speed: Depends on engine and tuning
Weight: n/a
Value Now: Depends on quality of build

The first successful importer for Triumph motorcycles was Reggie Pink's dealership in New York City.

 The 1938 model year marked the first time that Triumph offered a twin-cylinder engine.

 Huntington Station, New York, to visit 20th Century Cycles, where you can hang out with singer Billy Joel. The "Piano Man" appreciates old bikes, and no doubt he'll produce an ivory smile when he sets his eyes on this early twin.

 ★ ★ ★
Wear your leather with pride because this was Edward Turner's first twin-cylinder design for Triumph.

Engine: Air-cooled, 498cc, four-stroke, vertical twin
Horsepower: 26 at 6,000 rpm
Top Speed: 100 miles per hour
Weight: 365 pounds
Value Now: $$$

**The first (along with the Tiger 100) twin-cylinder Triumph**

The world didn't shift on its axis in 1937, but a rather noteworthy event took place that year among the world's motorcyclists—Triumph introduced its first twin-cylinder model. Edward Turner, Triumph's chief designer and managing director, launched the Triumph Speed Twin at the 1937 National Motorcycle Show as a 1938 model. Actually, there were two models, the 5T Speed Twin and the slightly faster Tiger 100, which came on line for the 1939 model year. Both models proved popular, establishing Triumph once and for all as a major player in the world's market, establishing the prototype for what would become the prototypical English motorcycle engine design.

# Triumph

## Thunderbird 6T

**The first Triumph motorcycle with a 650cc engine**
Edward Turner read the American motorcycle market well
when he gave orders to increase the size of Triumph's
500cc parallel twin engine in 1949. What rolled out of the
Meriden factory in England was a bike mimicking the size
of the lightweight Speed Twin but with an additional 150cc
under the overhead-valve cylinder heads. Thus was born the
Thunderbird, and to prove its mettle, Triumph sent three
of them to Autodrome de Montlhéry in France for a 500-
mile speed endurance test. All three bikes passed with flying
colors, averaging 90 miles per hour (with stops), and all
three bikes posted fast laps in excess of 100 miles per hour.

 Advertising literature in 1950 proclaimed that the Thunderbird
was "the motorcycle for which American riders have long
been waiting."

 The bike that Marlon Brando's Johnny rode in the movie *The
Wild One.*

 A ride into Hollister, California—the farm town portrayed as
Wrightsville in the movie *The Wild One.*

 ★ ★ ★ ★ ★
Wear them like Marlon Brando did in *The Wild One.*

Engine: Air-cooled, 649cc,
    four-stroke, parallel twin
Horsepower: 34 at 6,000 rpm

Top Speed: 100 miles per hour
Weight: 385 pounds
Value Now: $$$

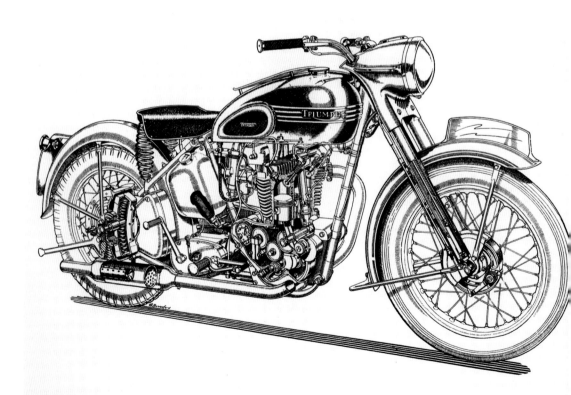

## TR5 Trophy

 The Fonz of *Happy Days* fame rode—well, sat on—a TR5 Trophy during scenes for the 1970s sitcom television show.

 The off-road model that was inspired by Triumph's three manufacturer team trophy bikes that won gold medals at the 1948 International Six Days Trials.

 Take a hot lap around Paramount Studios, where *Happy Days* was filmed. Quiet on the set, everybody!

 ★ ★ ★ ★ ★
Heyyyyyy, if it's good enough for Arthur Fonzarelli, it's good enough for us!

Engine: Air-cooled, 498cc,
   four-stroke, parallel twin
Horsepower: 25 at 6,000 rpm

Top Speed: n/a
Weight: n/a
Value Now: $$$

### A lightweight, agile, and powerful off-road bike for its time

Hot on the heels of winning three gold medals at the 1948 International Six Days Trials in Italy, Triumph brought out the TR5 Trophy. This off-road model was lightweight and nimble, and its engine was based on the proven 500cc Speed Twin. The TR5 Trophy led to more competition-based Triumphs too, including the T100 (pictured below with road going Daytona). Among Triumph's triumphs in America were wins at such notable races as the Catalina Grand Prix and Daytona 200. If you have any doubts about how cool the TR5 Trophy was, consider this: James Dean, a hardcore racing fan, selected a TR5 Trophy as his personal ride.

# Triumph

## 3TA Twenty-One

### A crying shame

Does "Twenty-One" stand for the number of years Triumph Engineering Company had been in business when the 3TA was launched, or was it a reference to the bike's displacement in cubic inches? We'll probably never really know for sure. Triumph advertised that the Twenty-One offered "brilliant performance" and set "a new standard in roadholding," but it wasn't enough. Dubbed "the Bathtub" because of its fully enclosed rear end, the 3TA was a sales failure in the United States. For some reason, the bulky bodywork and scooterlike under-seat storage compartment just didn't attract American buyers, despite the interesting new unit-construction engine. Altogether a pity, since the tool kit that came with the bike was superb.

 Many U.S. Triumph dealers replaced the cumbersome rear body panels and front fender in order to make the Twenty-One more appealing to buyers.

 This was the first Triumph with a unit-construction engine and gearbox.

 The B4110 south from Coventry, England.

 ★ ★
It has fender skirts. Skirts! Not cool.

Engine: Air-cooled, 349cc, OHV, four-stroke twin
Horsepower: 18 at 4,500 rpm
Top Speed: 80 miles per hour
Weight: n/a
Value Now: $$$

Back in the 1950s, a 650cc motorcycle was considered a big bike.

 Two carbs and a modified cylinder head made for more power—and speed.

 Highway 93 leading north from Las Vegas, Nevada, to Wendover, Utah, and the Bonneville Salt Flats.

 ★ ★ ★
A British bike named after an American landmark.

| | |
|---|---|
| Engine: Air-cooled, 649cc, four-stroke, vertical twin | Top Speed: 110 miles per hour |
| | Weight: 404 pounds |
| Horsepower: 46 at 6,500 rpm | Value Now: $$$$ |

### Built in England for Americans

If looks could kill, the Triumph Bonneville might have met its demise in 1959, the year it was introduced. The original Bonneville's rather stately styling—it had valance fenders, an ungainly headlight nacelle, and stuffy colors—wasn't well received. The following year, Edward Turner's crew in England returned with a more sporty-looking design. Not that the original was a complete flop; the twin-carb engine proved a hit, establishing the Bonneville among the fastest production models anywhere. It was named to pay tribute to the Triumph-powered streamliner built by Jack Wilson and J. H. Mangham that set a land speed record of 214 miles per hour in 1956 at the Bonneville Salt Flats.

# Triumph

## Tiger T100/R

**The bike that won the Daytona 200**

Some people consider Buddy Elmore's Daytona 200 victory a miracle win because he rode a bike that his mechanic, Dick Bender, rebuilt several times during Speed Week. Triumph's chief mechanic, Cliff Guild, described the cobbled-together race engine as "floor sweepings." Due to a poor qualifying speed, Elmore started 46th in the field for the race, having to work his way up for the win. It marked Triumph's second Daytona victory ever, and in the process, the rider from Texas bumped the race average from 94.833 miles per hour to 96.582 miles per hour.

 Buddy Elmore was 30 years old when he won Daytona. His "day job" was as an electrician.

 The T100/R was a new model—only six were built—intended specifically to win Daytona.

 Daytona International Speedway for the vintage races during the early part of Bike Week.

 ★ ★ ★ ★
The T100/R was capable of lapping Daytona at more than 100 miles per hour.

Engine: Air-cooled, 500cc, four-stroke, vertical twin
Horsepower: 46.5 at 8,000 rpm

Top Speed: 150-plus miles per hour
Weight: 315 pounds
Value Now: $$$$

During 1966, about the same time that engineers were developing the Trident, another Triumph-powered streamliner driven by Bob Leppan of Detroit, Michigan, upped the land speed record to 245.66 miles per hour.

Triumph's first three-cylinder *and* 750cc engine.

Highway 1 (Blue Star Memorial Highway) in Maine, where your eyes will feast on the coastal scenery while your ears enjoy the tunes from the Trident's exhaust.

★ ★ ★
One jacket for each cylinder.

Engine: Air-cooled, 750cc, four-stroke, inline triple
Horsepower: 58 at 7,250 rpm

Top Speed: 122 miles per hour
Weight: 482 pounds
Value Now: $$$

**This three-cylinder was crowded out of the market by a four**

Edward Turner was so enamored of his own Speed Twin design that he could not conceive of anyone wanting anything more from a motorcycle. Hence, initial development work on the Triumph T150 Trident took place during clandestine meetings in dark pubs, with designs sketched out on napkins. Triumph could have launched the Trident 750 before Honda unveiled its CB750 four, but serious development had to wait until the old man retired. As a result, while the Honda's overhead-cam engine captivated the world, Trident sales remained speared to the ground, and within a few years, the model was dropped.

# Triumph

## T120R Bonneville

The original T120 was Edward Turner's final production design before his retirement.

First of the oil-in-frame models that earmark Bonnevilles from the 1970s.

No matter where you ride this model, a few miles in its saddle will make you appreciate the original Bonneville even more.

★ ★
Triumph purists feel that this model lacks much of the original Bonneville's character because the frame creates an ungainly silhouette.

Engine: Air-cooled, 649cc, four-stroke, parallel twin
Horsepower: 40 at 6,700 rpm

Top Speed: 110 miles per hour
Weight: n/a
Value Now: $$

### An old name with a new frame

Anybody seeking the reason why Triumph went out of business in 1983 can trace the demise to the 1971 Bonneville. Most people identify the oil-in-frame design as the bike's biggest shortcoming—the 4-inch-diameter backbone/oil supply gave the 1971 T120R an overall height 3 inches taller than the original Bonneville, giving the bike a tall, ungainly profile.

# Triumph

## TSS

### Too little, too late to save Triumph

Even though the TSS' engine design shared the same basic bottom end with the Bonneville, it sported eight-valve cylinder heads developed by Weslake. After developing the head design throughout the latter half of the 1970s, Triumph introduced the TSS for the 1982 model year. The TSS and cruiser-styled TSX were the smoothest twins Triumph had built up until that time. Unfortunately the Meriden firm was in the process of going into receivership and lacked the resources to fully develop the eight-valve engine, resulting in a poorly executed brilliant idea and an unreliable motorcycle.

Only 112 of the TSS models were imported to the United States.

Four valves per cylinder and a 10:1 compression ratio made for the fastest Triumph up to that time.

An autumn ride up Vermont Highway 100 is in order, during which you can enjoy the TSS' powerful engine while soaking in the New England scenery.

★ ★ ★
Even though the bike itself isn't exactly cutting edge, there's something a little rebellious about a dying company that refuses to stop developing innovative new motorcycles.

Engine: Air-cooled, 748cc, four-stroke, parallel twin
Horsepower: 58 at 6,500 rpm

Top Speed: 126 miles per hour
Weight: 422 pounds
Value Now: $$

The original Trident (the bike on which the Hurricane was based) wasn't sold in England until 1969, a year after its release to foreign markets.

 Among Craig Vetter's first complete motorcycle styling exercises.

 A cruise down Melrose Avenue, considered the free-spirit district of Los Angeles.

 ★ ★ ★
Brown and Vetter were freethinkers, so wear the jackets with pride.

Engine: Air-cooled, 740cc, four-stroke, inline triple
Horsepower: 58 at 7,250 rpm

Top Speed: 122 miles per hour
Weight: 422 pounds
Value Now: $$$

**As American as, well, a Florida hurricane**

Two men, both Americans, were instrumental in the X75 Hurricane's development for the U.S. market. Don Brown, at the time vice president and general manager for BSA, Inc. (U.S.A), commissioned free-spirited designer Craig Vetter to give the BSA Rocket 3/Triumph Trident a new look. The project was a clandestine effort by Brown and Vetter because they knew that BSA/Triumph's corporate officers in England would disapprove. As it turned out, Vetter produced a prototype that eventually was absorbed by Triumph to become the X75 Hurricane. Bold and unabashed styling didn't help with sales, but the X75 laid the groundwork for future styles to come from motorcycle manufacturers everywhere.

# A Hurricane named Vetter
the story of the last BSA motorcycle
by Joe Parkhurst

# Triumph

## Trophy 1200

### The return of England's most famous marque

When John Bloor bought the remnants of Triumph motorcycles in 1983, he was hell-bent on producing modern, competitive motorcycles rather than just resurrecting the tired old vertical twins the company had produced throughout most of the twentieth century. All the rumors and speculation about what sort of machine the revived firm would produce were answered when the 1991 Trophy 1200 rolled out of the new factory in Hinckley, England. That the bike, which boasted a fresh design from engine to chassis, told the world that the new Triumphs were not going to be rehashes of old models. The new Trophy 1200 performed well in tests, which resulted in favorable reviews by the magazine editors, but it wasn't until Bloor relented and brought back the vertical-twin Bonneville in 2001 that the company really began to take a bite out of competitors' market shares.

 By 1995, Triumph had refined the Trophy 1200 into a sport-touring model.

 Among the first of the new Triumphs to roll out of the new Hinckley plant.

 Maryhill Loops Road in Washington, the "Road to Nowhere," because ultimately that's where the Trophy went.

 ★ ★
Riding a landmark model is always rewarding. Sort of like overnighting in the same bed that George Washington once slept in.

Engine: Liquid-cooled, 1,179cc, four-stroke, inline four
Horsepower: 141 at 9,000 rpm
Top Speed: 135 miles per hour
Weight: 589 pounds
Value Now: $$

# Triumph

## T509 Speed Triple

 First-year T509s had carburetors; 1998-and-later versions utilized electronic fuel injection.

 Proof that the born-again company was serious about its products.

 Take the Speed Triple to Deal's Gap in Tennessee to slay the dragon.

 ✱ ✱ ✱
Ride the Speed Triple hard. That's what it was made to do.

Engine: Liquid-cooled, 885cc, four-stroke, inline triple
Horsepower: 108 at 9,000 rpm
Top Speed: n/a
Weight: 431 pounds
Value Now: $$

**A street fighter with street smarts**

When John Bloor brought Triumph back from the grave, the original lineup consisted of solid but conservative bikes that, while they used modern technology, were anything but cutting edge. When the company introduced the second generation of its Speed Triple in 1997, the new street fighter represented Triumph's determination to be a leader in performance and technology. Electronic fuel injection highlighted the T509's specifications chart, but it was the bike's hooligan heart and soul that helped establish Triumph's current reputation for creating some of the best-performing motorcycles on the planet.

# Triumph

## TT600

### Intended for racing, yet built for the street

By 1996, the new Triumph motorcycle company was fully committed to creating some of the best bikes in the world. But to really prove their mettle, the folks in Hinckley knew they had to go toe to toe with the Japanese manufacturers in the 600cc sportbike class, so Triumph engineers embarked on the journey. The fruits of their labor were served to the world for the 2000 model year. Unfortunately, having the testicular fortitude to take on the Japanese didn't mean that Triumph had the manufacturing expertise to produce a competitive bike; the bike was overpriced, was underpowered, and suffered from glitchy fuel injection. It was gone within three years.

 BSA acquired the original Triumph motorcycle company in early 1951.

 Triumph's (and anyone's) first attempt at competing with the Japanese in the popular 600cc sportbike class.

 This bike deserves a lap around the Isle of Man TT course. Do it on Mad Sunday, and you'll have the Mountain Section closed to one-way riding, so you can ride 100 percent.

 ★ ★ ★ ★
While it was an unsuccessful motorcycle, at least Triumph had the cajones to butt heads with the Japanese on their own turf.

Engine: Liquid-cooled, 599cc, four-stroke, inline four
Horsepower: 110 at 12,750 rpm
Top Speed: 162 miles per hour
Weight: 375 pounds
Value Now: $$

# Triumph

## Bonneville

### The same as, only different from, the original classic

A few years after John Bloor resurrected the Triumph marque he decided it was time to bring back the Bonneville name. They tacked the old name badge onto an all-new model, and the Bonneville legend was reborn.

 Work on a prototype Bonneville began in 1997, and the following year the new DOHC engine was bench-tested.

 Retro concept with new technology.

 We're going Down Under to Narromine, NSW, Australia, stopping at the Lime Grove Café, just down the road from the world's largest lime grove—10,000 lime trees!

 ★ ★
The resurrected Bonneville is one of the nicest standard motorcycles available today, but "nice" is not the stuff of rebellion.

Engine: Air-cooled, 790cc, four-stroke, parallel twin
Horsepower: 61 at 7500 rpm
Top Speed: 112 miles per hour
Weight: 453 pounds
Value Now: $$$

The original Rocket III was BSA's 750 triple, introduced in 1968.

The largest-displacement engine in production.

Set your GPS for Parkfield, California—known as earthquake central because the San Andreas Fault runs right through town—to see if the Rocket's 150 lbs-ft. of torque can jolt the fault line!

★ ★ ★
Big is good.

Engine: Liquid-cooled, 2,294cc, four-stroke, longitudinal triple
Horsepower: 140 at 6,000 rpm
Top Speed: 140 miles per hour
Weight: 704 pounds
Value Now: $$$

**A Brit bike made famous the American way—with a huge engine**

*Outrage* is the key word when describing the Rocket III, and make no mistake about it, when John Mockett and his staff set out to design the bike, it was their intention to create outrage all along. Indeed, early concept drawings included a V-6 engine, and ray-gun-style mufflers were even considered. Fortunately, Triumph's marketing staff conducted focus-group surveys to get a feel for what consumers wanted, and the responses boiled down to a big-bore engine, which the Rocket III most certainly has, straddled in a rather conventional frame. Unfortunately, its crowning glory is a gigantic, chrome-plated-plastic candy dish on the left side of the engine.

# Triumph

## Thruxton

**The only thing missing is the checkered flag**

To say the Thruxton is little more than a Bonneville with low bars and a racy seat shortchanges its classic lines. The riding position, which can be painful for those old enough to remember the original Triumphs, requires some getting used to. Still, it's worth a little pain to experience the heritage that links this modern Triumph to one of the classic production races of all time.

The Thruxton was named after the British race circuit that was site of the 1960s Thruxton 500 production-bike endurance race.

A café racer that perpetuates the classic British style made famous 50 years ago.

Track Day at the 2.4-mile Thruxton circuit. The track is set on the remains of a World War II airfield.

★ ★ ★
Earns three leather jackets just for reflecting the rebelliousness of the original rockers who rode café racers back in the day.

Engine: Air-cooled, 865cc, four-stroke, parallel twin
Horsepower: 69 at 7,250 rpm
Top Speed: 125 miles per hour
Weight: 506 pounds
Value Now: $$$

# Triumph

## Scrambler

**It's a street scrambler—emphasis on street**

Back in the 1960s, street scramblers were popular, so the natural thing was for Triumph to build a modern version. Triumph even offered an accessory kit that included number plates with the number used by Steve McQueen on his Triumph when he competed in the 1964 ISDT.

Bill Baird won nine straight AMA Grand National Enduro Championships in the 1960s riding a Triumph T100.

Film star Steve McQueen raced a similar scrambler in Southern California desert races during the 1960s.

What the heck, take it out to the Mojave Desert in Southern California where Triumph desert sleds used to rule the roost.

★ ★ ★
If you keep Steve McQueen's numbers (optional kit) on the side plates, you'll be so cool you might have to stop for another jacket.

Engine: Air-cooled, 865cc, four-stroke, parallel twin
Horsepower: 58 at 6,800 rpm
Top Speed: 115 miles per hour
Weight: 451 pounds
Value Now: $$

The new Thunderbird's engine displacement is the most of any Triumph twin ever.

 Like a phoenix rising from the ashes, the new Thunderbird revives an old model name—again.

 Cruise the boulevard or take to the highway. Choose either route, and you'll be rewarded with a nice ride.

★ ★

Even though the original Thunderbird epitomized rebellion, the latest version is pretty tame.

Engine: Liquid-cooled, 1,597cc,
  four-stroke, parallel twin
Horsepower: 85 at 4,850 rpm

Top Speed: n/a
Weight: 746 pounds
Value Now: $$$

### Looking like a Bonneville on steroids

Don't confuse the 2010 Thunderbird with the 'bird of the 1950s, the most prominent example of which was ridden by Marlon Brando in *The Wild One*. For starters, Triumph created the original Thunderbird by boring out the engine of a 500cc Speed Twin to 650cc because the firm believed it needed a *big* bike for the American market. Today's version measures 1,597cc, almost two-and-a-half times larger than Triumph's original big bike. Like Marlon Brando himself, each iteration of the Thunderbird has packed on a few pounds, but this latest version still exhibits all the good qualities of a large-bore cruiser with the benefits of a lighter, more compact bike.

# Triumph

## Daytona 675

**A larger engine ups the ante for the middleweight class**

It's only fitting that some people consider the Daytona 675 to be in a class by itself. First, there's the fact that it's a triple, a three-cylinder competing against an army of angry four-cylinders from Japan. Next, consider the oddball engine displacement of 675cc. What happened to the traditional 600cc and 750cc limits? No big deal, really, because the 675 can take on both camps. The bike has the agility of a 600 and the performance of a 750. Best of both worlds? Perhaps. But even if you find yourself riding a country road all by yourself, you'll feel that you can't be beat on this bike.

 The Daytona's three-cylinder engine produces a wider powerband than most inline fours.

 A three-cylinder middleweight!

 Any road with tight curves and high-speed straights; this bike begs to be ridden hard.

 ★ ★ ★ ★
In good hands, the 675 can keep up with much larger bikes.

Engine: Liquid-cooled, 675cc,
   four-stroke, inline triple
Horsepower: 123 at 12,500 rpm

Top Speed: n/a
Weight: 363 pounds
Value Now: $$$

# Tul-aris 800

## Two-stroke Road Racer

Before putting the Tul-aris on the racetrack, Dr. Rob Tuluie built a 500cc racer called the Tul-Da.

A home-built racer that was competitive and capable of winning road races in America.

The Tul-aris is a native of Minnesota, so a track day at Brainerd Raceway makes sense.

★ ★ ★ ★
With a power-to-weight ratio of less than 1:2, this should be an interesting ride.

Engine: Liquid-cooled, 772cc, two-stroke, parallel twin-cylinder
Horsepower: 183 at 8,700 rpm

Top Speed: n/a
Weight: 263 pounds
Value Now: $$$$

### An advanced design that was behind the times

Just when the racing world was about to toss out the two-stroke engine, along came free-thinking Dr. Rob Tuluie with his batch of two-stroke-powered road racers. Dr. T. built several racers that took advantage of various engine displacements, but perhaps his crowning glory was the 800 that placed a bike with a power-to-weight ratio of less than 1:2 on the race tarmac. The engine was based on a modified Polaris snowmobile engine, and the chassis was designed by the good doctor himself. The sum total was nothing short of stunning and remarkable.

# Ural

## Gear-Up

### Two-wheel drive for you and your comrade

It's slow, its design was based on one that helped Adolf Hitler lose the war, it's cumbersome and unwieldy, it's rather expensive, and did we mention that it's slow? Despite these and other shortcomings too numerous to address here, the Ural Gear-Up has endeared itself to motorcycle enthusiasts and outdoorsmen around the globe.

 Even without the Ural Gear-Up, communism was destined to lose the Cold War.

 It outlasted Stalin, the Politburo, and many a long, cold Russian winter.

 The foothills of the Ural Mountains, packing an AK-47 for a caribou hunt.

 ★ ★
Make that two fur-lined leather jackets.

| | |
|---|---|
| Engine: Air-cooled, 749cc, four-stroke, opposed twin | Top Speed: 62 miles per hour |
| Horsepower: 40 at 5,600 rpm | Weight: 739 pounds |
| | Value Now: $ |

# Ural

## Red October

### The hunt for Red October ends here!

The Red October was commissioned as a special edition (only 30 were made) to celebrate the 25th anniversary of the book *The Hunt for Red October*. Even though the Red October (the motorcycle, not the book) lacks the Gear-Up's two-wheel drive, the big red machine offers the same frivolous fun—and at the same glacial speeds. The eco-political system that spawned the Ural may have gone from ruble to rubble, but this hearty motorcycle design has gone on to prosper.

 Red October is a Russian celebration that commemorates the month in which the Bolshevik (Communist) government came to power.

 Perhaps the only motorcycle to be named after a novel.

 Mark your calendar for May Day when you and your comrade will proudly parade through Moscow's Red Square with a Red October.

 ★
The revolution is over, comrade—we're all capitalists now.

| | |
|---|---|
| Engine: Air-cooled, 749cc, four-stroke, opposed twin | Top Speed: 62 miles per hour |
| Horsepower: 40 at 5,600 rpm | Weight: n/a |
| | Value Now: $ |

# Velocette

## Venom

 In the early 1920s, Velocette produced a model with an overhead-camshaft, 350cc engine known as the K.

 In 1961, a modified Venom became the first motorcycle to cover 2,400 miles in a 24-hour period (100 miles per hour average).

 A winding English country road, lined with hedges and green pastures.

 ★ ★ ★ ★
Any bike that could do the ton for 24 hours on 1950s-era tires has the testicular fortitude to earn at least four leather jackets.

Engine: Air-cooled, 499cc, four-stroke single-cylinder
Horsepower: 34 at 6,200 rpm

Top Speed: 100 miles per hour
Weight: 390 pounds
Value Now: $$$$

### Setting the standard for classic British single-cylinder engines

Velocette introduced the single-cylinder Venom, conceived by Eugene Goodman and designed by Charles Udall, in November 1955. The Venom's 449cc engine had an alloy cylinder with a cast-iron liner, a high-compression piston, and a light alloy cylinder head—top-shelf equipment for the time. The engine's high camshaft with short pushrods was simpler to produce than an OHC engine, and the clutch was located between the gearbox and gearbox sprocket, an unusual layout for the time. The Venom's transmission also had cutting-edge technology, using constant-mesh, close-ratio gears. Perhaps most of all, though, the Venom was known for its rock-steady handling, thanks to its stout, brazed-lug frame. No doubt, the Venom ranks as one of the all-time great British single-cylinder motorcycles.

# Velocette

## Thruxton

### The original bike with the name Thruxton

How do you improve on an already-successful motorcycle? If it's Velocette's Venom, you give it a little more horsepower so that it goes a little faster, which Velocette did in 1965 to create the Thruxton, perhaps the most recognizable name in the company's 67-year history. Velocette's designer, Bertie Goodman, boosted the Venom's 499cc, single-cylinder engine's performance using a race-spec cylinder head equipped with larger valves. An oversize Amal Grand Prix carburetor helped give the Thruxton its most distinctive feature: a cutaway section under the gas tank to make room for the large-mouth carb. The Thruxton proved to be a popular and successful clubman racer, but even that wasn't enough to save Velocette from going out of business in 1971.

 Thruxton was named after the Hampshire track used for long-distance production races.

 The last Velocette to be made before the company went out of business in February 1971.

 Nothing short of a lap around the famous Thruxton track will do.

 ★ ★ ★ ★
If you care anything about road racing's heritage, you'll care about this bike.

Engine: Air-cooled, 499cc, four-stroke single-cylinder
Horsepower: 40 at 6,200 rpm

Top Speed: 120 miles per hour
Weight: 390 pounds
Value Now: $$$$

Polaris Industries has been in business since 1954.

Victory's first motorcycle.

Across the Great Plains, where no one can see you aboard the ugly thing.

*
Polaris gets one leather jacket for having the nerve to build such a homely motorcycle.

Engine: Air-cooled, 92-cubic-inch, four-stroke, 50-degree V-twin
Horsepower: 65 at 6,800 rpm
Top Speed: 115 miles per hour
Weight: 637 pounds
Value Now: $$

### A first effort that led to better products

For Victory's first effort, the V92C wasn't bad. The four-valve, overhead-cam engine offered plenty of torque, and overall ride comfort was on par for a cruiser, but it was the V92C's handling that proved to be its shortcoming. That, and the fact that it looked like it had been dropped on its watery head before its fontanel had fully hardened.

The V92SC was presented with *Easyriders'* V-Twin Excellence Award for Sport-Cruiser of the Year in 2001.

Victory's first performance-oriented model.

Cross over into "enemy" territory with a ride along the Mississippi River, following the Great River Road (Route 35) from St. Paul to Prairie du Chien, Wisconsin.

*
The Victory V92SC was only slightly better than the turdlike bike that preceded it.

Engine: Air-cooled, 92-cubic-inch, four-stroke, 50-degree V-twin
Horsepower: n/a
Top Speed: n/a
Weight: 630 pounds
Value Now: $

### A (baby) step in the right direction

When Victory entered the motorcycle market in 1998, the fledging company (actually a new subsidiary of Polaris Industries, established in 1954) had a lot of ground to make up on its competition, chief among them Harley-Davidson, with roots dating back to 1903. The V92C wasn't an especially great motorcycle to ride (to paraphrase one motojournalist who rode a V92C, "It could break into a low-speed wobble just cruising through the parking lot!"), and it was downright painful to look at. The Sport Cruiser, the second model from Victory, might not have been much prettier than its heinous forefather, but it did provide evidence that the Minnesota-based company was on the right track in terms of improved handling. By shaving nearly 30 pounds from the V92C, Victory had its first model that could leave a parking lot without weaving like a drunken sailor on Saturday night.

# Victory

## Vegas

**The folks from Minnesota hit the jackpot**

It didn't take Victory's engineers long to figure out how to build a reliable motorcycle that performed well in all categories. It took a couple more years to dial out the ugly. Victory exorcised the ugly with the introduction of the lovely Vegas in 2003. Suddenly the new motorcycle company from Minnesota was a serious player in the hard-fought cruiser-bike market.

 The Vegas serves as the platform for the Kingpin model line too.

 The first new Victory design since the V92C was launched in 1998.

 Where else but the Las Vegas Strip?

 ✳ ✳
It's the kind of ride you expect from a stylish cruiser.

Engine: Air-cooled, 100-cubic-inch, four-stroke, 50-degree V-twin
Horsepower: 85 at 6,800 rpm

Top Speed: 115 miles per hour
Weight: 642 pounds
Value Now: $$

---

# Victory

## Hammer S

**A hot rod in every sense of the term**

When you look at Victory's Hammer S, the words *hot rod* come to mind. In addition to an upgraded suspension, the engine of the Hammer S received more than a few hot rod tweaks, resulting in a bike that offers customlike styling with muscle-bike performance.

 The Hammer S engine was remapped, at an expense of $28,000, so that it would comply with CARB standards, making it a 50-state model.

 One of the best-handling cruiser bikes in the world.

 California State Highway 22 from Borrego Springs to Highway 79. The twisty, uphill road puts the spotlight on the Hammer S' engine and handling.

 ✳ ✳ ✳
It looks like a cruiser but behaves like a sportbike.

Engine: Air-cooled, 106-cubic-inch, four-stroke, 50-degree V-twin
Horsepower: 97 at 4,900 rpm

Top Speed: 120 miles per hour
Weight: 669 pounds
Value Now: $$

# Victory

The 849-pound Vision has an optional reverse gear.

The Vision is the motorcycle of choice for that most infamous of Hells Angels, Sonny Barger.

Follow the lead of the Victory product manager, Gary Gray, and chase down an Iron Butt SaddleSore 1000—he was the first to do it aboard a Vision.

★ ★ ★
Despite its Flash Gordon lines, the Vision is a remarkable bike to ride.

Engine: Air-cooled, 106-cubic-inch, four-stroke, 50-degree V-twin
Horsepower: 92 at 5,500 rpm

Top Speed: 115 miles per hour
Weight: 849 pounds
Value Now: $$$

**Literally, a touring bike like no other**

Victory Motorcycles engineers had two primary goals when developing the Vision: they wanted the bike to be the equal of any other touring model on the market, and they wanted people to notice it right away. In case you haven't noticed, Victory succeeded in both categories. Indeed, the Vision brings many innovative features to the touring bike world, among them a stout, aluminum frame that supports suspension fit for a more sporting motorcycle. In terms of comfort, the Vision's sleek fairing was tested in a wind tunnel to minimize wind turbulence on the rider, and other creature comforts include heated seats and hand grips with easy-reach switches and controls, an electrically adjustable windscreen, an optional anti-lock braking system, and an easy-access air valve to set air pressure for the rear shock absorber. You can decide for yourself about the Vision's cutting-edge styling.

# Vincent

## Series A Rapide

**Guaranteed 110 miles per hour at a time when 90 miles per hour was considered fast**

The logical follow-up to the success of the 500cc single-cylinder engine that powered Vincent-HRD's Meteor and Comet was to build a twin-cylinder engine that utilized the single's top-end design. Thus was born the Rapide, a bike powered by a V-twin engine that was most extraordinary for its time. When the Rapide bowed in 1936, Phil Vincent guaranteed that it would go 110 miles per hour, setting the standard for all future V-twins to roll out of the small factory in Stevenage, Hertfordshire, England.

 The Series A Rapide was dubbed the "Snarling Beast" by corporate figurehead Bill Clarke.

 When it was introduced in 1937, the Rapide was the fastest production machine on two, three, or four wheels.

 The letter roads that lace the Mojave Desert north of Los Angeles, where you can ride the Rapide WFO.

 ★ ★ ★ ★
Go ahead, take it up to 110 miles per hour. We dare ya.

Engine: Air-cooled, 998cc, four-stroke, 50-degree V-twin
Horsepower: 45 at 5,500 rpm
Top Speed: 110 miles per hour
Weight: 430 pounds
Value Now: $$$$

PHOTO "MOTOR CYCLING"

In 1947, Phil Vincent crashed a test bike while not wearing a helmet; his injuries weren't life threatening, but they prevented him from ever riding again.

 The first Vincent-HRD to exceed 100 miles per hour.

 Any fine English country road will do, eh, mate?

 ★ ★
To fully enjoy the experience, you really must ride a twin-cylinder Vincent.

Engine: Air-cooled, 499cc, four-stroke single cylinder
Horsepower: 26 at 5,600 rpm

Top Speed: 90 miles per hour
Weight: 385 pounds
Value Now: $$$$

### The swinging single of the family

After Vincent's ill-fated attempt to race at the Isle of Man TT in 1934 (all three bikes experienced engine failure), Philip Conrad Vincent and Phil Irving gave their 500cc single-cylinder engine a facelift, resulting in the Meteor and the Comet. A TT replica based on the Comet competed at the fabled Brooklands motordrome, where it posted a top speed of 101 miles per hour. In the process, Vincent-HRD became a key player in the horsepower game.

# Vincent

## Black Shadow

### A bike whose legend continues to grow

Vincent's Rapide changed the face of motorcycling, earning a reputation as the fastest production motorcycle built for its time, so it's little wonder that Phil Irving and fellow Vincent employee George Brown modified a Rapide to go even faster. That original high-performance prototype evolved into the Black Shadow, introduced to the market in 1948. The Black Shadow was intended to be a sport-touring bike, though any doubts about its status as a high-performance machine were erased by the 5-inch-diameter, 150-mile-per-hour Smith speedometer that was mounted in front of the rider. A legend was born.

 The very first Black Shadow prototype, affectionately dubbed *Gunga Din* by *Motor Cycling* magazine, still exists.

 The model that established, once and for all, Vincent's reputation for speed.

 Load the Black Shadow onto a train to traverse the Chunnel; we're going to Germany to give our Black Shadow free rein on the autobahn. Any bets that we can do 129 miles per hour?

 ★ ★ ★ ★ ★
The Vincent Black Shadow is so badass it's had a song written about it.

Engine: Air-cooled, 998cc, four-stroke, 50-degree V-twin
Horsepower: 55 at 5,700 rpm

Top Speed: 128 miles per hour
Weight: 458 pounds
Value Now: $$$$$

Despite heroic efforts attributed to the Black Shadow and Black Lightning, Vincent-HRD went into receivership in 1949.

 The Vincent that makes the Black Shadow pale by comparison.

 Gairdner Lake in Australia (Vincent designer Phil Irving's home country) for a shot at Rollie Free's 1950 land speed record.

 ★ ★ ★ ★ ★
How cool would it be to ride a Black Lightning to 150 miles per hour?

Engine: Air-cooled, 998cc, four-stroke, 50-degree V-twin
Horsepower: 70 at 5,600 rpm
Top Speed: 150 miles per hour
Weight: 380 pounds
Value Now: $$$$$

**Proof that less can be more—in this case, more speed**
The Black Lightning was essentially a stripped-down Black Shadow that also sported a few engine modifications for more horsepower—and speed. Inspiration for the Lightning came from American hot rodder Rollie Free, whose modified Black Shadow set speed records at the inaugural Bonneville Nationals in 1948. The Black Lightning amounted to nothing more than a factory racer, and records indicate that only 31 were built between 1948 and 1954. Among the features that set it apart from the Black Shadow was its 180-mile-per-hour speedometer.

# Vincent

## Grey Flash

**Not all fast Vincents had V-twin engines**

Like the Black Lightning, the Grey Flash was based on an existing model, in this case the Comet. And, like the Black Lightning, the Grey Flash's engine was given a heavy dose of hot rod parts that boosted its performance enough to make it competitive in various forms of racing. The Grey Flash was available as a stripped racer or in two road-legal configurations, one that included a bevy of even more speed parts. And, finally, like the Black Lightning, only 31 Grey Flashes were built.

 John Surtees, the only man to win Grand Prix World Championships with motorcycles *and* cars, raced a Grey Flash.

 A race-ready Vincent for the popular 500cc class.

 A lap around England's fabled Brands Hatch road-race circuit will do.

 ★ ★ ★ ★ ★
If you can master this bike on a road-race course, you deserve all five jackets.

Engine: Air-cooled, 499cc, four-stroke single-cylinder
Horsepower: 35 at 6,200 rpm
Top Speed: 110 miles per hour
Weight: 330 pounds
Value Now: $$$$$

Four years after Free's remarkable feat, Tommy Smith wore the same attire at the Salt Flats during his ride on a Triumph. He crashed at 140 miles per hour, sustaining considerable road rash that led to numerous skin grafts. Kids, don't try this at home.

The first motorcycle to top 150 miles per hour in America.

Bonneville's Salt Flats, of course; swimsuit is optional.

★ ★ ★ ★ ★
Think about it. Rollie Free rode this thing 150 miles per hour. On salt. Wearing a bathing suit. Do the math.

| | |
|---|---|
| Engine: Air-cooled, 998cc, four-stroke, 50-degree V-twin | Top Speed: 150.313 miles per hour |
| Horsepower: n/a | Weight: Less than 458 pounds |
| | Value Now: $$$$$ |

### Think of it as Vincent-HRD's swimsuit issue

One of the most famous motorcycle racing photos of all time shows a guy wearing only a bathing cap and swimsuit, lying prone on a Vincent while at speed. That's Rollie Free aboard a modified Black Shadow during his fabled record run of 150-plus miles per hour. The Vincent belonged to John Edgar and was sponsored by Mobil Oil when it broke Joe Petrali's American land speed record of 136 miles per hour, setting the new mark at more than 150 miles per hour. Free stripped to his swimsuit because he felt that his racing leathers were creating too much drag. He was right; prior to the swimsuit run he could only muster 148 miles per hour.

## Black Prince

**Sporting body armor before body armor was fashionable**

For some reason, Phil Vincent felt the need to envelop a Black Shadow in a full-piece body, resulting in the Black Prince. The model sparked controversy, to which Vincent himself responded in his autobiography years later: "To hear riders getting heated about the looks of machines frankly bores me. Motorcycles are supposed to be ridden—and one cannot see the model when one is riding it." True, but one must "see the model" before mounting it to ride.

 The Black Prince wasn't well received when it was offered in 1954. But then, you probably already knew that.

 The Black Knight (based on the Rapide) joined the Black Prince, and they were, mercifully, the only Vincents with fully enclosed body systems.

 Even though the Black Prince might resemble a carnival ride, we'll keep it on the public highway nonetheless.

 ✴ ✴
For obvious reasons, this bike just doesn't look "Vincent tough."

Engine: Air-cooled, 998cc, four-stroke, 50-degree V-twin
Horsepower: 55 at 5,700 rpm

Top Speed: 125 miles per hour
Weight: 460 pounds
Value Now: $$$$$

# Yamaha

Yamaha sold performance parts—known as GYT Kits—for the YL-1 and other models.

Perhaps the first Japanese-made multi-cylinder engine under 125cc.

Enter the little Yammie in the Moto Giro, USA. This is the perfect all-day ride for that event.

★ ★

There's something compelling about riding a bike with a 100cc two-cylinder engine.

| | |
|---|---|
| Engine: Air-cooled, 97cc, two-stroke, parallel twin | Top Speed: 65 miles per hour |
| Horsepower: 9.5 at 8,500 rpm | Weight: 180 pounds |
| | Value Now: $$$ |

**A "teacup" engine with "teapot" performance**

Advertisements in 1966 proclaimed that the YL-1 was based on Yamaha's Grand Prix–winning 125cc road racers. That was probably a stretch, but it didn't matter; the little roadster, powered by its own twin-cylinder 100cc engine, was and still is a classic. The two-stroke engine made use of Yamaha's new-at-the-time Autolube oil injection system that eliminated the need to pre-mix the oil with gasoline. If you kept the oil reservoir filled, you were good to go simply by topping off the gas tank.

# Yamaha

## DT-1

**The bike that gave dual-purpose singular meaning**

Yamaha could have paraphrased Honda's legendary advertising slogan to read "You Meet the Nicest People Off Road" when it launched the DT-1 in 1968. No other motorcycle had such an impact on off-road riding as this little dual-purpose wonder. The DT-1 was all things at once: it was affordable, street legal, off-road-capable, and easy to ride in all conditions. It may not have been the best dirtbike on the market, and it didn't necessarily excel on the public roads, either. But let the record show that its dual purpose in life opened the doors for a whole new market for the motorcycle industry.

 The White Brothers—Dan and Tom—got their start racing a modified DT-1. Their racing success allowed them to open their first shop in Garden Grove, California.

 This was the first of the Japanese-made enduros, making this a landmark motorcycle for off-roaders.

 Follow Silverado Canyon Road in Orange County, California, to its end, where it melds into a fire road leading up and over Santiago Peak. Turn left onto Ortega Highway to Lake Elsinore, where you'll pay homage to the original Elsinore Grand Prix of *On Any Sunday* fame.

 ★ ★ ★
Trade your leather for an authentic Belstaff jacket; you'll almost feel the clock tick back in time if you do.

Engine: Air-cooled, 246cc, two-stroke single-cylinder
Horsepower: 18 at 6,000 rpm

Top Speed: 70 miles per hour
Weight: 231 pounds
Value Now: $$$

# Yamaha

## RD350/400

Eddie Lawson raced an RD350 before he aspired to become a four-time 500cc Grand Prix world champion.

Amateur club racers across America relied on this affordable pocket rocket to win races—sometimes against bikes with engines having three times as much displacement.

Angeles Crest Highway—with no traffic either direction.

★ ★ ★ ★
Despite its diminutive size (engine and chassis), on a twisty road and with a capable rider on board, this bike can give fits to larger bikes.

| | |
|---|---|
| Engine: Air-cooled, 347cc/399cc, two-stroke twin-cylinder | Top Speed: 98 miles per hour (400F) |
| Horsepower: 30 (400F at rear wheel) at 7,500 rpm | Weight: 355 pounds (400F) |
| | Value Now: $$$ |

### The giant-killer of the 1970s

The term *punk racer* gained significance when Yamaha launched the R5 (piston-port engine) in 1970 and later the RD350 (reed-valve induction) in 1973. The two-stroke engine and chassis were based on hardware that the factory had tried, tested, and won with on the road-race courses of the world in the guise of the RD56 (250cc Grand Prix racer) and later the TD and TR production racers (250cc and 350cc, respectively). That the street-legal RD350 (and its 250cc sister and later the RD400) shared so much of the purebred racers' technology said a lot about Yamaha's commitment to its customers. And RD customers responded, not only with stellar sales, but they also won countless races all across America.

# Yamaha

## XS-1

**Just when the British wanted out of the 650 vertical twin market, Yamaha jumped in**

Yamaha's XS-1, powered by a 650cc, twin-cylinder engine, hit the market at precisely the wrong time—Honda had just launched its 750cc inline four and Kawasaki startled the world with its potent three-cylinder Mach III. Yet of all those models, the Yamaha lasted the longest, with the final edition—in the guise of the XS-650—rolling off the assembly line in 1985.

 Yamaha originally considered marketing a 650cc, vertical-twin two-stroke, but research revealed that American riders preferred the throaty sound of a four-stroke engine over the oil-burner's annoying popping noise.

 Kenny Roberts won his two AMA Grand National Championships racing bikes with modified versions of the XS-1 engine.

 Little Tokyo in London, England—if there is such a place.

 ★ ★
Every year, Yamaha's 650 twin gains even more fans, but how rebellious can you be aboard a clone of a British classic?

Engine: Air-cooled, 654cc, SOHC, four-stroke, vertical twin
Horsepower: 53 at 7,000 rpm

Top Speed: 100 miles per hour
Weight: 450 pounds
Value Now: $$

# Yamaha

## XS-650G Special II

**Spoke-laced wheels, bobbed fenders, trumpet mufflers, teardrop gas tank—it all adds up to Fonzie cool with a shot of saki.**

A contingent of Yamaha's American motorcycle designers—led by sales marketing maven Ed Burke—cut up an otherwise stock XS-650 in 1977 and created a new genre of bike: the crusier. The fruits of their labor resulted in the XS-650 Special, which signified Yamaha's interpretation of what an American cruiser should be.

 By the time Yamaha ceased production of its 650 twin-cylinder model, it had built nearly a quarter-million units.

 The 1977 XS-650 Special was the first Yamaha to don chopper-like styling.

 Any tree-lined road that leads to a diner serving vanilla milkshakes made with real ice cream.

 ★ ★ ★
It may be a lackluster bike, but in reality, the XS-650G did a pretty good job of executing the custom theme.

Engine: Air-cooled, single overhead camshaft, 654cc, four-stroke, vertical twin
Horsepower: n/a

Top Speed: 110 miles per hour
Weight: 463 pounds
Value Now: $$$

## Production TD, TA, TR, and TZ Road Racers

Don Emde's 1972 Daytona 200 win aboard a TR3 350 was the first time a two-stroke won the prestigious race.

Affordable production-based road racers for privateers.

Any road-racetrack in America, nay, the world, where the Yamahas dominated for so many years.

★ ★ ★ ★
You'll get a full five-leather-jacket salute if you wheelie across the finish line.

Engine: Air- or liquid-cooled; 125cc, 250cc, 350cc, two-stroke; single, parallel, twin-cylinder
Horsepower: n/a
Top Speed: n/a
Weight: n/a
Value Now: $$$$

### Race-winning heritage from the early TD up to the remarkable TZ models

For more than four decades, Yamaha offered what no other motorcycle company could match: race-ready motorcycles for privateers. From the TD models of the mid-1960s through the latest TZ250 that was sold in the twenty-first century, the crate racers won countless national and world road racing championships.

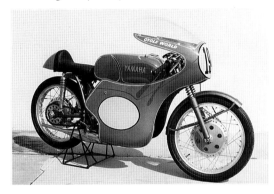

## TZ700/750

Kel Carruthers, 1960 250cc Grand Prix world champion, was among the first non-Japanese racers to ride the TZ700 during its developmental stage in late 1973.

This model dominated road racing throughout the 1970s, effectively changing the face of the sport in the process.

Any road-race course on the planet, and you can bet that you'll scare yourself silly.

★ ★ ★ ★ ★
Make 'em big, round, hairy leather jackets too.

Engine: Liquid-cooled, 700cc, two-stroke, inline four
Horsepower: 145 at 10,000 rpm (700cc)
Top Speed: 180 miles per hour
Weight: 345 pounds
Value Now: $$$$$

### Horsepower, not handling, was its forte

Make no mistake, a few hot laps aboard a well-tuned TZ750, and you'll grow hair on the palms of your hands. This bike places 145-plus horsepower into a spindly frame that's supported by wobbly suspension that relies on second-rate tires for traction. But in the skilled hands of pro racers like Kenny Roberts, Steve Baker, and a handful of others, the big two-stroke conquered the world.

# Yamaha

## TX500

### Third time's a charm

The company's third foray into four-strokes, the TX500 was Yamaha's first attempt at giving each cylinder four valves. As it did with the XS650 motor, Yamaha seems to have studied the British version of a 500cc vertical twin and then made it better. Or maybe the TX500's engine owes more to the 180-degree-crankshaft twin Honda used in its CR77. Then again, its pentproof cylinder head could be based on an old Offenhauser racing engine. Wherever it came from, *Cycle* magazine thought it worked. The writers also liked the bike's handling: "Circular freeway on-ramps are especially enjoyable!" they gushed. And not without reason—the TX500 was a fun bike to ride. It could even get you into trouble.

 Because of its 180-degree crankshaft, the TX500's power was kind of sneaky.

 The first DOHC Yammie.

 The Great River Road along the Mississippi River, all the way from Itasca State Park in Minnesota to the End of Road marker in Venice, Louisiana.

 ★ ★ ★
Cool new engine, nice-handling frame, excellent brakes. But it still seems like an imitation of something.

Engine: Air-cooled, 500cc, DOHC, four-stroke twin
Horsepower: 50 at 9,000 rpm

Top Speed: 110 miles per hour
Weight: n/a
Value Now: $$

Yamaha was considering marketing a similar street model powered by a four-cylinder, two-stroke engine.

This was Yamaha's first 750cc, four-stroke engine design.

Pennsylvania's stretch of U.S. Highway 15 that parallels the lazy Susquehanna River would be a great ride. Among the sights are closed-down steel mills.

★ ★ ★
The Yamaha's throaty exhaust note made the bike sound tougher than it really was.

Engine: Air-cooled, 744cc,
   four-stroke, vertical twin
Horsepower: 63 at 7,500 rpm

Top Speed: 105 miles per hour
Weight: 518 pounds
Value Now: $

## The right idea at the wrong time

At a time when multi-cylinder engines were in vogue (thank Honda and Kawasaki for that), Yamaha elected to jump into the fray with a pair of twins, the TX500 and TX750. Of the two, the 750 certainly offered more bang for the buck, and in truth, the overhead-cam engine produced good low-end torque. Good thing too, because over time the engine's crankshaft assembly proved vulnerable to complete destruction when exposed to sustained high rpm, meaning that the engines in most TX750s have been beaten into duck butter by now. Part of the TX750's mechanical woes could be traced to its Omni-Phase counterbalance system that was intended to smooth out the twin-cylinder engine's vibration harmonics. Otherwise, the TX750 was a very pleasant motorcycle to ride, at least before its engine disintegrated.

# Yamaha

## SC500

**Yamaha's first motocross entry into the Open Class**

*Dirt Bike* magazine stated in its test of the 1973 Yamaha SC500: "A classic Japanese approach to something they have never done before—get all the details right and utterly fail on the basic concept of the package. As it stands now, the SC500 doesn't fit anywhere. But the forks don't leak." Writers also pointed out how the big 500cc engine had practically no low-end power, but spool it to redline, and it could dig a trench deep enough to bury the bike. Even so, the SC500 marked Japan's entry into the Open Class for motocross racing, and within a few years, bikes from Japan would dominate that class.

 Heikki Mikkola of Finland won Yamaha's first 500cc motocross world championship in 1977.

 Yamaha's first big-bore motocrosser. It was fast, and it was a handful to ride fast.

 Watching your buddy ride the bike, pulling an unplanned wheelie in the process.

 ★ ★ ★
A big, pipey, two-stroke engine cradled in a motocross chassis with very little suspension travel. You do the math.

Engine: Air-cooled, 496cc, two-stroke single-cylinder
Horsepower: 40 at 6,800 rpm
Top Speed: 70 miles per hour
Weight: 236 pounds
Value Now: $$

The design team's motto was "a yen for every gram." The idea was to make the XT500 as light as possible.

 Won the Paris–Dakar Rally in 1979, the first year it was held.

 From Paris, France, to Dakar, Senegal (but you'd better wear bulletproof riding gear).

 ★ ★ ★ ★ ★
Mel Hannah rode one.

Engine: Air-cooled, 499cc, SOHC, four-stroke single
Horsepower: 32 at 6,500 rpm
Top Speed: 101 miles per hour
Weight: n/a
Value Now: $$

**First take's a keeper**

Bob Hannah learned to ride from his dad, Mel. Bob got pretty competent, so it's safe to surmise he might have had a good teacher. Mel rode a Triumph 650 in the desert near their home, and Bob started tagging along on a homemade minibike when he was old enough. The point of all this is that Mel Hannah knew a thing or two about bikes, and he got an XT500 when they came out. That should be all you need to know. If you're still not convinced, consider this: Cyril Neveu won the motorcycle division of the very first Paris–Dakar Rally on an XT500. It's altogether not bad for the first four-stroke single the tuning fork people ever built.

# Yamaha

## YZ250

### A very bad business decision

Yamaha caused quite a stir at the 1973 Belgian Grand Prix
when the team showed up with a bike that, apparently,
had no rear shock absorbers. Internally coded the YZ637,
the Yamaha YZ250 was the first monoshock factory
works motocross bike. It's fitting that its debut was in
Belgium because a Belgian, Lucien Tilkens, developed the
monoshock. Suzuki was the dominant force in motocross
racing at the time, so he took his idea to that company first.
He altered a spare works frame Suzuki gave him and took
it to a secret test. It performed better than the dual-shock
version, but Tilkens couldn't explain it in mathematical
terms to the Suzuki engineers. Suzuki passed. Turns out,
there was no magical explanation except that it just had lots
more travel. Lucky Yamaha was Tilkens' next stop.

Dr. Tilkens first experimented with the monoshock rear
suspension design on a Sylvain Geboers 1969 factory
works YZ380.

The YZ250 was the first production motocrosser to use the
monoshock rear suspension design.

Beating a twin-shock RM250 from the same year would
be perfect.

★ ★ ★ ★ ★
It changed the whole world of motorcycling.

Engine: Liquid-cooled, 249cc,   Top Speed: n/a
   reed-valve, two-stroke single   Weight: n/a
Horsepower: 46.8 at 8,800 rpm   Value Now: $$

# Yamaha

## RD400F Daytona Special

The Daytona Special was the only RD model that had footpegs mounted above the mufflers for maximum cornering clearance.

The Daytona Special was the last of the air-cooled, RD-powered Yamahas.

Not Daytona Beach, Florida! We'll fill the oil reservoir with Yamahalube before heading out to the roads near Malibu, California, stopping, of course, at the Rock Store so that people can admire our ride.

★ ★ ★
In capable hands, the RD400F can stay with many larger bikes on a twisty road.

Engine: Air-cooled, 399cc, two-stroke, parallel twin
Horsepower: n/a
Top Speed: 100 miles per hour
Weight: 355 pounds
Value Now: $$$$

**America quit smoking after 1979—temporarily, that is**

Federal clean-air laws were the deciding factor in removing two-stroke motorcycles from America's highways, but Yamaha didn't go without a fight. Witness the RD400F, an oil-burner that was awash in clean-air technology. Those emission monitors didn't throttle back the Daytona Special's performance, though, and this model checked in as the best-performing RD of all time.

# Yamaha

## RZ500 Daytona

Kenny Roberts won the 500cc Grand Prix World Championship the first three seasons he competed in Europe (1978–1980).

The first 500cc Grand Prix two-stroke replica-racer from Japan.

Laguna Seca Raceway, where Kenny Roberts won his final AMA Grand National road race in 1984 aboard a square four OW69.

★ ★ ★ ★ ★
King Kenny, step aside and make way for King (your name here).

Engine: Liquid-cooled, 499.7cc, two-stroke, 50-degree V-4
Horsepower: 90 at 9,500 rpm
Top Speed: 136 miles per hour
Weight: 439 pounds
Value Now: $$$$$

**Excuse me for the next few miles while I pretend that I'm Kenny Roberts**

Back in the motorcycle industry's Dark Ages, many of the replica-racers that Japan et al. offered weren't allowed on America's public roads, thanks to stringent EPA regulations. Among the bikes banned from the United States was Yamaha's RZ500, a bike that was the closest thing to a 500cc GP bike as you could get back in 1984. The RZ500 actually used reed-valve induction (versus rotary valves used on Yamaha's factory GP bikes), but that didn't matter. That spunky V-4 engine served up the same on-track gratification as you imagine those factory-tuned racers would give. And that was good enough for any frustrated wannabe racer back in those dark days.

# Yamaha

## XV920RJ

**It's like a Ducati, only cheaper and easier to maintain**

By the early 1980s, Japan's motorcycle manufacturers recognized that American riders were becoming more and more enamored with the V-twin engine layout. Yamaha was first to answer the call with its Virago 750 Special in 1981. A pair of bikes powered by a 920cc version of the same engine soon followed. One of those bikes was the XV920RJ, a motorcycle touted by some members of the American press as the Euro Virago, a name you won't find on any sales brochure, however. The bike was predictable in steering and handling through corners, and it offered a firm, steady ride in a straight line. It also was styled differently enough that you either wanted it for your very own or wouldn't give it a second glance on the showroom floor.

 The original Virago 750 V-twin engine was adapted by Mert Lawwill and Kenny Roberts in 1981 to compete in the AMA Grand National flat-track series.

 A Ducati in Samurai clothing, the XV920 offered the agility of the Italian marque but at a more affordable price.

 California's State Highway 166 north of Santa Maria offers the gentle twists and turns that make riding the XV920 so rewarding.

 ★ ★ ★ ★ ★
The XV920 isn't known for its rebel factor, but rest assured, when you pull up at the local roadhouse, that air-cooled V-twin engine should muster a curious crowd.

Engine: Air-cooled, 920cc, four-stroke V-twin
Horsepower: n/a

Top Speed: 112 miles per hour
Weight: 509 pounds
Value Now: $$$

Sales were poor for the 1982 model, so Yamaha returned the following year with a full touring fairing for this middleweight bike. It didn't help sales.

 The 550 Vision was the first Japanese motorcycle to utilize a downdraft carburetor.

 Take the Vision to the Hill Country east of Austin, Texas, where you can spend the day meandering over the winding roads while you drain the 550's 4.5-gallon gas tank.

 ★ ★
Yawn . . . it's a 550 that's slow to wake up (road tests from the time emphasize how cold-blooded the liquid-cooled engine could be).

Engine: Liquid-cooled, 553cc, four-stroke V-twin
Horsepower: 65 at 9500 rpm
Top Speed: 112 miles per hour
Weight: 467 pounds
Value Now: $

**High in style and technology, low in sales**

The 550 Vision was hailed by most technophiles in 1982 as an engineering masterpiece; a V-twin alternative to the four-cylinder models that dominated the market during the early 1980s. The V-twin engine's 70-degree cylinder placement promoted a compact package that also looked high tech, especially given that it was liquid cooled at a time when air cooling dominated most engine designs. The narrow motorcycle handled well through the turns, was predictable in steering, and scored high marks in braking. The chink in the Vision's armor proved to be a hard-starting engine during cold start-ups. The problem was later traced to a casting error inside the downdraft carburetor and was rather easy to fix. But the fix came too late, and the Vision was blindsided by poor sales in the United States.

# Yamaha

## XJ650 Turbo

### Oh, what might have been

According to *Cycle World*, "The Turbo Seca transforms itself from motorcycle to superbike and back again with ease, and the transformation is simply controlled by the right wrist." Yamaha introduced the XJ650 Turbo in 1982 as an answer to Honda's CX500 Turbo. But it wasn't quite the correct answer, so Yamaha engineers fiddled with the turbocharger, and the 1983 model got it right. However, an air-cooled engine was seen as a strange choice for turbocharging. How would the turbo cope with the heat? Just fine, it turned out. If the engine hadn't simply been thrown into a stock XJ650 frame, the XJ650 Turbo might have changed the world. But it was, so it didn't.

 Model year 1982 XJ650 Turbos were so anemic that Yamaha distributed "Power-Up" kits free of charge to owners. Enterprising riders just disconnected the wastegate vacuum hose and plugged up the holes instead. Boost jumped from 7 psi to 14.

 This bike made Yamaha give up on turbocharging.

 Someplace close: it eats gas.

 ★★
Turbocharging is cool. Fast bikes that don't handle well are not.

Engine: Air-cooled, 653cc, turbocharged, DOHC, four-stroke, inline four
Horsepower: 90 at 9,000 rpm

Top Speed: 126 miles per hour
Weight: n/a
Value Now: $$

# Yamaha

## FJ1200

**The "Big Easy"**

Yamaha introduced the FJ1100 in 1984. It was well received and became the standard for sport-tourers. In 1986, Yamaha gave it a bigger engine and better suspension. The FJ1200 is still regarded as a capable sport-tourer today, even though it's been out of production for almost a decade and a half. Its secret is the ease with which it does its job. Other bikes were lighter, faster, and more powerful, but none could rack up miles like the FJ. Well, they could, but they left their riders wishing they had an FJ after a day and longing for their La-Z-Boys after three.

In a surprising move, when Yamaha engineers designed the new FJ engine, they opted for air cooling rather than liquid.

First of the real sport-tourers—bikes with powerful engines, good handling, and actual comfort.

Someplace very far away.

★ ★ ★ ★
Good performance and actual all-day riding comfort.

Engine: Air-cooled, 1,188cc, DOHC, four-stroke, inline four
Horsepower: 130 at 9,000 rpm
Top Speed: n/a
Weight: n/a
Value Now: $$$

# Yamaha

## FJ600

**A competent ride that will satisfy but not thrill you; the engine's mechanical noise is a bonus**

When taken at face value, it's hard to see the appeal of Yamaha's FJ600. By the time Yamaha brought the bike to the market, its air-cooled, two-valve-per-cylinder engine was already antiquated technology. But there's something to be said about a middleweight sportbike that doesn't necessarily dazzle your senses but nonetheless rewards you with a pleasant ride no matter where you take it. Yamaha's FJ600 is such a bike. This mid-1980s midweight offers plenty of power from its inline four engine, and handling is on par with what you expect from a 1980s-era bike. The basic platform proved so sound that it lived on for many years as the budget-priced Yamaha Radian 600, then with a mild reworking experienced yet a third lease on life as the Yamaha XJ600 Seca II.

 *Cycle Guide* magazine compared five middleweight sportbikes in its July 1984 issue, and the FJ600 posted the quickest quarter-mile time.

 The FJ600 represented Yamaha's entry into the middleweight market that was becoming so popular during the mid-1980s.

 Tour north-central Minnesota to take in the state's finest hardwood forests and dine on fresh walleye fish during a cruise around famous Mille Lacs Lake.

 *
The FJ600 is a worthy ride and is representative of what was offered back in the 1980s, but it's about as rebellious as a church pew.

Engine: Air-cooled, 598cc, four-stroke, inline four-cylinder
Horsepower: n/a
Top Speed: 126 miles per hour
Weight: 435 pounds
Value Now: $

The Fazer FZX700 was imported to America for only two years, 1986 and 1987.

Scary quick like a V-Max but with a much more affordable price tag.

On the same roads that you'll find Mr. V-Max, where the lanes are straight and narrow.

★ ★ ★ ★
Inadequate brakes and soft suspension make the ride even more thrilling.

| | |
|---|---|
| Engine: Liquid-cooled, 698cc, four-stroke, inline four | Top Speed: 130 miles per hour |
| | Weight: 440 pounds |
| Horsepower: 85 at 9,500 rpm | Value Now: $$ |

### "The start of a new generation of motorcycles."— Cycle News

The Fazer FZX700 was sold elsewhere in the world as the FZX750, but for the U.S. market, the engine sported de-bored cylinders to keep it under 700cc so that it wasn't subject to the federally imposed import tariffs on motorcycles with engines larger than 700cc. The tax was created to counter the price dumping that had taken place prior to 1984 by various Japanese brands. Losing 50cc did little to hamper the Fazer 700's performance, however; magazine tests from the era report that this tariff-fighter held its own in terms of acceleration against bikes with much larger engines. The reason: the Fazer 700 shared the same basic five-valve cylinder head that was used on the FZ750 sportbike. The Fazer's cam timing gave the engine slightly more low- and midrange power, though.

# Yamaha

## V-Max

**Superfast flexi-flyer**

Of Yamaha's original Godzilla-like 1985 V-Max, Jeff Karr wrote, "I saw Jesus so many times, I started using him as a braking marker." What Mr. Karr so eloquently alluded to was the bike's tendency toward a high-speed weave, courtesy of a chassis several steps behind its engine, technology-wise. That hardly mattered to customers. While the V-Max might have been cavalier about stability, it was heart-attack serious about acceleration. A claimed 140 horsepower made it the quickest motorcycle a consumer could buy 20-plus years ago. Its brutal, hairy-chested approach to speed kept it in Yamaha's lineup until a replacement finally arrived in 2009.

 The V-Max has outlived every one of its contemporaries—achieving a near-25-year lifespan, which is virtually unheard of for motorcycles or cars.

 In its day, the V-Max was the quickest motorcycle you could buy.

 Down any quarter-mile-long strip of asphalt.

 ★ ★ ★ ★
In its day, *nothing* threatened the V-Max in terms of speed. Handling? Well, that was another matter entirely.

Engine: Liquid-cooled, DOHC, 30-valve V-4
Horsepower: 140 at 8,500 rpm (claimed)

Top Speed: 140 miles per hour
Weight: n/a
Value Now: $$

# Yamaha

## Royal Star

Yamaha generated a great deal of friction with its dealer network by forcing dealers to purchase expensive displays for their (slow-selling) Royal Star motorcycles.

The protobike of Yamaha's Star line of cruisers.

Cruise Death Valley during the springtime when the wildflowers are in bloom and the temperature isn't so deathly hot.

*
A liquid-cooled V-4 engine that cranks out the same level of power as an air-cooled V-twin just isn't that rebellious.

Engine: Liquid-cooled, 1,294cc,
    four-stroke V-4
Horsepower: n/a

Top Speed: n/a
Weight: 725 pounds
Value Now: $$

### Long, low, and wide

It seemed like a good idea at the time: combine classic American cruiser-bike styling with a modern liquid-cooled V-4 engine. Such was Yamaha's formula for the Royal Star in 1996. Styling-wise, the Royal Star was a success, but oddly enough the V-4 engine produced some annoying vibration, especially to the floorboards. Worse yet, despite the vibration, the big V-4 engine didn't produce much power, mostly because styling considerations had forced engineers to choke the engine with inadequate airflow. Later adaptations of the basic Royal Star platform improved on this situation somewhat by mounting external air boxes inside the lower fairing.

# Yamaha

## FZR400

### Forerunner to the much-heralded FZR600

Swing a leg over Yamaha's FZR400, and you'll learn right away what it's like to dash into a corner, heel the bike over for the apex, then accelerate smoothly out and onto the awaiting straight section to conquer the next turn. This 385-pound bike feels light and agile, making it easy to flick from side to side, and the engine, seasoned with a 12,000-rpm redline, gives plenty of kick—provided you keep the revs high.

 Although built between 1986 and 1994, the FZR400 was only imported into the U.S. market between 1988 and 1990.

 This bike dominated the lightweight class in club racing for a decade or more.

 Glendora Mountain Road near Glendora, California. Its twists and turns will keep you entertained on the FZR.

 ★ ★ ★ ★
The FZR400 is small but rewarding to ride fast; one jacket per 100cc.

| | |
|---|---|
| Engine: Liquid-cooled, 399cc, four-stroke, inline four | Top Speed: 133 miles per hour |
| Horsepower: 59 at 12,000 rpm | Weight: 385 pounds |
| | Value Now: $$ |

---

# Yamaha

## TDM850

### A versatile oddball

The TDM850 proves agile in the turns and offers a rather inviting ride in terms of sport-touring. You can enjoy the sights and the TDM850, thanks to its high seating position. Besides, anyone with a credit card and a set of spanner wrenches can replace a crappy stock shock.

 The original 1991 model was a disappointment, but a few years later Yamaha brought out a revamped version that has been a success.

 Proof that you don't need a squadron of engine cylinders to produce an adequate sport-touring motorcycle.

 Pack your passport, we're heading to Switzerland where we'll tackle the Oberalp Pass. Bring wool socks; the TDM doesn't offer leg protection.

 ★ ★
Nothing stellar about this bike, but nothing disappointing, either.

| | |
|---|---|
| Engine: Liquid-cooled, 849cc, four-stroke, parallel twin | Top Speed: n/a |
| Horsepower: 80 at 7,500 rpm | Weight: 436 pounds |
| | Value Now: n/a |

# Yamaha

## GTS 1000

James Parker originally tested the RADD front end on a Honda XL600.

First mass-produced bike of the modern era not to use telescopic forks.

New Mexico Highway 475 through the Santa Fe National Forest.

★ ★ ★ ★ ★
Scrapping telescopic forks and starting over is quite rebellious.

Engine: Liquid-cooled, 1,002cc, DOHC, four-stroke, inline four
Horsepower: 102 at 9,000 rpm
Top Speed: 141 miles per hour
Weight: n/a
Value Now: $$$

### Considerably ahead of its time

The GTS was something you stared at, wondering how it worked. What was up with that front end? Did it signal a seismic change in the motorcycle universe, or would James Parker's RADD front end be relegated to the footnotes of history? The idea was to separate steering duties from suspension duties so that bumps didn't affect your line in a corner. That goal was achieved, and the GTS, more stable than agile, was hailed for its composed nature at speed—which was surprisingly hard to find, what with the FZR Genesis engine having been radically detuned in the search for low- and midrange power. Sadly, even electronic fuel injection and ABS brakes couldn't compensate for its overall weirdness, and the GTS was a showroom flop.

# Yamaha

## VX 1700 Road Star Warrior

**Form shares the rider's seat with function**

The cruiser segment of the American motorcycle market experienced huge growth in the 1990s. Yamaha recognized that, but response from focus groups also told them that cruiser riders desired bikes that performed and handled well too. Yamaha responded with the Road Star Warrior, a hot-rod model that blends custom styling with snappy performance. Unfortunately, the Warrior never sold in the numbers Yamaha had anticipated, and it disappeared from the lineup after the 2009 model year. Apparently what cruiser buyers told focus groups they wanted and what they really wanted were two very different things.

 Yamaha formed its Star line in 1994.

 The Road Star Warrior was one of the first cruisers to offer good handling too.

 Take a ride on Sepulveda Boulevard as it meanders through Los Angeles. Measuring 42.8 miles in length, it's one of America's longest urban roads.

 ✶ ✶
This bike is capable of 12.7-second quarter-mile times, so hang on.

Engine: Air-cooled, 1,670cc, four-stroke, 48-degree V-twin
Horsepower: 85 at 4,500 rpm

Top Speed: 118 miles per hour
Weight: 606 pounds
Value Now: $$

The R6 is a rider's bike and encourages high cornering speed.

 With a redline of more than 16,000 rpm, the R6 has one of the highest-revving engines intended for street use.

 No question, the best place to ride this bike is at your local road-race course during open-track day—or for a race.

 ★ ★ ★ ★
Riding a 600cc sportbike quickly is one thing—launching it to a sub-11-second quarter-mile run is another matter entirely.

Engine: Liquid-cooled, 599cc, four-stroke, inline four
Horsepower: 108.5 at 14,250 rpm
Top Speed: 161 miles per hour
Weight: 366 pounds
Value Now: $$$

**Small on size, yet big on performance in every category**

Do you want to know what it feels like to be a pro road racer? Look no further than Yamaha's R6, a pocket rocket that's powered by a 600cc, inline, four-cylinder engine with a redline above 16,000 rpm. Thanks to a sturdy Deltabox aluminum frame, hefty disc brakes, and gobs of race-bred hardware, including fully adjustable suspension, the R6 easily harnesses its 100-plus rear-wheel horsepower so that you can command it through the turns and onto the straights as if you were, well, a pro road racer. The ride gets even more thrilling when you steer the R6 onto a road-race track where you can ride it at its limits, which is exactly the point.

# Yamaha

## R1

**Leaner, faster, snappier handling—all you want in a sportbike and more**

Yamaha's R1 was a no-nonsense motorcycle, and although engineered to be a streetbike, it was built purposefully for the racetrack too. Indeed, many enthusiast publications touted the first R1 as a race bike in street livery. The R1 package broke new ground, checking in at about the same physical size as a typical 600cc sportbike. The secret was its Deltabox II aluminum twin-spar frame that allowed for a compact package stiff enough to contain the 998cc engine's 150 horsepower. The net result was a stable ride at practically any speed on the racetrack or on the street.

 Yamaha didn't win a World Superbike Championship until 2009, when Texan Ben Spies rode his 2009 R1 to the title.

 The R1's signature was its Genesis-based engine, delivering 150 horsepower and buckets of torque at the mere twist of the throttle.

 Pick the road-race track of your choice; whatever you choose, you'll be satisfied at the end of the day.

 ★ ★ ★ ★ ★
Despite its race-bred heritage and minimalist design, riding the R1 can be tricky. One publication said a ride on the R1 would "wring the rider's adrenal glands dry."

Engine: Liquid-cooled, 998cc, four-stroke, inline four-cylinder
Horsepower: 150 at 10,000 rpm
Top Speed: 186 miles per hour
Weight: 390 pounds
Value Now: $$$

*Cycle World* named the Star Roadliner the best cruiser for 2006.

A cruiser with an aluminum frame!

Take the scenic route around San Francisco where the Roadliner's low center of gravity and gobs of engine torque will make for a pleasant ride.

✶ ✶
Keep the jacket liners zipped in—San Francisco can be cold, even during the summertime!

Engine: Air-cooled, 1,854cc, four-stroke, 48-degree V-twin
Horsepower: n/a

Top Speed: 120 miles per hour
Weight: 749 pounds
Value Now: $$

**A cruiser that combines handling with engine power**
The cruiser-bike world keeps getting better and better, and the Star Roadliner S is proof of that. The Roadliner's V-twin engine generates massive torque—it peaks at only about 2,500 rpm—so you don't have to over-rev the engine nor tap dance through the gears to enjoy performance. A solid chassis that's based on a lightweight, aluminum frame offers a firm, steady ride, and who can argue about the comfort factor when you settle into the large saddle? If it's time for you to go low and slow, this might be the bike for you.

# Yamaha

## R1

**At last, Yamaha builds a winner for the World Superbike Championship!**

Yamaha's crossplane technology—what members of the motorcycle press referred to as the big-bang engine—found its way onto America's public roads when the R1 bowed for 2009. Crossplane technology is based on a unique firing order that's similar to what's found on Ben Spies' superbike—the same superbike that he finished first with in the World Superbike Championship for 2009. The technology allows the power pulses to be spread evenly to the rear tire for gentler, more predictable acceleration out of a corner. Result: in the case of Ben Spies, a world championship. For you? One of the most pleasant and fastest rides offered today.

 Though this bike marks the first use of a big-bang engine in a streetbike, that type of engine has long been used in MotoGP.

 Ben Spies won the 2009 World Superbike Championship in his first year in the series.

 Any racetrack where Ben Spies trounced the competition during his quest to the 2009 WSC crown.

 ★ ★ ★ ★ ★
You get all five leather jackets only if you can keep up with Ben Spies on the track.

Engine: Liquid-cooled, 998cc, four-stroke, inline four-cylinder
Horsepower: 146 at 11,800 rpm
Top Speed: 186 miles per hour
Weight: 390 pounds
Value Now: $$$

# Yankee

## 500Z

 Two-time AMA Grand National Champion Dick Mann was instrumental in developing the 500Z's frame.

 An off-road bike developed by Americans.

 Let's hit the trail with Dick "Bugsy" Mann. The Mann will be leading, of course.

 ★ ★ ★
An American off-road bike developed with input from an all-American rider.

Engine: Air-cooled, 488cc, two-stroke, parallel twin-cylinder
Horsepower: 40 at 6,500 rpm

Top Speed: 85 miles per hour
Weight: 349 pounds
Value Now: $$$

**An off-road bike for Mann-size riders**

Despite a rather heavy frame and a wide engine (by off-road standards), the Yankee 500Z proved to be a capable trail bike 40 years ago. The frame was stout, and the twin-cylinder engine's 360-degree firing order coupled with massive flywheels translated into a wide powerband. The 500Z project began in 1967, but an unusually long developmental period meant that when the bike finally made it to the showroom floor a few years later, the competition had gained even more of an advantage through their own advancements.

# Acknowledgments

## Photo Credits

The bulk of the photography for this book was selected from the archives at *Cycle World* magazine, which is easily the most amazing collection of motorcycle photography on the planet. We would like to thank the many fine staff photographers who have helped to create that collection over the past fifty years.

But even the best collection is not complete. The following companies and photographers provided the images missing from the archives:

Kevin Ash
Big Dog Motorcycles
Dave Bush
Confederate Motors, Inc.
Ducati North America
Mush Emmons
Fischer Motor Company
Harley-Davidson Motor Company, Inc.

Jerry Hatfield
Darwin Holmstrom
Honda Motor Company
KTM North America
Kawasaki Motor Operation
John Lamm
Randy Leffingwell
Henry N. Manney III
MV Agusta Motor S.p.A.
Zack Miller
*Minnesota Motorcycle Monthly*
Mission Motor Company
Piaggio Group USA
Rick Schunk
Stan Sholik
Triumph Motorcycles
Dr. Robin Tuluie
Geoffrey Wood
Yamaha Motor Company